Defining Visions

Defining Visions
Television and the American Experience in the 20th Century

Second Edition

Mary Ann Watson

Blackwell
Publishing

BLACKWELL PUBLISHING
350 Main Street, Malden, MA 02148-5020, USA
9600 Garsington Road, Oxford OX4 2DQ, UK
550 Swanston Street, Carlton, Victoria 3053, Australia

First published 2008 by Blackwell Publishing Ltd

1   2008

Library of Congress Cataloging-in-Publication Data has been applied for

ISBN 978-1-4051-7054-3. (hardback)
ISBN 978-1-4051-7053-6. (paperback)

A catalogue record for this title is available from the British Library.

Set in 11/13.5 Dante MT Std
by Newgen Imaging Systems. (P) Ltd, Chennai, India
Printed and bound in Singapore
by Markono Print Media Pte Ltd

For further information on
Blackwell Publishing, visit our website:

www.blackwellpublishing.com

For Al and Jane, Sam and Lucille—
who gave their baby boomers every opportunity

Contents

List of Illustrations

Photo Section

Acknowledgments

The first edition of this book was published in 1998 as part of a series on post-WWII America under the editorial guidance of Distinguished Professors of History Gerald D. Nash and Richard W. Etulain of the University of New Mexico. Their encouragement of historical studies that strive to be explanatory and engaging, rather than arcane, was heartwarming. I'm grateful for the privilege to have worked with such wise men.

Then, as now, Dennis Beagen, the head of my department at Eastern Michigan University, has provided steady moral support and too many kindnesses to count. The award of a research grant from the College of Arts Sciences was an uplifting recognition of the importance of cultural studies in a liberal arts education.

Many friends who share my enthusiasm for media history, especially Lawrence W. Lichty and Cary O'Dell, discussed, debated, and argued in wonderfully helpful ways. Randal Baier, the Multimedia Arts librarian at EMU, assisted this project not only as a technical perfectionist, but also as a curious intellectual.

Heroic measures are standard operating procedure for archivist Michael Henry of the Library of American Broadcasting. He has my deep appreciation for his professionalism as well as his vast knowledge and understanding of broadcasting in the 20th century. Professor Douglas Gomery of the University of Maryland and Resident Scholar of the Library of American Broadcasting has made a great contribution to the field by taking the lead in processing the massive amount of material in the Don West *Broadcasting and Cable* Photo Archive. It was a resource of tremendous value to me and will undoubtedly inform the work of students and scholars yet to be born.

I am indebted to Senior Editor Elizabeth Swayze of Blackwell Publishing and Project Editor Ken Provencher for sharing my vision of this book and for understanding an author's concerns.

In the last two decades, every published sentence that I've written has been read, proofread, re-read—and in many cases improved—by Tom Mascaro. It is a collaboration and friendship based on kindred visions of how the world should be. Writing will always be lonely and hard, but Tom owns my immense gratitude for making it less so.

Not one day has passed in thirty years of marriage that my wonderful husband, the other half of my heartbeat, didn't say or do something that made me laugh out loud. Of the four million Americans born in 1953, I am certain that Dennis Watson is the funniest and I'm the luckiest.

Fig. 0 In the mid-20th century, television was redefining American family life. (Author Photo.)

Prologue

The 20th century opened and closed with wireless technology redefining the nature of human communication. On December 12, 1901, the transmission of the letter "S" in Morse code—three dots sent through the ether across the Atlantic Ocean—generated worldwide speculation on the possibilities of annihilating time and space in the dissemination of information. On September 11, 2001, citizens around the globe saw live television pictures of an attack on America and were soon privy to telephone messages from victims in the throes of the disaster.

The years between Guglielmo Marconi's experiments in wireless telegraphy and the live transmission of 9/11 have been called "the American Century" and "the Broadcast Century." Both are fitting labels, because the connections are numerous and intertwining between the rise of America's power and influence in the world and the growth of mass culture in the United States through communication networks.

During the first decade of the 20th century, military applications were considered the primary value of the "ethereal telegraph." Freed from wire, coded point-to-point communication between ships was a significant breakthrough. But two prominent experimenters were working independently on the wireless transmission of voice that promised to eliminate the need for the bewildering strings of dots and dashes.

On Christmas Eve 1906, wireless operators, on ships in the Atlantic carrying bananas for the United Fruit Company, were startled to hear a woman singing, violin music, and a man reading Bible passages from the Book of Luke. Canadian Reginald Fessenden, striving to improve the vacuum tube needed for such a miracle, was at the point of origination, his experimental station in Brant Rock, Massachusetts. Days later,

American Lee De Forest also accomplished the successful delivery of uncoded messages and music through the air. Their achievement was called radio telephony.

De Forest eventually perfected a glass bulb called an audion tube, which became a technological foundation of the emerging medium. Being a scientist, but also a skillful self-promoter, De Forest deemed himself "the father of radio" and called his transmissions from New York and later the Eiffel Tower in Paris "broadcasts." "Broadcasting," an agricultural term, was an apt analogy and it quickly caught on. The radio broadcaster, like a farmer scattering seeds over a wide area, cast a signal not knowing how many connections would be made with listeners. The farmer knew not every seed would take, but enough would sprout for cover crops and lawns. The radio operator knew the odds were good of attracting a critical mass.

Although scientific research during World War I improved the quality of voice reception, few, save a handful of visionaries, grasped the profound social implications of point-to-mass communication. Radio was first regarded as a substitute for the telegraph, a form of point-to-point communication, therefore it was criticized for its lack of privacy. The ability of many people to hear the same message was considered a disadvantage. Some wondered whether the potential for eavesdropping would limit the commercial value of the medium.

By the second decade of the 20th century, though, people began to appreciate radio's ability to reach great numbers of people. Three radio stations were on the air in the United States in 1920; by 1923 there were more than five hundred. The country was enthralled with the new medium. "Radio mania" had been unleashed and communal listening experiences began to transform American society. Class distinctions diminished as mass appeal became the goal of radio programming. People in every socio-economic stratum listened to the same ballgames, prize-fights, popular music, and comic characters. Neither a person's station in life nor his or her geographic location guaranteed isolation.

By the end of the 1920s, the foundations of radio broadcasting were in place and the medium was poised to become an industry of enormous power and influence: advertising would be the means of financing programming, the formation of networks would allow all communities access to high-quality broadcasts, and government regulation would eliminate the technical confusion of overlapping frequencies.

At the same time radio began its ascent and was still considered miraculous by most listeners, other inventors were envisioning the wildest of dreams—radio with pictures. One was a youngster who dreamed of "capturing light in a bottle." Philo T. Farnsworth, a 14-year-old Idaho farm boy, was plowing a potato field when he had a "Eureka!" moment. Farnsworth was a math prodigy, who was born in a log cabin and rode to school on horseback. He realized that in the same way he was plowing horizontally row by row, an image could be scanned by electrons.

By 1927, at the age of 21, Farnsworth had attracted investors for the work he was doing in his San Francisco laboratory, with a few assistants and the constant help of his bride Pem. On September 7, he demonstrated an experiment for a potential backer. Farnsworth covered a piece of glass with a layer of black paint. He then scratched a straight line through the paint in the center of the glass. Pem's brother placed this "slide" between Farnsworth's invention, the "image dissector," and the bright light of a carbon arc lamp. In another room, Philo and Pem Farnsworth, along with an investor named George Everson, watched the receiver as the slide was turned. They saw it move. "There you are," the inventor said, "electronic television." Later, Everson sent a telegram to another investor in Farnsworth's vision: "The damn thing works!"

The president of the Radio Corporation of America (RCA) could also imagine radio with pictures. David Sarnoff, the son of Russian immigrants, hired Vladimir Zworykin to help RCA get a foothold in television. Zworykin, a Russian-born scientist with a doctorate in electrical engineering, was sent to visit Farnsworth's lab, where he saw the image dissector. A few years later, Zworykin claimed to have perfected the "iconoscope," an invention essentially the same as Farnsworth's. The two men filed similar patent applications.

Even during the Great Depression, Sarnoff had the wherewithal to engage in endless litigation while promulgating the misconception that RCA was fully responsible for the creation and development of electronic television. Broadcast historians have characterized the corporation's fight as fierce and unfair. The underdog Farnsworth would eventually win the battle when the U.S. Patent Office decided in his favor in 1939, but RCA had gained the upper hand. Although RCA was required to pay royalties to Farnsworth, he was never able to reap the rewards of his success. When America entered World War II, the government suspended the sale of TV sets. By war's end, Farnsworth's major patents were near expiration. His financial limitations and deteriorating mental health allowed RCA to take advantage of the circumstances and spring quickly into the manufacturing leadership role of the new medium.

World War II was a shining victory in a righteous cause, and as the war faded from a constant worry to a memory, Americans took pride and comfort in the certain knowledge their sacrifices were not made in vain. Optimism for the future was the most meaningful tribute that could be paid to those whose lives were given for democratic principles.

The generation that grew up during the Great Depression and survived World War II was motivated by the unswerving belief that the lives of their children would be happier than theirs. Protecting their sons and daughters from the trauma they had endured was a natural instinct. And in 1945, after so many years of forbearance, they were ready to step into the future. The promise of express highways, quick-frozen foods, affordable single-family homes, air-conditioning, automatic washers and dryers, and, most of all, television sets was dazzling. Life in the second half of the century would surely be easier and better.

The astounding sense of common purpose Americans felt during World War II was engendered in large measure by radio. The medium bound its listeners in a universally shared experience. Pioneering live news broadcasts, such as Edward R. Murrow's dramatic accounts of the bombing of London, riveted audiences. Patriotic themes permeated the airwaves. Storylines in popular radio shows, such as *Fibber McGee and Molly*, frequently dealt with subjects like the rationing of sugar or the conservation of gasoline and rubber. Fans of the serial *Ma Perkins* cried when her son John was killed "somewhere in Germany." Listeners were urged by the biggest stars, including George Burns and Gracie Allen, Eddie Cantor, Kate Smith, Jack Benny, and Bob Hope, to help win the war through the purchase of war bonds, contributions to the Red Cross, and sacrifice at home.

Radio, one of the most powerful weapons in the arsenal of democracy, was there for the duration. And when it was over, radio provided the national catharsis. On V-E Day, May 8, 1945, the day Germany finally collapsed and the Allied forces achieved victory in Europe, the CBS network aired a celebratory and reflective broadcast called *On a Note of Triumph*. It was an epic aural mosaic that brought the Golden Age of radio to its zenith. The collective high emotion of the moment was captured perfectly in the words of the program's writer, Norman Corwin: "Take a bow, G.I. Take a bow, little guy. You had what it took and you gave it, and each of you has a hunk of rainbow round your helmet. Seems like free men have done it again."

Three months later, the news of Japan's surrender brought the painful years of World War II to their conclusion. In August 1945, with the mushroom clouds of atomic bombs as a profound punctuation mark, Americans entered a new phase in the evolution of the republic.

At the dawn of the postwar era, radio was the dominant cultural medium. Church, family, and government, though, were still the strongest institutions in the weave of the American fabric. But in short order the advent of television would change the equation. More than any other aspect of American life, the history of television reveals the story of the reorientation of culture and the shift in American values that occurred after World War II.

Within a year of the war's end, twelve million GIs were back home ready to make up for lost time—building and buying and making babies at a dizzying rate. As the country boomed in postwar prosperity, an abundant home life became part of a new nationalism. All the marvels arrived as predicted and changed not only the physical landscape of the country and household, but the social and psychological contours as well.

Vast suburban areas sprouted to accommodate the throngs of Americans—those not restricted by race or income—pressing out from the cities. People were marrying at an earlier age and the population continued to swell. Superhighways were laid across the country like so many ribbons of pavement, and two-car families were hardly a rarity in many neighborhoods. New supermarkets and shopping centers with lots of easy parking, brimming with quantities of food and merchandise that would be simply unbelievable in other parts of the world, were most often the destination of mom's car. But long vacation drives were also becoming a new summer ritual, making travel and recreation a growth industry.

So many developments came along and made a difference, from the blessing of antibiotics to the wonder of fiberglass. Among them was television, which by mid-century was becoming central to modern life in the United States. Soon it would be the common reference point, a palpable force in creating a national consensus on what was important. In the postwar decades, so momentous in the life of the nation, television defined what mattered most—setting our country's agenda for debate and action, giving us our myths and stories.

It is the premise of this book that in the second half of the 20th century, TV has been the primary means by which Americans have defined themselves and each other. In the three decades after World War II, free, over-the-air network television provided entertainment, information, and advertising for the mass of American viewers. The by-product of this programming, however inadvertent, has aptly been called "social glue."

Network TV reminded us we had a common national destiny. When the program *See It Now* made its debut in 1951 and broadcast simultaneous views of the Atlantic and Pacific Oceans on a split screen, the concept of nationhood, of states united, lost any sense of abstraction.

Social scientists grappled with the impact of television. Eventually, Professor George Gerbner's Cultivation Theory gained wide acceptance. Gerbner posited that television acts as a socializing agent. Viewers, though, innately understood TV was becoming the principal forum for national dialogue, and the medium was encroaching on the educational role of parents, teachers, and clergy.

From the start, groups of citizens, particularly those marginalized in American culture, wanted to have a say in their own portrayals on television. They intuited correctly the pictures of the world the new medium transmitted would be defining. To the black viewers who protested the *Amos 'n' Andy* show and the Native Americans who took issue with the way TV Westerns portrayed Indian cultures, the debate over whether television reflected or shaped society was academic. They knew, as do the countless other groups who have fought for access and input to American television ever since, that TV confers status on ideas, quite apart from their legitimacy or accuracy.

In postwar America, commercial television's most obvious function has been to sell products, but its most significant function has been to give viewers common ground with which to start a conversation. Even casual discussions of TV are really interpretations of American life. Contemporary archetypes come from the small screen, which is why so many people understand precisely what is meant when someone is referred to as "a real Eddie Haskell," "a regular Barney Fife," or a "Bart Simpson kind of kid."

Public television too has provided programming that defines. Historical series such as *Vietnam: A Television History* and *Eyes on the Prize: America's Civil Rights Years* created a common context for understanding critical events. *American Masters* has explored our highest artistic aspirations, *American Experience* our shared history, and *Sesame Street*, virtually inseparable from American childhood, develops not only basic reading and arithmetic skills, but also social and emotional concepts.

While public television, known in its early days as educational television, welcomes its function as an educator, the commercial television industry has always resisted the notion that its programming offers tacit lessons about what is valued in our culture and how to behave in it. "Nobody elected us to be the agents of social change," a network entertainment president once protested, "if you're looking for truth, go to God, go to your guru." Despite such glib dismissals of responsibility, the record of postwar America offers abundant proof that television has been a catalyst in social change, both constructive and detrimental.

One of the sweeping transformations in recent history centers on the role of women at home and in the workplace. Any student assessing these tremendous changes would naturally consider many critical factors, such as government and industry labor policies, the technology of housework, and the availability of contraception. But what about TV? If it's not included in the analysis, the picture is incomplete.

An understanding of women and American culture in the 1970s, for instance, requires a consideration of *The Mary Tyler Moore Show*. By anyone's standards, it is a landmark television series featuring bright scripting, outstanding performances, and precision directing. But its significance has less to do with creative artistic values than with its cultural resonance. *The Mary Tyler Moore Show* is a social milestone that redefined American life. What it means to be an unmarried woman over the age of 30 was forever altered in the national consciousness by Mary Richards, who became a model for millions of young women eager to put their talents to use in the professional world.

News narratives, too, offered public symbols and unified themes about the American way of life to postwar viewers. Nightly newscasts were, in the words of correspondent Daniel Schorr, "a national evening séance." Watching television became a qualification of engaged citizenship. The sight of our astronauts bouncing on the moon in 1969 was a salve on the painful divisions that existed at that moment in history. Americans were, however fleetingly, all members of a nation that could unquestionably define itself as triumphant.

The heyday of network television coincided with the postwar joyride of prosperity, which many assumed was a natural state. TV fueled a consumption culture and Americans began to base their expectations on materialistic rather than spiritual tenets. The American Dream, as typically defined on television, was fulfilled through the acquisition of possessions. Presuming affluence, though, the first TV generation came into adulthood in a stagnant economy.

The oil shortage and soaring inflation of the 1970s jolted America's sense of security. Citizens had come to expect that not only the pursuit of happiness, but happiness itself, was a birthright. Gone, though, was the ability of an American family to sustain itself decently on a single blue-collar income. Socioeconomic class divisions that had been blurring during the first phase of the television age now grew more pronounced. And an influx of Hispanic and Asian immigrants was changing the face of America—just as television itself was fragmenting.

In the 1980s, the television industry experienced a dramatic upheaval with the spectacular rise of cable and the public's energetic embrace of VCRs. The growing number of video rental stores and the increasing channel capacity of cable systems multiplied viewing choices exponentially, decreasing the probability that any two neighbors had watched the same program on a given evening. Bruce Springsteen released the album *Human Touch* in 1992, with a track lamenting the state of American television— "57 Channels (And Nothin' On)." Home satellite dishes brought the number of viewing options into the hundreds. Instead of sharing in the culture of broadcasting, more Americans were subscribing to narrowcasting.

Early adopters of technology were replacing their VCRs with DVRs (Digital Video Recorders), such as TiVO, portals for organizing and controlling massive amounts of program content. As the year 2000 approached— or, as it was called in the mass media, "Y2K"—Americans were buying more personal computers than television sets. The term "convergence" came into wide use to describe the melding of the two technologies. To the millennial generation, there was no significant difference between a TV screen and a computer screen. The question "What's on TV tonight?" was evolving into a quaintness of the mass era.

At the turn of the 21st century, Americans had the ability to program their viewing to their own special interests—perhaps prejudices—and to shut out whatever was disparate. Narrowcasting was evolving into *sliver*-casting. This was a grave concern among educators, clergy, sociologists, political scientists, and many other thoughtful people. When common values and common knowledge are threatened—the essence of American empowerment during the 20th century—does America as a community of shared ideas begin to come apart?

A horrific test of that question presented itself on the morning of Tuesday, September 11, 2001. Americans riveted to TV coverage witnessed a shift in the definition of their nation from "superpower" to "vulnerable." Future generations will judge the strength and character of the United States at this juncture in history. And, no doubt, the role of television will be included in the deliberations.

There are many lenses that can be used to take a careful look at the United States since the end of World War II, but television offers an especially telling scope. The struggles for a more fair republic, the wars won and lost, political metamorphoses, and cultural revolutions have been remarkably chronicled by television. But the medium has been much more than a detached witness. Its imprint can be detected on every episode of consequence in contemporary American history.

The snapshots of programming presented in *Defining Visions* have been selected to illustrate a sixty-year panorama of television. Certainly other examples might be chosen, including some that appear to counter the historical point being made. But, rare exceptions notwithstanding, the potency and direction of television's influence on America since the end of World War II are consistently observable. The chapters that follow, each about a different facet of American life, explore representative evidence that confirms the significance of television as a cultural and historical force.

Fig. 1 *The Texaco Star Theater*, starring Milton Berle, debuted in 1948 and became the nation's first TV sensation. (NBC publicity photo.)

CHAPTER 1

Television Enters the Picture

In the month before the opening of the 1939 New York World's Fair, several big companies were preparing their exhibits. The General Motors pavilion featured remote-controlled cars and Westinghouse's centerpiece was a cigarette-smoking robot named Elektro. But no display better captured the Fair's theme, "The World of Tomorrow," than the Hall of Television sponsored by RCA, the Radio Corporation of America.

The New York Times proffered a grim prognostication about the invention that would soon be demonstrated to the public for the first time: "The problem with television is that people must sit down and keep their eyes glued to the screen. The average American family hasn't the time for it. . . . If for no other reason, television will never be a serious competitor of radio broadcasting." David Sarnoff's prediction proved a little more accurate. Though hardly a detached observer, the president of RCA, who had a vested interest in TV's development, claimed that what was being introduced to America that April 30th was "a new art so important in its implications that it is bound to affect all society."

The National Broadcasting Company (NBC), owned by RCA, was using President Roosevelt's remarks opening the World's Fair as the inaugural broadcast for its "new deal in communication"—regular television service from its transmitter atop the Empire State Building. There were approximately two hundred TV sets within about a forty-mile radius of the fairgrounds in Flushing Meadow, Queens. Most were owned by RCA executives. But scores of onlookers seated before TV receivers at the company's Radio City headquarters in Manhattan, eight miles away, were also watching the festivities. And on sidewalks outside several department store windows, passers-by also witnessed history in the making as they stopped to view the TV sets that were displayed with the hope of generating a market for the RCA receivers going on sale the next day.

Visitors to the Fair were invited to stand in line to appear in front of a camera while a friend or family member stood at a monitor a short distance away. People shouted and waved in wonder to confirm that a live image was indeed being relayed. Back to the end of the long line, their places were alternated and the process reversed.

Even though the public was enchanted by television, not many sets were being sold. For most families, the few hours of programming being offered each week didn't justify the major investment. Price tags ranged between $199.50 for a set with a screen smaller than a postcard to $600 for the larger, 8-by-10-inch picture. For a person lucky enough to have a good job during the Depression, that could be a few months' pay. For the millions out of work and with little money for food, television surely was not a top priority.

Before the attack on Pearl Harbor, television was a curio for the wealthy. Only several thousand sets were sold. Then, for all practical purposes, World War II halted television's expansion. The raw materials needed to manufacture TV receivers and transmitters, like aluminum, cobalt, and copper, were instead put to military use. Station construction was also halted. Most Americans were unaware that a skeleton schedule of TV programs was even being offered by the fledgling medium.

There were, however, a handful of experimental stations on the air in New York City, Schenectady, Philadelphia, Los Angeles, and Chicago. In 1940, the Balaban and Katz Theater Corporation, the subsidiary of Paramount Pictures, that brought movie palaces to Chicago, opened test station W9XBK in the Windy City. Before long, the station began losing its staff of male technicians, whose expertise was needed by the military. In September 1941, a classified ad appeared in Chicago newspapers: "WANTED: Telegenic talent girls for technical work in television studio. Mechanical experience unnecessary. Apply Box 151." More than one hundred women responded. Eight were selected to become the Women's Auxiliary Television Technical Staff, called the WATTS.

The group was given a crash course by the station's chief engineer, who had not yet moved over to U.S. Navy radar school. One of the WATTS, Fran Harris, remembered, "We were taken on a tour of the station and shown each piece of equipment and told how it worked—and that was our training. And then we went to work!"

The station was on the air on Monday and Wednesday afternoons and during the evening hours on Tuesdays, Thursdays, and Fridays. The WATTS produced, directed, and often appeared in talk shows, puppet shows, cooking programs, and newscasts. There was even an exercise show called *The TeleSlimmer*. Not many viewers were able to enjoy their creativity, however. There were fewer than 400 television sets in Chicago during the WATTS era, which ended in August 1945. The group was never officially disbanded, but as soldiers returned from overseas, men were hired as permanent technical staff.

TV's apparent dormancy to most Americans during the war was deceiving, though. Technological strides were being made. Many scientists who had been involved with developing television entered the military to study high-frequency electronics. Innovations in electronic gear, including walkie-talkies, field transmitters, and especially radar, were directly applied to television development.

At war's end, factories that were producing electronics for the military were ready to convert to mass production of TV sets. And a multitude of Navy-trained radar operators were ready to assume a new occupation in civilian life nonexistent before the war—TV Repairman. But to fuel the mass consumption of TV sets, programs had to be produced that people wanted to watch.

Rearranging the Furniture

At the end of World War II it was still radio that kept the mass audience informed and entertained with the top talent of the country night after night. The most popular postwar radio programs tended toward escapism and domesticity. *The Adventures of Ozzie and Harriet,* for instance, a comedy about the idyllic household of "America's favorite young couple," was rife with innocuous trouble.

Television stations couldn't yet compete. Their programming was still locally produced and not up to par with the quality of network radio shows. And even though the image orthicon tube perfected during the war greatly improved the picture quality of studio cameras, filling the hours of a broadcast day was a challenge. Sports broadcasts, especially boxing and wrestling, were a natural fit. But the key to television's future was the interconnecting of stations into a nationwide network. In December 1945, the first steps were made when NBC telecast the Army–Navy football game on WNBT in New York using a coaxial cable link from the Philadelphia game site.

In 1946 another sporting event advanced the state of networking. The championship heavyweight boxing match at Yankee Stadium between Joe Louis and Billy Conn was broadcast on an ad hoc network to four cities on the East Coast. The spectacle reached as many as 150,000 viewers. Skeptics were convinced—TV was here to stay.

When the first postwar sets went on sale in 1946, many buyers of RCA's 15-by-20-inch large-screen model were making the purchase not for home, but for their businesses. Watching the TV set at the corner bar was the way many Americans became acquainted with the new medium. Signs saying "We Have TV" were a sure lure when a major sporting event was in the offing. The 1947 World Series between the Brooklyn Dodgers and the New York Yankees was a bonanza for TV-equipped taverns in the Big Apple. An estimated four million viewers watched—very few from their own homes.

In 1947 about 60 percent of TV airtime was devoted to sports, but some innovative programming began to show a glimmer of television's potential for bringing the world into the living room. A total eclipse of the sun took place on May 20, 1947. NBC sent correspondent Ben Grauer to Brazil with a crew of engineers and cameramen to film the event from an ideal vantage point. The film was telecast some sixty hours after the eclipse. NBC declared it a "scoop."

By the end of 1947, TV was beginning to take permanent hold. Twelve stations were broadcasting to about 14,000 households. The wartime shortage of raw materials eased and the federal government granted permits to build fifty-five new television stations. The turning point came in 1948—year one of the modern age of television. When major advertisers launched big-league programs, a mass audience was ready to watch. In fall of that year, the medium's first sensation detonated on American culture.

The Texaco Star Theater was an old-fashioned vaudeville variety show starring a brash comic of middling celebrity. Milton Berle was a virtuoso of sight gags. Appearing at the beginning of each show in a bizarre costume became his trademark. An intro like "And now the man with jokes from the Stone Age" would precede Berle's grand entrance dressed as a caveman. It was supremely corny and the audience adored it.

Berle's popularity became a bona fide phenomenon. On Tuesday nights between eight and nine o'clock, movie theaters, restaurants, and nightclubs in cities with an NBC affiliate experienced a marked decline in business, while neighborhood taverns with TV packed them in. Appliance stores could garner crowds of potential TV buyers to their windows by showing *The Texaco Star Theater*. One enterprising laundromat proprietor advertised: "Watch Berle while your clothes whirl."

Of course many factors came into play for families contemplating the purchase of a television set or a kit to build one, but being able to watch "Mr. Television," as Berle was soon called, was an added incentive. In 1948, Electro-Technical Industries of Philadelphia was one of several companies offering home tinkerers the chance to own a TV set at a bargain price. The Telekit for a 7" tabletop model with a walnut cabinet came to a little under $150. Magazines such as *Popular Mechanics* and *Radio and Television Broadcasting* offered encouragement and guidance to those ambitious enough to try to assemble their own set.

After the decision to buy and the selection of model, where to put the television set was the big question. Typically, stately radio consoles made of finely finished wood were moved aside to make room for the new TV cabinet holding a device that would transform family interaction.

There was status involved in being the first member of the clan or neighborhood to own a TV, but the distinction came with a responsibility. A wonderful part of contemporary American folklore revolves around the visits of non-TV-owners to their more progressive friends and relatives. Where and how to seat the inevitable visitors was the next issue. Since owning a TV felt like having a miniature motion picture theater in the house, sometimes chairs would be arranged accordingly. It didn't take long to figure out, though, that a straight row of seats placed in front of the screen was not the most comfortable position for viewing. Soon the chairs were fanned out in a semi-circle, reminiscent of a group huddled around the hearth.

Eventually recliners, specially designed for viewing, settled into a permanent spot in front of the set and stackable TV-tray tables could be purchased so snacks didn't have to be balanced on a knee or drinks perched on coasters. But for a brief period in the late 1940s and early 1950s, watching TV at someone else's home or welcoming visitors into yours was a custom that required social effort.

Generally it was considered a serious breach of decorum for anyone but the host to initiate a re-tuning of the set. Lacking an outdoor antenna on the roof, "rabbit ears" were placed on top of the TV. Carefully positioning the base and delicately adjusting the antennae were mandatory every time the channel was changed. Precision tuning a TV set having two doors, four big knobs, and a speaker covered with brown mesh was a feat that could be complicated by the time of day, weather conditions, and the next-door neighbor's vacuum sweeper.

Although the taboo would quickly ease, talking during a program, as it was in a movie theater, was considered rude. But offering opinions after the fact was not. A New York housewife recalled her days as a TV hostess: "I remember *Milton Berle* was on and my friends came over to watch and then said 'What a crazy thing. What do I need that in the house for?' They said they would never bring such a thing in their house—but later they didn't have one TV, they had two! It grows on you. We made friends with the people in the neighborhood when we got our TV, even the rich dentist on the corner."

In 1949, television sets made their first appearance in the Sears, Roebuck catalog, and anyone looking for an excuse to order one had plenty of reasons besides Uncle Miltie, Berle's familiar nickname. There was Ed Sullivan's *Toast of the Town*, John Cameron Swayze's nightly news roundup, *The Camel News Caravan*, and coverage of special events like President Truman's inauguration. Enormously popular radio stars like Arthur Godfrey tried the new medium. Several radio favorites, comedies like *The Aldrich Family* and *The Life of Riley*, were adapted as well.

For many families, though, the most compelling reason to take the plunge into television ownership was children. Even the most loving parents who enjoyed spending time with their little ones appreciated an uninterrupted hour now and then as the kids watched TV.

It's Howdy Doody Time!

In a stroke of brilliant timing, Dr. Benjamin Spock was writing *The Common Sense Book of Baby and Child Care* in 1945 just as the American population was about to explode. Over the next two decades seventy-six million children, who would be known as "Baby Boomers," were born. Postwar parents placed tremendous trust in the easy-going, nonauthoritarian approach espoused by Spock. Sternly regulated feeding and toilet training, he advised, were apt to make a child "balky and disagreeable." Young parents, themselves raised under a more rigorous no-nonsense regimen, appreciated the new relaxed technique of bringing up baby.

Unlike previous generations, these kids learned early that they could actually exert some control over the way things would be in the household. They could negotiate with casual parents, or perhaps dictate, matters like bedtime and vegetable consumption. One concept that children of the postwar era could not yet grasp, though, was that their sheer volume gave them a collective buying power that could launch entire industries overnight. It was a fact not lost on television executives.

It was no mystery of marketing that growing families would be more likely to buy TV sets if there were programs on the air that appealed to kids. In 1947, after NBC's first broadcast of *The Puppet Playhouse* – which was soon renamed *Howdy Doody*—the show biz trade paper *Variety* explained to its readership: "In the middle-class home, there is perhaps nothing as welcome to the mother as something that will keep the small fry intently absorbed and out of possible mischief. This program can almost be guaranteed to pin down the squirmiest of the brood."

Set in a Western land known as Doodyville, with a studio audience of children called the Peanut Gallery, the show starred a freckle-faced marionette whose best friend was a human named Buffalo Bob. Every afternoon at 5:30 Howdy and Bob presided over a cast of puppets and people who were at the root of gleeful mayhem.

Clarabell was a mute clown in a zebra-striped billowy suit who could toot a sweet "yes" or a sour "no" with a bicycle-horn box, but expressed himself most articulately with a well-aimed squirt of his seltzer bottle. The villain of Doodyville was Phineas T. Bluster, an elderly man-puppet dressed formally with a vest, spats, and a bowler hat. He was a humorless, boring old coot, a horrible crime in and of itself. But as Mayor of Doodyville he sometimes stood in the way of the other residents having unbridled fun, and that was the most unforgivable offense.

In Hoboken, New Jersey, in 1948, bar owner Parkey Radigan felt bad for the kids who didn't have TV sets to watch *Howdy Doody*. At show time he would cap the beer taps at his tavern, ask the adults to leave, and let children from the neighborhood have the run of the place. "Most of them come from poor families," he explained, "and besides, it seemed like a good way to keep them off the streets." Two months later the New Jersey Liquor Board nixed his brand of community service. But no authority of any sort was about to slow down the *Howdy Doody* juggernaut.

In the national election of 1948, Thomas Dewey and Harry Truman were the adult candidates, but American kids had their own presidential hopeful, who came with strings attached. In a grand publicity scheme, NBC cooked up a contest for president between Howdy Doody and Phineas T. Bluster. *Time* magazine even ran Howdy's platform promises: "Cut-rate banana splits, two Christmas holidays and one school day each year, double sodas for a dime, plenty of movies, more pictures in history books, plus free circus and rodeo admissions." Howdy won in a landslide of ballots that came from the labels of Wonder Bread, a happy sponsor of the show.

Mothers preparing dinner while *Howdy Doody* was on might not have paid too much attention to their progeny sitting stoop-shouldered in front of the tube watching pie-chase pandemonium. Maybe it was later, at a family gathering, that an aunt or grandmother first noticed the increasingly rounded stance, patted the child on the back, and said, "Stand up straight."

One alumnus of the show's first crop of viewers recalled its impact: "*Howdy Doody* was bad for both my posture and my self-restraint. The show was unrestrained; it suggested a world wonderfully out of joint. . . . 'Naughty!' one of my friends shouted when Clarabell squirted Buffalo Bob. Naughty was to my age group what a martini was to our parents: intoxicating. *Howdy Doody* distilled naughtiness and dispensed it from the seltzer bottle. No child could watch *Howdy Doody* without entering the conspiracy; there was only one rule governing the peanut gallery, and that was have fun."

The ostensible lessons presented in each show—brush your teeth, obey your parents, do your homework, say your prayers—were completely overwhelmed by the antic, frantic high jinks that made Doodyville a blast. The message to young viewers of *Howdy Doody* was exhilaratingly obvious: Life is a party and you're the guest of honor.

But although the children in the audience defined themselves as VIPs, advertisers and marketers defined the kids as fair game, a market to be cultivated without compunction. Radio targeted children too, but not with the same ferocity. *Howdy Doody* was the show that best demonstrated just how high the stakes were in the postwar pitching of products to kids.

A few months after the program went on the air, a toy buyer for Macy's, who had been getting requests for *Howdy Doody* dolls, got the idea to have some made. It was the first drop in an incredible flood of licensed merchandise. Soon Buffalo Bob was making department store appearances in which thousands of kids would be ushered past display counters overflowing with *Howdy Doody* salables: dolls, comic books, T-shirts, earmuffs, suspenders, phonograph record albums, and a rocking chair that played "It's *Howdy Doody* Time!" "We also had a *Howdy Doody* beanie," recalled Buffalo Bob, "we'd have every kid in the Peanut Gallery wear one. The next day, stores would run out of them."

The show's sponsors, including Colgate Dental Cream, Mars Candy, Ovaltine, Welch's Grape Juice, and Tootsie Rolls, loved the drawing power of *Howdy Doody* and the shameless persuasiveness of Buffalo Bob. He told the kids point-blank to nudge their parents into submission. In a shoe commercial, for instance, Buffalo Bob told his peanuts how they could get a swell full-color cutout of *Howdy Doody*, "All you do is have your Mom or Daddy take you to the store where you get Poll-Parrot shoes, and ask for YOUR *Howdy Doody* cutout!"

In commercials for all sorts of products children were instructed not to ask their parents, but to "have" or "tell" their parents to buy them exactly what they saw on the *Howdy Doody* show—no reasonable facsimiles allowed. Schoolchildren learned early to become brand name consumers. "We were real hucksters," Buffalo Bob acknowledged candidly years later, "You might say we were real whores."

The program *Howdy Doody* symbolized the first generation of Americans nurtured on television. Its cultural aftershocks became the subject of much speculation. Some social critics see a connection between the zeitgeist of Doodyville and the rebelliousness of baby boomers in the 1960s and their self-centeredness in the 1970s and 1980s. People less inclined to analyze popular culture are likely to roll their eyes in disdain at such esoteric ruminations on media and history. But who could deny that the experiences of childhood echo in adult life?

A half-century later, when *Newsweek* magazine asked prominent Americans to reflect on the contributions of the World War II generation, author James Michener, full of praise for the accomplishments of his peers, wrote: "I must in fairness admit that we failed conspicuously in meeting one vital obligation. We did a wretched job in raising the children we produced, for we did not prepare them to assume the responsibilities of citizenship. We threw them into the world as an undisciplined gang, and our nation suffered. Starting about 1960, the flood of children born after the end of World War II and properly labeled the Baby Boom began behaving in mysterious ways." Those who agree with Michener's perception point directly at lenient and indulgent postwar parents as the source of the problem. Perhaps, though, it's only fair to share at least some of the blame with *Howdy Doody*.

The Marvelous World of the Ordinary

As the war wound down in 1945 and broadcasters geared up for the expansion of television, another sales strategy, one as fundamental as targeting families with children, was implemented. The plan was to convince upper-income, well-educated men and women, those who could most easily afford TV, that their purchase of a television would be an enlightened investment. The appeal of live drama to urban sophisticates lent impetus to the sponsorship of several anthology series by manufacturers of TV sets, automobiles, and upscale consumer products.

The first postwar dramatic series, *The Kraft Television Theater*, made its debut in 1947. The sponsor had just introduced to the market a premium line of cheese called McClaren's Imperial. At one dollar per pound, sales were sluggish. But during commercial breaks on *The Kraft Television Theater*, viewers saw a pretty model displaying the product and heard the rich voice of announcer Ed Herlihy waxing lyrical about McClaren's Imperial. Within two weeks, there was not a single package of the pricey cheese left for sale in New York City.

Attracting affluent viewers had its rewards, and living-room theater flourished in the early postwar period. Although some in the legitimate theater disparaged the upstart medium, calling TV drama "summer stock in an iron lung," in its first few years television became a nursery for the talents of young unheard-of performers, directors, and, most of all, writers. With as many as a dozen original scripts offered by the networks each week on series like *Ford Television Theater* and *Studio One*, writers for the small screen were producing a new body of American literature—the teleplay.

The nature of live television posed limitations for scriptwriters, though. The type of action seen in feature films, such as car chases and shoot-outs, was not an option. TV characters were studio-bound, forced to live in a world of three or four sets. So, in its first decade, television drama resembled New York theater much more than Hollywood movies.

Since dialogue mattered most, live television drama became the perfect canvas for exploring internal landscapes. A common thread running through many of the hundreds of original television plays written in this era was the focus on small situations. Unexceptional people with unremarkable problems made for extraordinary storytelling. Matters of personal honor often propelled the plots. Characters who, in their own ways, sought dignity and decency and some respect from society prompted an empathetic response from cerebral viewers.

The most celebrated drama from the period nostalgically referred to as the Golden Age of Television—when writers were actually thought of as stars—is Paddy Chayefsky's *Marty*. The simple story of a lonely Bronx butcher aired on the *Philco Television Playhouse* in May 1953, a broadcast regarded as the high-water mark of live television drama. "I set out in *Marty* to write a love story, the most ordinary love story in the world," Chayefsky said of his seminal script. "I didn't want my hero to be handsome, and I didn't want the girl to be pretty. I wanted to write a love story the way it would literally have happened to the kind of people I know."

The thirty-six-year-old, average looking-at-best, bachelor Marty Pilletti, played by Rod Steiger, lives at home with his Italian-immigrant widowed mother. Worried that her oldest child will "die without a son," she urges him to take a shave, put on his blue suit, and go out to the Waverly Ballroom, a respectable dance hall where he might meet a nice girl. But Marty, stung so often by the rejection of women, has made peace with his fate. "Sooner or later," he tells his mother, "there comes a point in a man's life when he's gotta face some facts, and one fact I gotta face is that whatever it is women like, I ain't got it. I chased enough girls in my life. I went to enough dances. I got hurt enough. I don't wanna get hurt no more."

Even though he would rather stay home and watch Sid Caesar on television, Marty relents for his mother's sake. He assures her, though, that he already knows the evening's outcome: "I'll put onna blue suit and I'll go! And you know what I'm gonna get for my trouble? Heartache! A big night of heartache!"

At the Waverly Ballroom, Marty meets a plain-looking school teacher who has been dumped reprehensibly by her blind date. Clara, played by Nancy Marchand, has experienced the same kind of anguish as Marty. "I can recognize pain a mile away," he tells her as they navigate the crowded dance floor, "my brothers, my brother-in-laws, they're always telling me what a good-hearted guy I am. Well you don't get good-hearted by accident. You get kicked around long enough you get to be a real professor of pain. I know exactly how you feel."

Before seeing Clara home on the bus, Marty takes her to his house, where his mother, returning from an evening at her sister's, interrupts an awkward kiss. Mrs. Pilletti, primed by her sister's warning that when Marty marries she'll likely find herself unneeded and unwanted, takes an irrational dislike to Clara.

The next day at his neighborhood bar hangout, Marty is taunted by his buddies about the homely girl he got stuck with the night before. In a moment of epiphany he recognizes he has a chance for happiness in life with a kindred spirit, but he must summon the courage to disregard what other people think. With an uncharacteristic intensity that shocks his pals,

Marty tells them: "If you don't like it it's too bad. She's a dog and I'm a fat, ugly little guy. Well I had a good time last night. And I'm gonna call her up tonight and if I have a good time tonight and enough good times I'm gonna get down on my knees and I'm gonna beg that girl she should marry me and I don't care whether you like it or anybody else."

The television audience loved *Marty*. But advertisers were growing less enchanted with the genre Chayefsky called "the marvelous world of the ordinary." "There is far more exciting drama in the reasons a man gets married," the scriptwriter believed, "than in why he murders someone." To sponsors, the trouble with such an introspective approach was that it defined most human problems as psychologically complex. The premise of successful advertising was exactly the opposite. In commercials, problems were easily solved by the purchase of the product.

Rather than Marty accepting the fact that he was not blessed with good looks, an advertising agency's version of the story might have him try a new shampoo to put luster in his hair, a new toothpaste to brighten his smile, and a new aerosol cream for a smoother shave. The best way for him to beat the blues, of course, would be to buy a big, impressive new car.

Advertisers *wanted* viewers to worry about what other people thought. Characters who could ultimately be at peace with themselves without buying things to achieve their personal harmony were not setting a good consumer example. Ordinary wasn't supposed to be marvelous. In commercials, ordinary was embarrassing—deluxe was marvelous.

By mid-decade, encouraging people to invest in the purchase of a TV set no longer required special efforts. Every day between 1954 and 1956, ten thousand American households were installing television receivers. And as the audience grew more demographically and geographically diverse, programming that had a New York-theater feel to it and that artistically elevated little people and the problems from which they suffered had less strategic value to the networks.

Madison Avenue was more interested in broadly rendered programming with elements of power, fame, wealth, youth, and adventure. By 1955 the major motion picture studios in Hollywood—20th Century Fox, Columbia, Republic, MGM, and Warner Bros.—decided that television couldn't be licked, so it might as well be joined. They began to play into the admen's desires by producing formulaic half-hour and hour-long filmed series specifically for the home tube.

With a steady supply of situation comedies, action-adventure series, and Westerns, the networks had less need for live anthology dramas and less tolerance for scripts that might invite controversy with viewers or displease sponsors.

Increasingly, advertiser interference was making the work of television dramatists more frustrating as the Golden Age began to wane. Some of it was just silly. A manufacturer of a breakfast food, for instance, insisted that the line "She eats too much" be cut from a script. It might give viewers the wrong idea about the wisdom of eating the product in moderation.

Much of the sponsor and network intervention was more devastating, though. In 1954, when Reginald Rose wrote a teleplay for *Studio One* entitled *Thunder on Sycamore Street*, he was forced to make a major change before the drama could air. His original story dealt with a black family moving into a white neighborhood and the efforts of the residents on the block to keep the newcomers out. Rose was informed, however, that it was unacceptable to present a black man as the hero. In the final version, the character was changed to an ex-convict. Although he felt the compromise would weaken his play, Rose agreed to it hoping "the principle under observation was strong enough to rouse an audience."

By the end of TV's first decade, the authors of the medium's most sensitive and lovely dramas could no longer sell their wares to the networks. In 1958, Chayefsky complained bitterly: "Our country is racing as fast as it can into anonymity. We're all trying to be conformists these days. The highly individual drama, the experimental show . . . will never make the grade here, never. If I have to sit down and go to work to write for a bunch of poker-faced fellows walking around with a horse, I'll give up the trade."

In 1961, the Museum of Modern Art officially recognized television as a contemporary art form capable of yielding masterpieces such as *Marty*. By then, prime-time drama had already been completely redefined, though. The successful TV writer of the 1960s, as one programming executive explained, "should be someone who doesn't have the burning desire to make an original statement."

Test Patterns, New Patterns

In the early days of radio, people would happily listen to amateurish programs, but in the early days of television some viewers were so fascinated that they actually sat and watched the screen before the station even signed on the air. "I remember my favorite test pattern," a child of the era recalled. "It was the one with the Indian's head in the middle, on Channel 13 from

New Jersey." "I would sit spellbound," another TV tyke remembered. "Sometimes I would watch the test pattern, which looked like an Art Deco record label, for ten minutes."

"Once that television arrived my whole life changed" is a typical reflection of those old enough to remember the first TV set being delivered to the home. For their younger siblings it was just part of the natural order of things. But TV's initial presence in the household was more intrusive than radio had been, because TV was not as naturally integrated into the rhythms of daily life.

In the immediate postwar period, more people than ever before were listening to radio and going to the movies. The sale of radio advertising and radio receivers broke records in 1946. That same year the average weekly motion picture attendance reached an all-time peak of nearly ninety million. But as more people moved out of the cities and away from their neighborhood movie theaters, box office receipts began to decline. Television made it easier to stay away. Once the family owned a TV set, evening hours were likely to be spent in front of the tube. Television's arrival also put a sizable dent in the readership of general interest magazines, such as *Saturday Evening Post*, *Collier's*, *Look*, and *Life*, which in a six-month period in 1954 lost nearly one-quarter of its newsstand circulation.

Television wasn't simply replacing the time Americans spent with other media, though; it was changing their everyday patterns in fundamental ways. Mealtimes and family conversations experienced obvious strain. Yet, advertisements for TV sets in consumer magazines highlighted increased family contact as a wonderful benefit, showing moms, dads, brothers, and sisters enjoying each other's company while watching a TV show.

Parents, especially those who had experienced long separations during the war, wanted to believe in TV's ability to strengthen family ties. Popular literature fostered the notion that TV togetherness did indeed make families stronger, a view that some social critics considered naïve. As the author of one study in the 1950s concluded, "increased family contact brought about by television is not social except in the most limited sense: that of being in the same room with other people."

School teachers quickly detected changes when the youngsters under their tutelage got hooked on TV. More restless and rambunctious, they were harder to control in the classroom. In 1950, Mrs. Allison Palmer, greatly discouraged by recent discipline problems, resigned from her teaching position in New Jersey to move to Nevada, where mountains blocked TV reception. But of course she couldn't hide for long. Soon kids all over the country were reading less and watching more.

Although it was easier to do household chores while listening to the radio, the television networks aggressively targeted homemakers with daytime programming that wasn't attention-intensive—and their habits changed. Viewership became routinized. Programming patterns and living patterns merged. "My husband now dresses in the living room," an early fan wrote to NBC's *Today* show, confirming TV's ability to direct the activities of the audience. Clothing stores reported the sales of women's lounging apparel increased steadily with the rise of TV sets.

Within a decade after the end of World War II, TV dinners and *TV Guides*, products on which empires would be built, could be found in shopping carts everywhere in the country, purchased by consumers of every class and race. Television was shaping a national culture by providing equal access to entertainment, news, and commercials—programming that offered working definitions of the American way of life. The most egalitarian of media was dissolving differences, yet some divisions would not yield to the television age—and none was more intractable than race.

Fig. 2 A scene from *The Jack Benny Show,* with Rochester (Eddie Anderson) as a Pullman porter and Mel Blanc as an Indian chief, reflects the prevalent assumption of white superiority in 1950s America. (Terrence O'Flaherty collection of the UCLA Theater Arts Library.)

CHAPTER 2

Television and the Melting Pot: Race and Ethnicity

During World War II, black soldiers were not allowed to eat a meal, ride on a bus, get a haircut, or watch a movie alongside white soldiers. Yet more than one million African Americans served in the armed forces. Their fight against the racist policies of Nazi Germany endowed them with the moral strength to return home, not embittered, but determined to achieve racial justice.

The war produced a bounty of good-paying industrial jobs in the North, which attracted a massive migration of Southern blacks to the Northern cities in the early 1940s. The democratic rationale of the war, coupled with the opportunity to earn real wages, transformed the expectations of black citizens. Pride and activism soared. Between 1940 and 1944, membership mushroomed in the National Association for the Advancement of Colored People (NAACP) to 500,000.

A great country willing to sacrifice so much in a commitment to freedom abroad, black citizens believed, could no longer deny one group of Americans the basic rights guaranteed to everyone else. It was understood changes would not come overnight. But the Allied victories created a groundswell of hope that a new chapter in American history, one in which the republic was true to its founding promise, was about to begin.

While black and white soldiers were fighting a common enemy, a number of radio programs dealt with the glaring contradiction of American segregation. In 1943, after a race riot in Detroit left thirty-four dead and seven hundred injured, CBS aired an elegant call for civil thinking entitled "An Open Letter on Race Hatred," written and directed by William Robson.

But despite such efforts, the most popular commercially sponsored network shows relied on racial stereotypes inherited from the blackface minstrelsy, developed long before the Civil War, as a way to rationalize and justify the enslavement of African people. The comedy of *Amos 'n' Andy*, performed on radio by the white actors Freeman Gosden and Charles Correll, revolved heavily around the characters' misuse and misunderstanding of the English language—suggesting not just lack of education, but also lack of intelligence. Rochester, the valet and chauffeur on *The Jack Benny Show*, played by Eddie Anderson, was the most successful black actor on the air. Rochester was not ignorant but he was depicted as rascally, with a strong penchant for alcohol, shooting craps, chasing women, and "totin' a razor."

The advent of commercial television brought high expectations among black opinion leaders that these damaging images could be reversed. Publications that served the black community reflected an optimistic view of the medium's potential to be an outlet for outstanding talent and to present black Americans in a variety of roles.

There were early indications, though, that those who harbored such idealism would have their mettle tested. In October 1947, the DuMont stations in New York and Washington, D.C., carried a variety program called *Look Upon a Star*. When a white girl and a young black man danced together as members of the Katherine Dunham troupe, the stations were barraged with angry protests against the interracial routine.

Despite President Truman's 1948 Executive Order of full integration in the armed forces, racial polarization was a prominent feature of America's postwar growth. The Housing Act of 1949 offered contractors financial incentives to build single-family homes in suburban areas. The government wanted to alleviate the housing shortage caused by the decline in residential construction during the Depression and the war. The sharp rise in postwar marriage and birth rates worsened the situation.

Communities blossomed featuring prefabricated Cape Cod and ranch-style homes. But the practice of restrictive covenants in mortgages and redline zoning, intended to protect property values, precluded black citizens from purchasing a piece of the American Dream.

The model development of postwar housing, the famous Levittown in Long Island, turned away black applicants without compunction. In 1949, black war veteran Gene Burnett saw an advertisement for affordable housing in Levittown and drove to Long Island with his fiancée. The salesman rejected outright the possibility of their purchase, saying, "The builders have not at this time decided to sell to Negroes." Even rental contracts in Levittown prohibited "the premises to be used or occupied by any person other than members of the Caucasian race." Years later, Burnett told a reporter, "I'll never forget the ride back to East Harlem."

There were no government-sanctioned racist guidelines preventing black consumers from purchasing television sets, however. And they did so in great numbers. In November 1950, *Jet*, a national magazine directed to the black audience, began a special section that listed the appearances of black performers on television. Variety programs, notably Ed Sullivan's *Toast of the Town*, frequently featured black entertainers like Louis Armstrong, Pearl Bailey, Count Basie, Harry Belafonte, Ella Fitzgerald, and Lena Horne. Each appearance, warmly received by the studio audience, seemed to confirm that television was indeed an instrument that could dissolve racial barriers.

But, although black performers gained acceptance as guests on variety shows hosted by white TV personalities, integrated acts still set off alarms. In 1952, Governor Herman Talmadge of Georgia urged Southerners to boycott the sponsors of television shows in which "white and Negro performers are shown together." His attempt to muster a campaign was prompted by the regular appearance on *The Arthur Godfrey Show* of The Mariners. The quartet consisted of two black and two white men, all of whom served in the Coast Guard during World War II. Talmadge claimed he was "not opposed to Negro performers, as long as they appear alone." "Many of them are top-notchers and have wonderful ability," he conceded. But an act like The Mariners, the governor believed, brought "whites and Negroes too close together on a social basis."

A headline in the *Chicago Defender*, one of the nation's prominent black newspapers, explained succinctly the industry reaction to the threat of a sponsor boycott: "CBS, Godfrey Thumb Noses at Talmadge." The liberalism of variety shows was gratifying to black viewers. A new entertainment ethic seemed to be emerging. In a skit on *The Texaco Star Theater* entitled "The United Nations of Show Business," guest star Danny Thomas congratulated host Milton Berle for offering the country a program that was not just a showcase for talent, but "a showcase for democracy." "Danny, there's no room for prejudice in our profession," Berle replied. "We entertainers rate a brother actor by his colorful performance, and not by the color of his skin."

Comic Throwbacks

By the beginning of the 1950s, television was making real progress in integrating the variety show genres and presenting black performers in respectful ways. Situation comedies were another matter entirely, though. Several radio programs were adopted by television, and some made the transfer with racism intact.

In 1947, Hattie McDaniel, who had won the Academy Award for her performance as Mammy in the film *Gone with the Wind*, was cast in the title role in the radio show *Beulah*. The stories were built around her life as a domestic servant for the Henderson family—Mr. Harry, "Miz" Alice, and Master Donnie. Plots often concerned the problems Beulah had with her boyfriend Bill, who was depicted as lazy, devoid of manly qualities, and generally irresponsible. Much of the comedy hinged on Bill's avoidance of marrying Beulah.

In October 1950, *Beulah* made its television debut with Hattie McDaniel continuing in the lead. She stayed with the series until her death in 1952. Three other accomplished actresses also played the character of Beulah before the series left the air in 1953—Ethel Waters, Amanda Randolph, and Louise Beavers. The role of Oriole, the dim-witted maid next door, was played first by Butterfly McQueen, who had also starred in *Gone With the Wind*, and then by Ruby Dandridge, who added a signature high-pitched giggle to punctuate the character's simplemindedness.

Although the show provided employment to some of Hollywood's best black actresses, it also reinforced the definition of black life in America perpetuated by the movies and radio. Beulah, like the character Aunt Jemima, was portly, ever jolly, and, above all, loyal to her employers. Their happiness was her motivation.

Black critics, while still hopeful that television could portray the range and shade of their people's experiences, were energetic in their objections about *Beulah*. "Like all other people, Negroes appreciate humor," one commentator wrote. "But they resent caricature. Especially offensive is such stuff as minstrels, blackfaced comedians, 'yuk yuk yuk' laughs, lawsy-me eye rollers, superstitious beliefs and happy-go-lucky attitudes. But some TV shows persist in these very things. . . . The most flagrant violator is *Beulah*."

Just nine days after *Beulah* premiered on TV, the video version of *The Jack Benny Show* took to the air. For the previous thirteen years, radio audiences had looked forward to Rochester's sparring with his vainglorious and cheap boss. Even though Rochester could one-up Jack Benny in most debates, he was still the servant and could be shooed away at will.

In making the transition to television, writers who had never before considered the feelings of the black audience were forced to acknowledge negative reactions to the character of Rochester. In February 1950, a radio episode of *The Jack Benny Show* caused an unexpected flap. Residents of Harlem protested vehemently to CBS about dialogue that characterized them as crap shooters and petty thieves. An editorial in the black press explained the significance of their grievances:

> To some whites, such protests seem unjustified and they insist that Negroes are too sensitive, too thin-skinned about this race and color business. They point out that jokes are made about the Irish, Scotch and other nationalities and racial groups and no offense is taken. These whites do not know what a Negro experiences when he tries to get a job or a promotion in his position. If they did, they would understand why those racial jokes and clownish characterizations are not funny. For years white America has been propagandized into believing that most Negroes are natural clowns on the one hand or natural criminals on the other. . . . There is nothing funny about being a second-class citizen and being denied opportunities for economic and cultural advancement.

Though his criminal proclivities were toned down in the TV version of *The Jack Benny Show*, Rochester remained of questionable moral fiber. For the next fourteen years he was a sassy but dutiful butler-chauffeur-valet-chief cook and bottle washer on one of the top-rated series in prime time. Eddie Anderson became an institution in American show business. But he always maintained a defensive posture when criticized for his professional choices, claiming he was merely playing the part of one person, not the race as a whole.

In 1951, less than a year after Beulah and Rochester made their TV entrances into American homes, the transformation of another radio show became part of postwar culture. A generation of radio listeners already knew the backstory of Amos and Andy, of the Fresh Air Taxi Cab Company Incorporated, and their friends and neighbors in Harlem. Amos Jones was an honest and devoted family man. Andrew H. Brown was altogether different. He was shiftless, lazy, and not very smart. Andy's energies were spent eyeing women and making feeble attempts to get a fast buck.

A third main character was written into the storyline to add interest to the plots. George Stevens, known as the Kingfish, was president of the local Lodge of the Mystic Knights of the Sea. He was an outright confidence man who bamboozled the gullible Andy. In the later years of the radio series, Kingfish eased Amos out of the spotlight. On television the role of Amos continued to be minimal, as the program centered essentially on the adventures of Kingfish and Andy.

The casting of black actors to play the characters on television was undertaken through a much publicized talent search. Fans at the highest level took an interest. President Truman suggested the producers audition students at Texas State University, a black college with a highly regarded drama department. General Dwight Eisenhower recommended a black soldier he had been acquainted with during World War II. The roles were ultimately given, though, to experienced performers. Alvin Childress played Amos, Spencer Williams, Jr., was Andy, and Tim Moore won the part of Kingfish.

Freeman Gosden and Charles Correll, who were paid $2.5 million by CBS for twenty-year rights to the show, helped coach the TV actors in the mannerisms of their characters. Once, when Gosden gave Spencer Williams some advice on the particulars of Andy's black dialect, the actor bristled that he "ought to know how Negroes talk, having been one all my life." The point of the tutoring was not accuracy, of course, but making sure the vast audience would get exactly what it had come to expect.

The same month Amos 'n' Andy premiered, the NAACP was meeting in Atlanta. The organization, which had already gone to federal court seeking an injunction to prevent CBS from televising the series, passed a resolution condemning Amos 'n' Andy and other shows such as Beulah for depicting "Negroes in a stereotyped and derogatory manner."

Despite the controversy, Amos 'n' Andy had many defenders in the black community. The influential newspaper the Pittsburgh Courier supported the show for providing "lucrative and continuous employment for many talented troupers who have waited a long time for this kind of open-door opportunity into the great and rapidly expanding television industry."

Alvin Childress reminded critics that Amos 'n' Andy "had many episodes in which Negroes played attorneys, store owners and so on, which they never had in TV or movies before." And when the plot occasionally focused on the relationship between Amos, his temperate wife Ruby, and their sweet daughter Arbedella, there were moments of genuine affection and tenderness between black characters that had never before been part of American popular culture. All of these positive elements, though, failed to dilute the corrosive racism of the series, which was written, produced, and directed by white men whose objective was just to make people laugh.

Familiar images, such as shrewish black women browbeating their men, foot-shuffling characters avoiding work, and eye-popping reactions to the most minimal degree of danger, were executed with brilliant comic timing by the actors, making Amos 'n' Andy an undeniably funny, often hilarious, television show.

Mispronunciations and the malapropisms of Andy and Kingfish were at the heart of the comedy. The word "ultimatum," for instance, was always pronounced "ultomato." When reading "The Legend of Hiawatha," by Henry Wadsworth Longfellow, Andy says, "Took three fellows to write this, huh?" "Andy, dat's a long poem," Kingfish replies. "Read that first credenza right dere." In another episode Kingfish explains the basics of nuclear fission: "Now you see, Andy, first the atom splits into what they call the monocle. And then the monocle busts and breaks down into what they call neutrons, potrons, fig newtons, and morons."

The unfortunate result of this type of comedy was that the aspirations of black Americans to get ahead in life seemed ridiculous. The characters on *Amos 'n' Andy* were depicted as simply mimicking how they thought white people would express themselves. They were clearly ill-equipped to compete in the professional, middle-class world.

During its two-year production and countless reruns in syndication, protests about *Amos 'n' Andy* continued, as did its high popularity in the ratings. It wasn't until 1966, as a result of NAACP activism, that the program was finally removed from syndicated distribution, long after its imprint on postwar America was securely set like an autograph in cement.

In the same time period that *Beulah*, *The Jack Benny Show*, and *Amos 'n' Andy* were on network television, another group of situation comedies derived from popular radio shows dealt with the lives of white immigrants and working-class people living in urban locales. Among them were *The Goldbergs*, starring Gertrude Berg as Molly Goldberg, the quintessential Jewish mother; *Mama*, set in turn-of-the-century San Francisco and featuring Peggy Wood as Norwegian-born Marta Hansen, wife of Lars, a carpenter struggling to make ends meet for his growing family; and *Life with Luigi*, a short-lived series about a newly arrived Italian immigrant learning to love his new homeland.

The contrast between these two groups of television series is stark—the laziness, greed, licentiousness, and complaisance of the black characters versus the sobriety, restraint, thrift, and strong work ethic of the white characters. Naturally there were complaints that the broad humor and exaggerations of immigrant life fostered harmful stereotypes as well. But the strivings and longings of these immigrant characters were presented as inspirational, what America is all about.

Molly Goldberg mangled metaphors, Marta Hansen expressed lofty notions in broken English, and Luigi Basco misunderstood American idioms and often took things literally. Yet, their linguistic shortcomings were charming. Audiences were meant to smile in gentle recognition, not hoot derisively at their pretensions of upward mobility.

By the mid-1950s, as the growing suburbs were severing the ties of second-generation European immigrants with their urban neighborhoods, ethnicity in American life was leveling and television itself was contributing to the homogenization of culture. National advertisers were interested in stimulating standardized appetites on a massive scale. In 1954, even Molly Goldberg's family left their Bronxville apartment and moved to Haverville, a fictitious suburban community.

As ethnic distinctness diminished in the lives of real Americans, it also diminished on television. By the end of TV's first decade, the most popular families on the tube, the Andersons, the Nelsons, the Cleavers, the Stones, were of unidentifiable nationality. And their middle-class communities were conspicuously white. The legitimizing power of television defined the most pernicious trend in postwar America—whites fleeing urban areas and leaving blacks behind in the inner cities—as a natural state of affairs that need not be agonized over or questioned.

The Incomparable Mr. Nat King Cole

Thanks in part to their many appearances on television variety programs, black recording artists were enjoying enormous postwar success, none more spectacular than that of Nat King Cole. By the mid-1950s he was a top night-club performer with several million-selling records, including "Nature Boy," "Mona Lisa," and "Too Young." He was a frequent guest on TV programs such as those hosted by Perry Como, Milton Berle, Dinah Shore, Jackie Gleason, Ed Sullivan, and Red Skelton. Cole was in the mainstream of American show business. He was, in fact, an international star revered for his talents as a jazz pianist and uniquely gifted vocalist. Cole's TV appearances delighted audiences. He seemed a natural for his own TV show, which he very much wanted.

Nat King Cole had experienced virulent racism in his life. During the early 1940s, when he was on the road with the Nat King Cole Trio, being refused service at hotels and restaurants was a recurring indignity. In 1948, when he and his wife purchased a home in Hancock Park, an exclusive section of Los Angeles, white neighbors were so incensed they formed the Hancock Park Property Owners Association and tried to derail the sale with threats of professional and physical harm to the real-estate agent.

In April 1956, while performing before an all-white audience in Birmingham, Alabama—the second show would be for blacks—five men bounded on stage and one of them hit Cole with such force that he staggered backward onto the piano bench, which split beneath him. Another of the thugs began assaulting Cole as the police finally managed to pull the attackers away and get the fracas under control.

To the disappointment of many social activists, Nat King Cole was reluctant to take on the role of crusader. When he was criticized for playing in segregated venues and accused of upholding the racist customs of the South, Cole responded by saying that he was an entertainer not a politician and felt he could best serve the cause of civil rights by performing for white audiences. Because of this intra-racial controversy, his bid for a TV show brought with it a personal sense of mission. "It could be a turning point," Cole realized.

Cole signed a contract with CBS in 1956, but the promise of his own program never materialized on that network. Later in the year, NBC reached an agreement with Cole's manager and agency. The first broadcast of *The Nat King Cole Show*, November 5, 1956, aired without commercial sponsorship. NBC agreed to foot the bill for the program, hoping advertisers would soon be attracted to the series. Cole felt confident that a national sponsor would emerge, but his optimism was misplaced.

Advertising agencies were unable to convince national clients to buy time on *The Nat King Cole Show*. It was one thing for black performers to appear as guests on white programs but quite another for a black man to be in charge and welcome white guests—especially white women—at his discretion. It was a definition of race relations still too jarring to many Americans.

Just the year before, Emmett Till, a fourteen-year old Chicago boy visiting relatives in Mississippi, was lynched for saying "Bye, Baby" as a prank to a white housewife in a grocery store. Defending the honor of Caucasian women against lustful black male predators was a cornerstone of Southern segregation. Race mixing on television was a frightening prospect to those who believed in the preservation of white masculine power.

Advertisers feared that white Southern audiences would boycott their products. A representative of Max Factor cosmetics, a logical sponsor for the program, claimed that a Negro couldn't sell lipstick for them. Cole was angered by the comment. "What do they think we use?" he asked. "Chalk? Congo paint?" "And what about a corporation like the telephone company?" Cole wondered. "A man sees a Negro on a television show.

What's he going to do—call up the telephone company and tell them to take out the telephone?" Occasionally the show was sponsored by Arrid deodorant and Rise shaving cream, but most often was sustained by NBC without sponsorship.

The program featured orchestra leader Nelson Riddle when the show was broadcast from Hollywood and Gordon Jenkins on weeks it originated from New York. Despite its musical excellence, *The Nat King Cole Show* suffered from anemic Nielsen ratings. Nonetheless, NBC decided to experiment. The network revamped the show in the summer of 1957, expanding it from fifteen to thirty minutes and increasing the production budget.

Cole's many friends and admirers in the music industry joined his determined effort to keep the series alive. Performers who could command enormous fees, including Ella Fitzgerald, Peggy Lee, Mel Torme, Pearl Bailey, Mahalia Jackson, Sammy Davis, Jr., Tony Bennett, and Harry Belafonte, appeared on *The Nat King Cole Show* for the minimum wage allowed by the union.

Ratings improved but still no sponsors were interested in a permanent relationship with the series. Some advertisers purchased airtime in particular markets. In San Francisco, Italian Swiss Colony wine was an underwriter; in New York, it was Rheingold beer; in Los Angeles, Gallo wine and Colgate toothpaste; and in Houston, Coca-Cola

This arrangement, though, was not as lucrative to the network as single national sponsorship. So, when the Singer Sewing Machine Company wanted to underwrite an adult Western called *The Californians*, NBC turned over Cole's time slot. The network offered to move his program to a less-expensive and less-desirable place in the schedule—Saturdays at 7:00 p.m.—but Cole declined the downgrade.

In the inevitable postmortem on the show, Cole praised NBC for its efforts. "The network supported this show from the beginning," he said. "From Mr. Sarnoff on down, they tried to sell it to agencies. They could have dropped it after the first thirteen weeks." The star placed the blame squarely on the advertising industry. "Madison Avenue," he said, "is afraid of the dark."

In an *Ebony* magazine article entitled "Why I Quit My TV Show," Cole expressed his frustration: "For thirteen months I was the Jackie Robinson of television. I was the pioneer, the test case, the Negro first. . . . On my show rode the hopes and tears and dreams of millions of people. . . . Once a week for sixty-four consecutive weeks I went to bat for these people.

I sacrificed and drove myself. I plowed part of my salary back into the show. I turned down $500,000 in dates in order to be on the scene. I did everything I could to make the show a success. And what happened? After a trailblazing year that shattered all the old bugaboos about Negroes on TV, I found myself standing there with the bat on my shoulder. The men who dictate what Americans see and hear didn't want to play ball."

Singer and actress Eartha Kitt, one of the program's guest stars, reflected many years later on the puzzling lack of success of *The Nat King Cole Show*. "At that time I think it was dangerous," she said referring to Cole's sophisticated image in an era when the only blacks appearing on television regularly were those on *Amos 'n' Andy*, *The Beulah Show*, and Jack Benny's manservant, Rochester. Nat King Cole's elegance and interaction with white performers as equals stood in sharp contrast. "I think it was too early," Kitt said, "to show ourselves off as intelligent people."

Discordant Definitions

By the early 1960s, television was an undeniable catalyst in the momentum of the nonviolent civil rights movement. While the few black characters seen on prime-time comedy and dramatic series—maids, butlers, elevator operators, janitors—were acquiescent about their subservience, network news divisions were providing another picture. In early 1960, four freshmen from North Carolina Agricultural and Technical School, an all-black institution in Greensboro, walked into the local Woolworth's, sat down at the lunch counter, and ordered coffee. When they were denied service, they refused to leave and inspired a wave of students to follow their lead.

Television was committed to covering every step of the unfolding drama of the civil rights movement. In nightly newscasts, numerous documentaries, and frequent special reports viewers saw a revolution in progress. They witnessed the courage of the Freedom Riders, black citizens excercising their right to travel on public transportation throughout the South; the hatred of a rioting mob on the campus of the University of Mississippi when a black man asserted his right to register; the atrocity of German shepherd police dogs and high-pressure fire hoses repelling peaceful demonstrators asking only for the right to use the same drinking fountains and rest rooms as white customers in the stores they also patronized; the quiet determination of Vivian Malone and James Hood challenging Governor George Wallace's promise to "stand in the schoolhouse door" at the

University of Alabama; the grief of Myrlie Evers after her husband Medgar, an NAACP field secretary in Jackson, Mississippi, was murdered in front of his home; the ringing spiritualism of Martin Luther King's "I Have a Dream" speech at the 1963 March on Washington; and the pure anguish of the congregation of the Sixteenth Street Baptist Church in Birmingham, Alabama, when a dynamite explosion killed an eleven-year-old and three fourteen-year-old girls attending a Bible school class.

While network news departments kept the civil rights movement firmly planted on the national agenda, prime-time entertainment programming paid little attention to the ground shifting beneath the status quo. Then, in the TV season following the crucial summer of 1963, there was a breakthrough. A remarkable number of dramatic series featured episodes in which black characters confronted bigotry.

The provocative series *East Side/West Side*, for example, which starred George C. Scott as a New York City social worker and Cicely Tyson as his secretary, offered an episode entitled "No Hiding Place." A middle-class, professional black couple, played by Ruby Dee and Earle Hyman, moves into an all-white Long Island neighborhood creating tension in the community and panic over declining property values. The program has a bleak ending as For Sale signs spring up along the block.

The realism of such stories, which pricked the conscience of many viewers, was discomforting, however, as reflected in the disappointing ratings of *East Side/West Side*. The experiments in blending pointed social commentary about race with entertainment were short-lived. Beginning with the next season, the networks and advertisers retreated.

By 1965 divisions deepened among civil rights groups over the future course of the movement. The Student Nonviolent Coordinating Committee (SNCC) drifted toward militancy and away from the gradualist policies of Martin Luther King and the Southern Christian Leadership Conference. Stokley Carmichael, a former Howard University student and new chairman of SNCC, repudiated the traditional chant of "Freedom Now" and pleas for nonviolent action. "The only way we gonna stop them white men from whippin' us is to take over," Carmichael declared. "We been saying freedom for six years and we ain't got nothin." A new chant, "Black Power!" became the rallying cry of Carmichael's angry young followers.

On a hot Wednesday afternoon in August 1965, Los Angeles police arrested a black man for drunk driving in the Los Angeles neighborhood known as Watts. A crowd gathered, a scuffle erupted, police, perhaps overreacting, called for military backup. By Friday morning, five thousand

National Guardsmen were on patrol with orders to shoot anyone on the streets after curfew. Over the weekend, residents responded with Molotov cocktails. By the following Tuesday, fifty-four square miles of South Central Los Angeles were ravaged, four thousand people had been arrested, and thirty-four were dead.

In the shadow of this nightmare, the hopes of established civil rights leaders and organizations to achieve voting rights and equal opportunities in employment, education, and housing seemed far less radical. Peaceful, incremental integration sounded eminently reasonable. But it was too late to contain the wave of violence that had been set in motion. The intransigence of social institutions was maddening to a generation raised on television commercials that promised faster, speedier, instant relief. Why was the remedy for injustice so slow? For the remainder of the decade, racial disturbances became commonplace in urban America and the cry "Burn, Baby, Burn" reverberated with a rage that made the blood of white liberals run cold.

During the mid- and late-1960s, issues of race—matters of black and white—were presented on television with an odd duality. News broadcasts showed cities like Detroit in flames and provocateurs like H. Rap Brown claiming that "violence is as American a cherry pie." Entertainment television, on the other hand, was now populated with professional, attractive, successful black characters who all shared a fundamental trait—faith in American institutions and ideals.

Bill Cosby played Alexander Scott, a government secret agent, in the groundbreaking series *I Spy*, which premiered in fall 1965. His partner in espionage, Kelly Robinson, portrayed by Robert Culp, posed as a top-seeded tennis pro and Scott assumed the role of his trainer and traveling companion. Cosby's character was a graduate of Temple University and an Oxford scholar. His knowledge of several languages came in handy as the team maneuvered around the globe. Implicit in the cloak-and-dagger action was Alexander Scott's willingness to give his life for the country he loved.

On *Mission: Impossible*, Barney Collier, played by Greg Morris, was also a government agent. The series, which debuted in 1966, revolved around the fantastic exploits of the Impossible Missions Force, an elite group of specialized operatives usually involved in disrupting a foreign power's attempt to damage America or the Free World. Collier was an electronics genius on whose skill rested the success of complex schemes requiring split-second timing. Like Bill Cosby's character, he too was a black man who put his life on the line for his country every day.

In July 1967, what was to that point the worst urban riot in American history erupted in the city of Detroit. The death and destruction were so devastating that President Johnson appointed a special commission chaired by Illinois governor Otto Kerner to study the violence. The following February the commission's report concluded that America was moving toward two societies—one black, one white, separate and unequal. On prime-time television, though, viewers saw a harmoniously integrated country.

The 1968 series *Julia*, with Diahann Carol in the title role, was about a beautiful widowed nurse raising a young son. The series was produced by Hal Kanter, who had written for the *Beulah* show. A Hollywood liberal deeply affected by the civil rights movement, Kanter viewed *Julia* as atonement of sorts for the earlier, hurtful representation of a black woman that he helped create. Like her prime-time peers, Julia believed in the American way of life. Although her husband had lost his life in Vietnam, she was not bitter, but proud of his sacrifice.

The same season *Julia* appeared so did *The Mod Squad*. Three young adults who had their own brushes with the law saw the light and became hippie cops—"one black, one white, one blonde," the promos advertised. Clarence Williams III played Linc Hayes, one of thirteen kids in a ghetto family who was arrested during the rioting in Watts. On probation and floundering, he was recruited by the police department for the special youth squad. Its purpose was to infiltrate the counterculture and bust adult criminals preying upon kids who had dropped out of square society. The differing cultural backgrounds of the trio caused friction at times, but they could only get the job done by working together. Separatism was a totally defeating option.

In 1969, *Room 222* was set in integrated, urban Walt Whitman high school. History teacher Pete Dixon, played by Lloyd Haynes, and guidance counselor Liz McIntyre, played by Denise Nichols, were black, middle-class, and attractive. Their lifestyle underscored the lesson that opportunity existed for those willing to work within the system. By example, students—and viewers—learned that indignation would not bring financial security or personal satisfaction. Professional achievement did not come easily to anyone, regardless of race, but, as evidenced by *Room 222*, success was absolutely attainable through a lifelong commitment to responsible action and self-respect.

During the second half of the 1960s, television news and entertainment were presenting such markedly different pictures of black Americans that it felt like a psychological split screen. Nonfiction broadcasts were documenting the growing belief among some that the American system, shaped by white values and institutions that could not be trusted, was beyond redemption. The disaffected had no desire to be "assimilated" into white society through the benevolence of "good" white people who set the pace of change by the clock of their own moral evolution.

The comedy and dramatic series that came on after the evening news, though, offered a more comforting definition of American democracy in action. Contrary to past representations, as if to make up for years of scarring ridicule, TV now presented black Americans as so intelligent, hard-working, and wonderful that they would be welcomed in any neighborhood or workplace. The color barriers of the past would not impede their progress or diminish their faith in the ideals of the republic. Hopeful viewers saw such programs as models of cultural possibilities, appealing examples of what America could become in the remainder of the century. Those whose optimism had been fully eroded, however—perhaps with the murders of Martin Luther King, Jr., and Robert Kennedy—believed that stories of racial harmony and a truly integrated America would always remain in the realm of fiction.

Villainous Accents and Threatening Looks

In the second half of the 19th century, hundreds of thousands of Chinese laborers performed some of the most strenuous and dirty jobs in the American West, including the construction of railroads and levees and working in factories and mines. Their sweat created an infrastructure that contributed to the growth of the national economy. Hostility grew, however, among native-born Americans who blamed foreign workers for keeping wages low and stealing their jobs, leading to the passage of the Chinese Exclusion Act of 1882, which prohibited the immigration of Chinese labor, and its renewal in 1892 and 1902.

Sixty years later, a World War II poster meant to fortify the resolve of American forces in the Pacific showed a buck-toothed, bespectacled rat, with its tail in a hideous coil, wearing a Japanese army cap. The motto read "KNOW YOUR ENEMY." Indoctrination in the belief that Japanese soldiers were dangerously rabid animals and that all Japanese citizens were subhuman allowed eradication of the enemy to proceed without debilitating pangs of conscience.

On the homefront, popular culture fertilized the racism so effectively that the internment of 110,000 Americans of Japanese ancestry in concentration camps, in which they were stripped of their land, businesses, and possessions as a wartime precaution, could actually proceed without public outcry. Moviegoers, for instance, saw cartoons like *Bugs Nips the Nips*. In the 1944 production, Bugs Bunny passes out ice cream cones with concealed bombs to a crowd of Japanese. "Here you go bowlegs," the star rabbit says. "Here you go monkey face, here you go slant eyes, everybody gets one."

Movies and cartoons of the war era that vilified and demeaned "the yellow race" eventually made their way to television in syndicated packages that local stations could purchase inexpensively and run in fringe time periods. In prime time, though, Asians were essentially defined out of the mainstream of American life by exclusion. Those few who did appear on network TV were in the service of Euro-American lead characters, as if their own lives were not worthy of examination.

The assumption of white racial superiority, so ingrained in the American consciousness, was apparent in TV's depictions of Asian characters. Sammee Tong as Peter, the helpful Oriental houseboy on comedy series *Bachelor Father*, was one of the more high-profile Asian roles of the 1950s. Peter looks after the household of a suave lawyer who becomes guardian to his orphaned niece. He is not family, though, he is a uniformed servant. Another Chinese domestic of the era was on the TV Western *Have Gun, Will Travel*. Actor Kan Tong played a hotel worker with the denigrating name of Hey Boy.

Throughout most of the television age, the small population of Asian characters—whether Japanese, Chinese, Korean, Fillipino, or Pacific Islanders—were subservient to white characters and were not created to be assimilated Americans. Rather, they were newly arrived foreigners or complete aliens to the American way. Media studies scholar Darrell Hamamoto refers to these roles as "controlling images": for example, the happy-go-lucky cab driver Kazuo Kim on the 1960s detective series *Hawaiian Eye* who spoke in pidgin English. This characteristic is, Hamamoto writes, "a material reminder of colonial subjectivity" and "a continual source of amusement to his superiors. The treatment of the Chinese servant Hop Sing by the Cartwrights on the classic TV Western *Bonanza*, he notes, represents "implicit white paternalism."

In the early 1970s, the geisha-like Japanese housekeeper Mrs. Livingstone on *The Courtship of Eddie's Father*, presumably a war bride, played by actress Miyoshi Umeki, was typical of a prime-time Asian character—an exotic oddity. In the short-lived 1976 series *Mr. T and Tina*, actor Pat Morita was Taro Takahashi, an inventor who moves his family from Japan to Chicago. Billed as "comedy of clashing cultures," it reinforced the notion of Asians being outside the mainstream of American culture.

A 1976 made-for-TV movie *Farewell to Manzanar*, however, offered a surprisingly different and rare depiction of Americans of Japanese descent. On the eve of Pearl Harbor, the Waktsuki family is celebrating the twenty-fifth wedding anniversary of parents Ko and Misa. Their guests are of different races, including white friends. Their food and music are a mix of Japanese and American favorites. Viewers watch a middle-class American family, not foreigners with strange customs, lose its freedom. The story chronicles the Waktsukis' internment for the duration of World War II.

Asian characters were so under-represented and generally so poorly portrayed on television that the 1994 debut of *All-American Girl*, starring stand up comedian Margaret Cho, was considered a landmark. The premise of the series about a multi-generational Korean family was that the strict traditions of the parents and grandparents cramped the style of the Westernized lead character. The high hopes for the show however turned to disappointment when poor writing led to stereotyping for easy laughs.

In television's first decade, the "red man" was a one-dimensional character, as he had been for generations in dime novels, Wild West shows, and motion pictures. On numerous Western series, such as *Gunsmoke*, *Cheyenne*, and *Wagon Train*, which inspired countless children in games of "Cowboys and Indians," Native Americans were portrayed as ruthless savages, their intent on plunder signaled by blood-curdling war whoops, or as trustworthy noble savages subordinate to white heroes.

The most famous Indian character of the era was Tonto of the *Lone Ranger*. The radio series came to television in 1949. The backstory was that a posse of six Texas Rangers was caught in an ambush and five were slaughtered. The sole survivor was nursed back to health by a friendly Indian. The two men bond, not as equals but as leader and sidekick in avenging the murders and righting the wrongs of the Old West.

Most Indians on TV were not played by Native American actors. Tonto was. Jay Silverheels was a Mohawk. Though Tonto was a stereotypical role, many Native Americans believed, nonetheless, it was a barrier broken. In later years, Silverheels founded the Indian Actors Workshop.

At the height of the Western series trend, the Association on American Indian Affairs offered consultation services to television producers in an attempt to assure more accuracy in the dramatization of frontier life. The executive director of the organization asserted that historical authenticity did not require that white men be presented solely as ruthless invaders. But it did require the American Indian to be presented as "a brave defender of his homeland and a way of life as good and free and reverent as the life dreamed of by the immigrants who swarmed to these shores."

Delegates of eleven Indian tribes even submitted a petition to President Eisenhower protesting television's false portrayals of Native Americans as bloodthirsty marauders. Their primary concern was that through "constant exposure" of such TV images American children "will be taught the Indian is not worthy of goodwill." Not only were Indians typically shown as fiendish, they were often depicted as drunken or stupid. In one episode of *Overland Trail*, for example, when two white men face twenty Indians on an opposite ridge, the men decide to scare the Indians away with a bit of mumbo-jumbo. They jump up and down and throw sand at each other as the primitives flee in terror. It wasn't until 1990, with *Northern Exposure*, that a TV series would feature real Native Americans playing complex and fully developed Indian characters.

The rise of television coincided with the Cold War. The rivalry between the United States and the Soviet Union was an all-consuming philosophical struggle, a contest between democratic Western society with a capitalistic economic system and the communist Eastern World with an authoritarian government and a collectivist economy.

As the U.S. government mobilized alliances and military resources to combat Soviet expansionism, television joined the crusade and energetically produced propagandistic entertainment. Americans rightly feared Soviet designs for the postwar world. Prudent national security required vigilance. But much of the rhetoric and intensity of the Cold War were incited by fears of communist infiltration, imagined to be in every nook and cranny of the country.

The Red Scare, a paranoia about domestic communism, spawned programs such as *I Led Three Lives*, which was syndicated between 1953 and 1956. The series followed an FBI agent, Herbert A. Philbrick, who worked as a counterspy inside the American Communist Party. Philbrick ingeniously defeated sinister plots to undermine the United States initiated by those who took their orders from the Kremlin, such as introducing low-cost narcotics to American youngsters. "Your best friend may be a traitor" was the underlying message. The treachery of TV communists appearing on the rash of spy shows like *Secret File*, *The Man Called X*, and *Passport to Danger* was so potentially damaging to America that real-life violations like the broadcast industry's blacklists and loyalty oaths could seem justified to fretful viewers.

Children of the 1950s who learned in school how to "Duck and Cover" in case of an air raid came to understand the stakes of the Cold War through science fiction kids' shows like *Space Patrol*, *Captain Video*, and *Commander Cody*. The villains in these shows generally hailed from an alien tyrannical regime that bore a strong resemblance to the Soviet Union. Slavic accents—like black hats in Westerns—were a tip-off of evil intentions.

The launch of the Soviet satellite *Sputnik* in 1957 shook America's confidence in its technological superiority and triggered widespread questioning about the quality of the educational system, especially in the sciences. At the close of the decade, the brilliant cartoon satire *Rocky and His Friends* confronted that fear. The program featured a flying squirrel and a lumbering moose named Bullwinkle who did battle with Boris Badenov and Natasha Fatale, venomous spies from Pottsylvania. The American heroes from Frostbite Falls, Minnesota, weren't always smart enough to outwit their adversaries. Often their victories were the result of happenstance. But in the war between the God-fearing and the Godless, the virtuous would always win.

In the three decades after World War II, America's continuing economic prosperity and the remarkable growth in the standard of living was a trump card in the clash with communism. No country in the world enjoyed the same levels of home ownership, automobile ownership, and access to higher education. Middle-class working Americans had confidence that the U.S. economy was an expanding pie that their children would share. Upward mobility was a defining characteristic of American life. But an oil embargo against the United States by the Organization of Petroleum Exporting Countries (OPEC), which lasted six months from the fall of 1973 through the spring of 1974, jolted America's sense of well-being. The price of oil doubled, which ushered in a long period of inflation.

Countries that most Americans regarded as minor powers were now directly influencing the lives of U.S. citizens in frightening ways. A loaf of bread that had cost twenty-eight cents at the beginning of the decade soon jumped to eighty-nine cents. The cost of an automobile increased 72 percent in just five years. Although only seven of the thirteen

OPEC members were Arab nations, in the American media, the acronym came to be synonymous with the Arab world. On prime-time television a new ethnic villain began to proliferate.

The Arab caricature was of a people, undifferentiated by country, who were all fabulously wealthy, yet crude and uncultured with exaggerated unattractive features. They engaged in terrorism and sexual perversion. If left unchecked, they would buy up America from under its citizens. Camels, sand, oil wells, and flowing headdresses became a quick read for identifying the bad guys.

In private eye and police shows, the titillating theme of Arab men abducting gorgeous American women into white slavery was recurring. In an episode of *McCloud*, for instance, Ramal, the Arab bad guy, kidnaps American beauty contest finalists and takes them to his kingdom, explaining that he likes his women "blond, beautiful, young and innocent." If his captives refuse to be "willing, docile, and loving" they will be forced to work in a bordello that charges "twenty-five cents per customer." When McCloud frees the enslaved women who are guarded by saber-wielding goons, the ruling Sheik metes out punishment to his nephew Ramal. The audience is left to presume the successful completion of an earlier order by the Sheik that the guards behead Ramal "on the day of my birth".

In 1979, a second oil shock hit the American economy when OPEC reduced production. A 50-percent rise in the price of crude oil caused a proportionate rise in the price of gasoline in American service stations. The prospect of not being able to gas up at all created a panic among American consumers that led to hours-long waits in lines at filling stations around the country. From the pinnacle of power after World War II, America seemed to have descended to the unenviable position of being at someone else's mercy. The frustrations with those who bedeviled the country continued to find popular expression on the small screen.

In an episode of *Cagney and Lacey*, an arrogant Arab, named Hassan Bin Moqtadi, whose vanity license plate affixed to his Rolls Royce reads "OILBUX," runs over Saul Klein, an American Jew, and nearly kills him. Since Moqtadi has diplomatic immunity, he cannot be arrested or forced to pay Klein's medical bills. Cagney complains, "You know what ticks me off, inspector? In this guy's country you steal a piece of fruit off a cart and they cut your hand off. He comes over here . . . nearly kills a man, and we can't even touch him." When the two detectives visit Moqtadi's embassy and are served strong Arabic coffee, the women share a laugh as Lacey dumps hers into the nearest flower pot.

Americans' anxiety over an imperiled economy surfaced in comedy programming as well. A sketch on the *Sonny and Cher* show in 1980 featured bearded Arabs wearing sunglasses and pulling up to a gas line in a big Cadillac. "Fill it up," one of the men orders the attendant. Instead of filling the tank with gasoline, the attendant fills the trunk to overflowing with bags of money.

In sitcoms, too, Arab rogues were legion. In an episode of *Alice* entitled "Florence of Arabia," the wisecracking waitress, whose signature insult was "Kiss my grits," is wooed by an Arab oil baron she meets in the checkout lane at the Quick Mart. "He had a roll of bills with pictures of presidents I never even seen," she tells her co-workers. When Florence realizes, though, she is to be part of a harem, she throws a $100,000 engagement ring into a bowl of soup and tells her Arab suitor to "Kiss my couscous."

Throughout the 1970s TV producers and writers grew more sensitized in their depictions of various ethnic groups, in part because of highly visible protests. During the 1972–73 season, for example, *Bridget Loves Bernie*, a sitcom about a Jewish boy and an Irish Catholic girl who fall in love and marry, was vociferously criticized by rabbinical groups and Jewish media commentators for what they considered to be an oversimplified praise of religious intermarriage.

Norman Lear, producer of several blockbuster series of the decade, earned the respect even of those who did not always agree with him because he actively solicited input about scripts and characters from groups such as the Congressional Black Caucus, the Jewish Anti-Defamation League, various Catholic organizations, and the National Institutes of Mental Health. Yet, despite this emerging climate of concern for fairness and diversity in the production community, Arabs were still considered a "safe" stereotype, unwelcome even in the pretend land of inclusion.

In 1979, Norman Lear was approached by the U.S. Department of Energy's Office of Conservation and by a citizens group called the Solar Lobby. They asked the producer to convey messages of energy conservation in his shows. As a result, an episode of *Archie Bunker's Place* included a segment on setting thermostats down from the usual 70-degree setting to 68. Although the show offered a positive model of conservation, it also presented Archie's denigration of "Ay-rabs" as an understandable outlet for frustration.

Professor Jack Shaheen, who conducted extensive interviews with television executives and creative personnel regarding Arab stereotypes, believes the negative images were tolerated in TV programming of the

1970s and early eighties "because they have run out of other villains." One of the scriptwriters he spoke with advised that Arabs hoping to change their portrayals should confront the networks: "Any minority group that has achieved anything [in broadcasting] has done it through organized pressure. The Jews, the blacks, the gays have, and the Chicanos. . . . You should get to a point where a broadcast standards division of any network will say, 'No, we will not accept any reference to camel jockey. We will not accept anything that can be construed as anti-Arab.' If that can be done, I think the battle is half won."

Through his work in documenting Arab stereotypes, Shaheen hopes that the distorted TV images of Arabs will eventually take their place "in video heaven alongside other stereotypes—the black domestic, the savage American Indian, the dirty Hispanic, and the Italian-American mobster." But in the waning TV seasons of the 20th century, new examples of racial and ethnic stereotypes were still being generated.

Drama requires villains, comedy requires a butt of the joke, and television entertainment deals in broad strokes. In postwar America this was an unfortunate combination for those who spoke, looked, or lived differently from the rest. Television definitions, once infused into the culture, are not easily retracted. Old stereotypes don't just fade away or evaporate in the heat of enlightenment; they get recycled and linger in the popular imagination.

Pluralism Unplugged

Television figures prominently in the memories of childhood. But for ethnic Americans who grew up in the 1950s and sixties, those recollections are often of TV's blind spots and their feelings of exclusion from the television programs they watched. "As a Chicana child growing up in the East Los Angeles Mexican American barrio," ruminated journalist Maria Elena Gutierrez, "my earliest and strongest memories of Anglos and other groups came from my exposure to them through television. . . . Where, I wondered, was someone on TV who looked like me? Where were my family and friends? When I did see someone who looked like me, they were disappointing stereotypes whose exaggerated Latin temperament and accents were the focus of jokes, setting the stage for ridicule. . . . Latinas never appeared on my childhood television, except for the few fat, happy mamacitas, sexy senoritas or Latin spitfires."

The actress who plays the familiar character Maria on *Sesame Street*, Sonia Manzano, recalls growing up as a Hispanic child in the Bronx. She never saw anyone on television who looked or talked like her. "I know that if a child spends his life not seeing himself reflected in society," she said, "which mostly means on television, it will wear him down."

For others, the mere appearance of a member of their ethnic group provided a sense of validation. A young actor remembers: "When we were growing up, when an Asian person came on TV, somebody would say: 'Come quick! Come into the living room. There's an Asian person on TV.' And everybody would run and go, with this bizarre fascination: 'Oh wow, look at that. That's amazing.'"

Even the fondest fans of the popular *Andy Griffith Show* had to wonder why, in 249 episodes, there weren't any black people in Mayberry. It was an outrageous invisibility given the biracial reality of the small Southern towns on which Mayberry was modeled. Throughout the run of the series, Mt. Airy, North Carolina, for instance, had a vigorous chapter of the NAACP.

In the early 1970s, though, the television industry discovered that younger and better educated viewers – those most coveted by advertisers— were attracted to programming that tackled highly charged social material, such as racial and ethnic issues. The phenomenal success of Norman Lear's *All in the Family*, which premiered in January 1971, spawned a tidal wave of prime-time "relevance," much of it generated by Lear's own company, Tandem Productions, with shows that included *Maude, Sanford and Son, The Jeffersons*, and *Good Times*.

With this new cultural temper, TV's Cold-War unitary view of American society was giving way to messages of pluralist tolerance for diversity. Audiences expected to see people of different races and ethnicities interacting on the small screen. The 1974–75 TV season offered a kaleidoscope of characters, from Rhoda Morgenstern—the obviously Jewish neighbor and best friend from *The Mary Tyler Moore Show*, who now had her own spin-off series, *Rhoda*—to Helen and Tom Willis, the interracial couple who lived in George Jefferson's Manhattan apartment building in *The Jeffersons*.

Public controversy followed, however, as various groups became more militant in challenging the accuracy and appropriateness of their TV portrayals. *Chico and the Man*, another of the series which debuted in 1974, was about a cranky, cynical owner of a run-down garage who takes on an enterprising young Chicano as a business partner. Mexican-American activists protested the casting of comedian Freddie Prinze, who was part Puerto Rican and part Hungarian – he called himself a "Hungarican"—in the role of Chico instead of a Mexican actor. They charged that the series was often stereotypical and demeaning. Lines of dialogue like "Take your flies and go," when the old man wanted Chico to leave the garage, were offensive. But being part of the American mix, even if in a flawed vehicle, was progress in the eyes of some. "I think the show has great potential," said an activist hired as a consultant to the series, "I am 70 percent happy with it."

A mid-season series, *Barney Miller*, was a triumph of middle-class pluralism. Set in the 12th Precinct police station in Greenwich Village, the ensemble of detectives was an ethnic potpourri. Detective Wojohowicz, called Wojo, was too trusting for his own good and had trouble expressing himself with precision. The erudite black detective, Ron Harris, was a novelist at heart. Phil Fish, the Jewish member of the team, complained constantly and was ready to retire at the drop of a hat. Nick Yemana was a philosophical gambler who claimed he was disliked by some members of the police force because Orientals spoiled the look of the St. Patrick's Day Parade. Arthur Dietrich, who joined the cast in the second season, was of German heritage and could always proffer a psychiatric diagnosis for every problem. A colorful parade of saucy female detectives appeared often in regular guest spots. The captain, Barney Miller, humane and usually exasperated, was the only one of nondescript persuasion.

As America prepared for its two hundredth birthday, *Barney Miller* provided an encouraging, although certainly contrived, view of how the melting pot works best. The characters shared common goals and basic values but maintained ethnic identities. With a low flame of patriotism simmering the melting pot, the tiles in the American mosaic softened and fused at the edges—malleable enough to yield to the greater good without dissolving the unique features of each face in the American portrait.

The observance of the national anniversary in 1976, replete with the popular *Bicentennial Minutes* on CBS—a nightly vignette highlighting an occurrence on that date in American history two hundred years earlier—was the last great unifying celebration of nationhood before the acceleration of America's slide into social fragmentation. As the oil embargo began to sour the economy, all parts of the country did not experience the same outcome. Oil-producing areas like Texas gained wealth, power, and confidence, while the automobile-producing Midwest suffered a devastating decline. Americans seemingly weren't all in it together anymore.

Inflation skyrocketed the price of homes, which meant property taxes increased dramatically and savings dropped. The middle class, receptive in the 1960s to the federal government looking after the general well-being by providing medical care and educational opportunities, now felt beleaguered. Claims of oppression from various groups—feminists, Native Americans, Chicanos—that had borrowed language and strategies from the civil rights movement engendered more resentment than soul-searching. A growing emphasis on personal freedom rather than social cohesion led author Tom Wolfe to dub the seventies the "Me Decade." By the beginning of the 1980s, the rise of cable television coupled with the rapid diffusion of VCRs contributed monumentally to American culture becoming less communitarian and more individualistic.

In his 1980 reelection campaign, Jimmy Carter's attempted to sell a prescription for national healing that would require Americans to live more modestly and with an awareness of how their consumption of resources affected the rest of the population. Voters found this option unappealing. Ronald Reagan's victory was a preference for rugged individualism. Social Darwinism—survival of the fittest—was the overarching theme of the new administration.

The top-rated series of the decade, *The Cosby Show*, began its eight-year run in 1984 and was a perfect fit with the mood of the Reagan years. Although it offered black viewers a positive and proud view of their heritage through details such as the Huxtables' collection of African-American art, it offered white viewers the false illusion that racial equality had been achieved in American life. Cliff Huxtable, a wealthy doctor, and his wife Clair, a successful attorney, who instilled in their five children the importance of education, had a simple formula for the comfortable life they lived—good humor and hard work. Unlike the topical sitcoms of the 1970s, racism was never introduced as a plot conflict.

Over time the show affected how white viewers defined the problem of race in America. As one study showed, white respondents believed affirmative action was no longer needed in the United States. "If black people fail," one of the study's authors explained, "then white people can look at the successful people on *The Cosby Show* and say they only have themselves to blame."

The divide between black and white Americans in the 1990s was amplified by the disparity in their choices of television programs. There was a widening gulf between what blacks and whites were watching each night in prime time. In the mid-1980s, fifteen of the top twenty shows among black viewers were also among the top twenty for whites. Ten years later, the lists were almost completely different.

The splintering of the audience, accommodated and promoted by the multi-channel marketplace, strained the tenuous bonds of a pluralist society. By the nineties, prime-time characters were much less likely than they once were to interact in meaningful or intimate ways with someone of a different race.

Los Angeles Times TV critic Greg Braxton pointed out in 1997: "The core casts of *Mad About You, Friends, Ellen, Murphy Brown, Frasier, Seinfeld, Caroline in the City, Cybill, Life's Work, Wings* and several other comedies are exclusively white. The core casts of *Family Matters, Martin, Living Single, Sparks, Malcolm and Eddie, In the House, The Wayans Bros.* and *The Jamie Foxx Show* are exclusively black."

The decade's biggest hit series depicted voluntary segregation as a self-evident aspect of American life. When actor David Schwimmer appeared as the guest host on *Saturday Night Live*, the network's promo featured Schwimmer telling the audience, "You'll see things I never do on *Friends*." To which *SNL*'s black repertory player, Tim Meadows, quips, "Like talk to a black man?"

"In prime time these days," *Newsday* TV critic Diane Werts observed, "white is white and black is black." This trend toward separatism was exacerbated later in the decade as the fledgling networks Warner Bros. (WB) and the United Paramount Network (UPN) aggressively targeted black audiences with programs starring African Americans. "The so-called ghetto-ization of TV," according to *Detroit Free Press* critic Mike Duffy, "actually began with the original baby network, Fox, which has long appealed to young, urban audiences with such shows as *In Living Color, New York Undercover, Martin,* and *Living Single*." Comedian Steve Harvey, star of the WB series *The Steve Harvey Show*, referred to the programming of the late nineties on the big three, ABC, CBS, and NBC, as "the bleaching of network television."

In the summer of 1999, when the slate of network TV shows for the fall season was announced, the paucity of significant roles for people of color led the NAACP to threaten a "sustained selective economic boycott" against one of the major networks and its advertisers. The organization's president, Kweisi Mfume, pledged "to begin the new century with old-fashioned activism." In response, ABC, CBS, Fox, and NBC agreed to do better and make earnest attempts to boost minority employment in front of the cameras and in the creative process. There was little follow-through, however, on the good intentions. Faced with slumping ratings and a faltering economy, the networks failed to make diversity a top priority.

At the turn of the century, television's diminished focus on creating programming that bound the separate communities of the mass audience was defining away the cherished notion of the American melting pot. Fragmented media were promoting racial and cultural separatism that were leading to more than individual myopia. It was threatening the potential of the American populace to come together, willing and able, to successfully undertake a sustained national effort.

Fig. 3 Marriage and home life on TV would undergo dramatic changes in the 1970s, but in the 1950s, *Father Knows Best* represented the model American Family. (*Broadcasting and Cable* collection, Library of American broadcasting)

CHAPTER 3

Home on the Screen: Gender and Family

In the 1930s, the vast majority of Americans, men and women alike, believed that a woman had no business working if she had a spouse capable of supporting her. Twenty-six states had laws prohibiting the employment of married women. America's entry into World War II changed that conventional wisdom overnight.

As men went to war, women were needed to replace them in the work force. Unworried about their femininity, the new workers operated cranes, cleaned blast furnaces, maintained roadways, greased locomotives, and toppled tall trees. Those who went to work in the munitions industries welded, riveted, and bound keels until aircraft carriers and fighter planes were ready for battle. Women who enlisted in the armed forces served as nurses, typists, switchboard operators, and parachute packers, but also as truck drivers, airplane mechanics, cargo pilots, test flyers for repaired planes, and as flying targets for artillery training.

Working women, as symbolized by Rosie the Riveter and her "We Can Do It!" promise, were heroines in the war effort. Victory would have been impossible without their labors. Initially inspired by patriotism, many women were transformed by their new roles—for the first time in their lives feeling power and independence.

Of the six and a half million women who joined the paid labor force during the war, four million were former full-time housewives, many with school-aged children. The assumption of the government, which had vigorously encouraged them to go to work through the War Manpower Commission, was that they would go back home once the war was won. The official policy line could be characterized as: "OK Rosie, you've riveted long enough, now go bake some cookies."

Masses of women were summarily dismissed from well-paying jobs they had proven they could do well. Some went down fighting, demanding to retain their positions and end discrimination based on gender. But popular sentiment was not on their side. Patriotism now demanded that women give up their jobs to returning soldiers.

Traditional definitions of a woman's place quickly resurfaced and saturated American culture. In radio soap operas, short stories in women's magazines, and especially on the programming of the new medium of television, the modern wife was glorified for devoting herself to raising children and doing all she could to support her husband's career. Career women, on the other hand, were typically depicted as lonely and emotionally unfulfilled.

In television programs of the 1950s, women's aspirations were something to be stifled. Lucy Ricardo's hopes for recognition in her own right on *I Love Lucy*, for instance, were presented as outlandish, not as a natural and appropriate longing. Wacky TV wives who persisted in wanting to work invariably ended up failing and disgraced by episode's end. A 1952 episode of *I Married Joan* opens with Joan's husband, Judge Bradley Stevens, counseling a couple on the brink of divorce. "Being a housewife ain't enough for her," the agitated husband complains. "She's gotta have a career. . . . How can I hold up my head in the business circles in which I move?"

After asking the wife to leave the room, the judge dispenses his wisdom man-to-man: "Every woman feels this way in the early stages of being a housewife. . . . I had the same problem. But I didn't make your mistake. I didn't fight her. I let her try having a career, because I knew she would soon realize the daily routine of having a career is a lot tougher than the daily routine of being a housewife."

A flashback scene follows in which Joan decides she'll pursue an acting career with the blessings of her spouse. But instead of the glamorous dramatic roles she dreamed about, Joan only manages to be cast as a frumpy scrub woman in a Magic Mop commercial. So, just as predicted by her husband, she gives up her ambitions and happily returns to full-time homemaking.

The concept of a working wife being a source of shame to the male head of the household was a common thread in 1950s situation comedies. In a 1955 episode of *The Honeymooners*, for example, Alice decides to get a job after Ralph is laid off from the bus company where he works. Even though there are no children to care for and money is extremely tight, when she broaches the subject, her husband explodes: "Don't start that again, Alice. No wife of mine is gonna work. I got my pride. You know, no Kramden woman has ever supported her husband. The Kramden men are the workers in the family."

Alice prevails and applies for a clerical job at the bus company. But since there is a policy against hiring married women, she must say that Ralph is her brother. Attracted to his new employee, the boss asks Ralph if he can get him a date with Alice. Although Ralph's initial objections to Alice getting a job were meant to seem unreasonable to viewers, he's now redeemed because his wife's foray into the workplace does indeed carry risks to the sanctity of marriage. As soon as the layoff is over, the "happy ending" is that things get back to normal. Ralph's ego is restored when Alice quits her job and is once again dependent on him.

A 1957 episode of *Date with the Angels*, starring Betty White as newly-wed Vicki Angel, buttressed the belief that married women who work outside the home—even before they have children—selfishly diminish the manhood of their mates. When Vicki's friend Dolly, who works in the bridal salon of an exclusive department store, tries to persuade Vicki to accept a sales job, Vicki says, "Even if I wanted to, you know how Gus feels about my working." The next morning, while in the store shopping for a necktie for her husband, Vicki stops by to visit Dolly and reiterates her refusal to accept the job, "It's just that I don't want to hurt Gus." But when customers need assistance, Vicki ends up agreeing to work just for the day to help out in a crunch. By mid-day, she's wracked with guilt, "I'm doing the very thing he asked me not to." That evening, when Gus returns home he finds a contrite bride resolved never again to defy her husband's wishes.

"Betty: Girl Engineer"

Throughout the 1950s, married women who wanted to work even in traditionally female support positions found little encouragement in the stories of popular culture. But young women of the era who were brash enough to aspire to professional careers were deliberately and actively discouraged—on television as well as in real life. A widespread conviction in American education was that students should prepare for future jobs, not sample various curricula that would be of limited value in their careers. Since all normal girls were presumed to be on a track to marriage and motherhood, those who went to college were urged to focus on subjects such as home economics, child development, and interior decorating.

A 1950 book contended that female college students should be steered away from male-dominated fields. *Educating Our Daughters* was written by the male president of the all-girls Mills College, Lynn White, Jr., who felt working girls threatened the livelihoods of men hoping to enter that field and would also hurt their own chances at happiness in marriage. Young women of the postwar era were told in myriad ways that there was virtue in being self-limiting. Television underscored the message in bold strokes.

A favorite prime-time series, *Father Knows Best*, starred Robert Young as Jim Anderson and Jane Wyatt as Margaret Anderson, the lovely, bright mother who had gone to college but never pursued a professional career. Margaret has no regrets about her life choices. Her three children and her husband, an insurance agent, provide all the fulfillment she needs. Critics praised the series for its realistic treatment of contemporary family issues.

In one episode, Betty, the older daughter affectionately called Princess by her father, decides after a series of vocational lectures at her high school that she wants to become an engineer. Before she arrives home to let her parents know about her new enthusiasm, they're discussing a dress that Margaret has just purchased for Betty on a whim. "Why do girls act so silly over dresses?" Jim asks his wife. "It's almost simpleminded." "So they'll look feminine and trap some simpleminded male and get him to pay for all their silly dresses," Margaret explains about the importance of attractive garments in a young woman's game plan.

Betty, played by Elinor Donahue, bolts in the house and with dramatic flair announces her intentions. Her parents react with apathy. "Didn't you hear me?" she asks her mother, incredulous at her lack of excitement. "Yes, I heard you," Margaret says distractedly as she folds the dress. "But you don't believe me?" Betty wonders. "Certainly not," Margaret smiles, "you're joking."

Despite her parents' lack of support, Betty tells them she'll be spending her spring vacation working with a county surveying crew. Later that evening as Margaret is setting the table for dinner and Jim is reading the newspaper, Margaret asks, "Jim, she can't possibly mean that, can she? This business of going out with a surveying crew?" Her husband assures her, "After a day-and-a-half of tramping through the dirt and lugging surveying instruments, she'll be ready to take up some nice vocation like crocheting."

Betty, overhearing the end of the conversation, vows that she won't give up. In response to her mother's entreaty, "Oh, Betty, this isn't the sort of life for you," the confident young woman claims, "Girls enter all kinds of professions now and why shouldn't they? Answer me that."

"I'm surprised they'd take a girl," Jim muses. Betty confesses they don't know she's a girl because she signed up for the program using her initials, B.J.

Her father cautions her against plunging head first into such a commitment. "I'm not plunging," Betty protests. "I went to all the lectures, I took all the tests. It appeals to me. I love the out-of-doors and I'm no dummy at math." "No," her father agrees, "what little you've had so far, but wait until you run into trigonometry, calculus ... Do you realize engineering schools are some of the toughest to get into?" "So," Betty rebuts, "you think I should give up a thing just 'cause it's difficult?"

The next morning, as Margaret prepares breakfast for the family, she says to Jim: "I don't see how you can be so complacent about it. I feel as though we don't have a daughter anymore. I hardly know what kind of towels to hang in her bathroom—His or Hers?"

At home Betty encounters only teasing from her father and brother, but on the job site, she is directly challenged by the project supervisor, Doyle Hobbs, a college student completing his degree in engineering. "Why are you taking this up?" he asks her harshly. "What are you running away from? You mad at your boyfriend? Don't you like your home?"

"Look, I signed up for a vocational experience in surveying," Betty protests, "not psychiatric counseling." "Why don't you go home where little girls belong," Hobbs says. "I'm not a little girl," she bristles. "You're a girl and a girl has an obligation to be one. A woman's place is in the home. . . . the plan of life was worked out long ago. The male has his job and the female has hers. Don't confuse them."

Betty holds her own and asks impertinently, "Did it ever occur to you that the world might be changing? Women vote now, you know?" "Yep," Hobbs agrees, "my sister votes, my mother votes and my aunt votes. But they wear skirts to the polls and they don't go until they cook their husband's breakfast." The implication that her interest in a male profession is abnormal disintegrates Betty's moxie and she leaves the site in frustration.

Returning home, Betty is angry at the way she was treated and embarrassed that she fled. "Maybe it's all for the best," Margaret counsels. But Betty decides she'll return the next day and prove herself. Determined, she decides to review some engineering text-books to familiarize herself with the basics.

Back at the site, Doyle Hobbs learns where Betty lives from one of the other high school students. Later that evening he shows up at the Anderson home carrying a box of chocolates wrapped with a fancy bow. While Betty hides from view, Jim greets Doyle, and the young man proceeds to offer his opinion on a girl taking up a man's job. "It's not that she couldn't be an engineer," he says. "She might be a darned good one, but think what a dirty trick that might be on some guy . . . some young engineer, some young guy who works hard all day in the dust and heat—Why does he do it? So when the day's over he comes home to some nice pretty wife. That's what makes working all day in the dust and heat worthwhile. That's why your bridges and roads and everything are built—to make a nice place for the guys, their wives, and their kids to live. But if your nice pretty girls are out working in the dust and heat too, who are the guys going to come home to?"

"You're wasting this talk on me," Jim says, "You don't have to sell me." Betty, after overhearing Doyle's homily, sneaks upstairs and changes into the new dress that Margaret bought for her. Just as Doyle is about to leave, thinking that she doesn't want to see him, Betty descends the staircase and greets him flirtatiously, "Well Mr. Hobbs, I didn't know you were here, who did you wish to see?" "Yeah, yeah, this is more like it," the young man confirms as he admires her dress with a form-fitting bodice. "I'm so happy you approve, that I fit into your blueprint," Betty teases coquettishly. As the story closes, viewers assume she's jettisoned her plans to return to the surveying crew. Instead of high hopes to excel in a challenging career, Betty has a box of chocolates and a date for Saturday night. Normalcy has returned to the Anderson household and all is well.

The 1958 "Betty: Girl Engineer" episode of *Father Knows Best* is a striking, but not at all rare, example of how young women in the postwar era were conditioned to believe their greatest value was in their auxiliary status to a man. Jim and Margaret Anderson, paragons of rational thought to millions of fans, had no qualms about imposing a ceiling on the aspirations of their daughter. Betty is not rewarded for her courage but instead made to look foolish. And Doyle Hobbs, whose discriminatory conduct would be considered criminal in later years, is presented as having done Betty a favor, dissuading her from a path that, even though she might have the requisite capability to be on, would surely bring her heartache.

The definitions of gender roles on prime-time TV in the 1950s were so categorical that women who, in their hearts, felt conformity was more suffocating than comforting were often deeply conflicted. The trailblazing women who became lawyers and doctors and engineers did so in the face of criticism and doubt. At the dawn of the 1960s, women who had ambitions beyond marriage and childbearing found little to nourish their goals on American television.

I Nurture; Therefore I Am

"Contrary to popular opinion," explained professor of history and family studies Stephanie Coontz, "*Leave It to Beaver* was not a documentary." During the 1950s and 1960s increasing numbers of married women with families entered the labor force. Yet, television continued to depict mothers as people whose lives were lived entirely vis-à-vis their husbands and children. Those women in real life who looked for personal satisfaction outside the home, or just as a break from full-time nurturing, had no prime-time counterparts to validate their feelings.

There could be no higher calling for television moms of the early 1960s than taking care of their brood. The assumption was that married women gave up their jobs at the altar, even though by 1960, 30 percent of American wives were wage-earners. A 1961 episode of *Leave It to Beaver* titled "Mother's Day Composition" opens with Beaver's class receiving the assignment to write a fifty-word composition on "what your mothers did before they were married."

"When you were a girl," Beaver asks his mother after school, "what did you do besides waiting around for Dad to come and marry you?" June has no career on which to report. She had been fired from a department store after five days because her sales slips were such a mess. And during the war, she worked with the United Service Organizations (USO), helping serve coffee and sandwiches every Thursday to the soldiers and sailors passing through Mayfield. "Gee Mom," laments Beaver, "didn't you ever do anything exciting before you stopped being a girl?" That she once won a blue bathing cap in a swimming contest at camp does not assuage Beaver's disappointment.

At school the next day, his classmates tell of their mothers' pre-marriage careers with pride. Larry Mondello's mother was a dental nurse. Judy's mother was the chief buyer for the dress department of a big store.

"She was going to be made general manager of the store before she decided to get married," the pigtailed girl brags. Richard's mother was in the Women's Army Corps (WACs) during World War II and was sent overseas. She has a medal for service to her country. When it's Beaver's turn to read his composition, he's so embarrassed by June's meager accomplishments that he says he doesn't have the assignment. He's given until the next day to present it to the class.

That evening, while watching a TV talk show, Beaver hears an interview with a Broadway star about her colorful rise to fame. Beaver borrows her story for his composition. The next day he tells his classmates and teacher about his mother's life as a chorus girl dancing in dives and being befriended by gangsters. Everyone knows he's fibbing and June is called to school for a conference about the incident. Beaver is spared punishment, though, because Ward believes his son was motivated by love.

It's hard to say what's sadder about this episode of a classic TV sitcom of the era—that June was not encouraged to develop her capacities more fully or that the other mothers who did reach a higher plateau of accomplishment were expected to retire their talents and skills prematurely. The message, one that surely sabotaged the self-respect of many female viewers, was that a woman's potential—like fossil fuel—could be frittered away without regret.

Anthropologist Margaret Mead concluded that in regard to gender and family, "TV more than any other medium gives models to the American people—models for life as it is or should be or can be lived." In the early 1960s, the models offered on prime-time television regularly belittled the notion of women actively engaged in a sphere of influence outside the household. An episode of *The Donna Reed Show* which aired in November 1962 provides an explicit example.

When Donna returns home one evening after a meeting of a group called WIVES, Women Independent Voters and Entertainment Society—"Entertainment" was just added, she says, because they needed the "E"—she reports to her family that one of the women in the group was asked to run for town council. "They asked a woman to run for town council?" her husband Alex smirks in disbelief. "Who did they pick?" Sheepishly, Donna admits she is the candidate. Her teenaged children, Mary and Jeff, are thrilled for their mother. But Alex isn't as enthusiastic, "Did they say how they happened to pick *you*?"

"I haven't even accepted yet," Donna says. She explains she's reluctant because of her lack of experience and because "I have a full-time job just taking care of my family." The kids urge her not to worry about them, they're grown up enough to look after themselves. Mary says, "This country needs you. . . . Remember you are representing all of American womanhood." Donna asks Alex what he thinks about her running. "I never discuss politics with strange women," he replies. When pressed, he concedes the kids should be able to manage and "it would give you something to do with your time."

After just three days of Donna attending early morning committee meetings and hitting the campaign trail, the Stone household is in disarray. The kids are squabbling about Jeff burning the toast and Mary's inability to make an omelet edible. Alex reminds them they're the ones who wanted their mother to run for office. Their excitement is renewed when they see the morning paper displaying a picture of the new candidate. She's identified as "Mrs. Donna Stone, wife of a prominent pediatrician of Hilldale, Dr. Alex Stone."

Later that evening, Alex is maladroitly trying to sew a button on his suit coat while Jeff is looking for his toothbrush under the sofa. When Donna returns home, though, the family feigns order and congeniality so she won't worry about them. In response, Donna pretends she is pleased at their ability to get along without her.

Before turning in for the night, Donna tells Alex she'd like him to join her at a candidates meeting at 3:00 the following afternoon. "All the candidates' wives will be there," she remarks. Alex takes umbrage at being put in that category and says he can't make the meeting because he has commitments at work. Donna says, "You can manage it if you really try."

The conversation is so disturbing to Alex that it leads to a vivid nightmare. Donna's success in politics is chronicled through a series of newspaper headlines: "Donna Stone elected Councilwoman"; "Donna Stone elected Mayor"; "Donna Stone elected Governor." When Donna is elected President of the United States, Alex experiences ultimate degradation. A reporter asks, "Tell me Mr. Stone, how does it feel to be the First Lady?" When asked what message he has for young people, Alex says, "This is the land of opportunity. Any boy can grow up to marry the President." And just as First Lady Jacqueline Kennedy had done earlier that year, Alex Stone gave a televised tour of the White House explaining his attempts to "preserve the historical charm."

Waking up in a panic, Alex quickly comes to his senses. He shouts for Donna. When she enters the room he points at her and says sternly, "Now you listen to me." "I thought you were asleep," she says. "Oh I was asleep all right, I've been sleeping too long," Alex replies. "We're going to settle this political business once and for all," he tells his wife. "Honey, there're people waiting for me," she says.

"But what about your family?" Alex insists, "I suppose everybody else comes first." Donna is surprised when Alex tells her, "I'm tired of losing my buttons, I'm sick of eating leathery eggs and carbon toast and I'm sick and tired of being the First Lady of the land."

"We need you more than the country does," Alex tells Donna. With sentimental music swelling in the background, Donna asks her husband to "say that again—that you need me."

With great relief, Donna says of her short time as a candidate: "Honey, I've learned lots of things—I'm not cut out for this campaign business. It takes experience. Enthusiasm isn't enough. I'll drop out of the campaign."

Hugging her close, Alex says, "At least that's settled, now all you have to do is concentrate on being a wife." "Well one good thing about being a wife," Donna jokes, "you don't get reelected every four years." "That might not be such a bad idea," Alex retorts.

Later, Donna explains to the head of the women's political committee, "I just can't hold down a public office and take care of my family at the same time." "To be honest with you Donna," the go-getting professional woman says, "If I had a family like yours, I'd give up all this dashing around. I hope you know how lucky you are." Giving Donna a pennant from her candidacy, the committee woman says, "Keep it as a reminder of how fortunate you are to be the center of a loving family, to have an adoring husband and two capable, intelligent children. You have everything."

The moral of the story is that a woman has no business trying to make a difference in the world and that a man is justified in feeling diminished by the success of his spouse. Single women past a "certain age" on prime-time television in the early 1960s were the most pitiable of characters. Most of them, as in this episode of *The Donna Reed Show*, were merely bit players whose barren personal lives are juxtaposed with the emotional richness of the married star.

But one such character, Sally Rogers on *The Dick Van Dyke Show*, was a more substantial and recurring fixture who fortified the cultural stereotype that career women sacrificed true happiness for professional success. Sally, who works with Rob Petrie as a comedy writer on *The Alan Brady Show*, is one of the guys. The only difference is that she always types the scripts.

Critic David Marc describes her this way: "With Sally Rogers, the image of the single working woman is pushed to a new level of pathos.

Sally desperately wants to get married, but she can't even get a date because she's too intelligent, too funny, too aggressive, has all the qualities no man will tolerate. 'Sally' episodes almost always end up with Sally rejected by a man for having acted too aggressively and left alone with her cat—that really pathetic image of the single woman." A man's affection was considered more valuable than her special talent—the gift to make people laugh.

In 1957, Betty Friedan was given an assignment by *McCall's* magazine on the occasion of the fifteenth reunion of her graduating class of Smith College—to survey their satisfactions and frustrations since leaving campus. The answers to questions such as "What do you wish you had done differently?" were surprising. Women expressed doubt and resentment about giving up their ambitions in life for traditional marriages. Raising children was isolating and unfulfilling in and of itself. Their husbands continued to grow intellectually, while they stagnated in suburbia.

Friedan, herself contemplative about whether she had wasted time and talent trying to be a good wife and mother, realized that she had uncovered a major secret about American life. "It was like a strange stirring," she would later write, "a sense of dissatisfaction, a yearning that women suffered in the middle of the twentieth century in the United States. Each suburban wife struggled with it alone as she made the beds, shopped for groceries, matched slip cover materials, ate peanut butter sandwiches with her children, chauffeured Cub Scouts and Brownies, lay beside her husband at night, she was afraid to ask herself the silent question—'Is this all?'"

McCall's was uninterested in Friedan's piece; neither were other women's magazines. Friedan was challenging the myths they had helped create. She decided to turn her ideas into a book, a medium not dependent on advertising. After gathering more material over several years, she finally published the results, *The Feminine Mystique*, in 1963. Its provocative ideas gained widespread attention just as a feminist awareness was emerging. As in the civil rights movement, activists were seeking reform legislation to end discrimination, on the basis of gender.

In February 1964, Friedan wrote a two-part article for *TV Guide*. In part one, "Television and the Feminine Mystique," she explained that the title of her book referred to a "sophisticated mishmash of obsolete prejudices" that had built up in American society since World War II. Ideas such as a woman's place is in the home, women are inferior and childlike, and females are incapable of independent thought, action, or contributions to society were promulgated by psychologists, sociologists, educators, marriage counselors, women's magazines, and advertising.

Postwar women, she argued, were robbed of their identities. "This whole process is projected on television to such an extreme," Friedan wrote, "that the question is not only what the feminine mystique and its stunted, dehumanized, sick image of women is doing to real women, and their respect for themselves, or men's love and respect for women—but what it is doing to television."

The following week in part two, "The Monsters in the Kitchen," Friedan wondered, "Why is there no image at all on television of the millions and millions of self-respecting American women who are not only capable of cleaning the sink, without help, but of acting to solve more complex problems of their own lives and their society?" She posed a question to the executive producer of *Mr. Novak*, a popular dramatic series at the time based on the life of a high school English teacher, "Why isn't one of the leads in a program like *Mr. Novak* a woman teacher?"

Producer Norman Felton explained: "If the action is led by a woman, she has to be in conflict—with men or women or something. She has to make decisions; she has to triumph over opposition. For a woman to make decisions, to triumph over anything, would be unpleasant, dominant, masculine. After all, most women are housewives, at home with children, most women are dominated by men, and they would react against a woman who succeeded at anything."

"Television badly needs some heroines," Friedan wrote. "And television decision makers need to take real women more seriously—not for women's sake, but for their own. . . . I've had letters from thousands of these real women and, for whatever reasons they tried to settle too soon for this narrow 'little housewife' image, a lot of them want a second chance to grow. Television could help them get it, not keep cutting them down."

No sooner had *The Feminine Mystique* begun to crystallize the concept of feminism in mainstream American thought when a curious genre of television sprang up. In shows like *Bewitched*, *I Dream of Jeannie*, and *My Living Doll*, women with *power* caused big trouble for men who didn't want the old order upset. Plots were propelled by male attempts to control how females used their supernatural gifts. The comic predicaments resulted from the women's sneakiness. But in every episode balance was restored when the gals inevitably deferred to the rightful authority of the guys.

In *My Living Doll*, Julie Newmar played Rhoda Miller, a robot maid in a shapely human form. She does whatever she is programmed to do by her male psychiatrist boss, Dr. McDonald, played by Bob Cummings.

The sexism inherent in the very premise of the program was disturbing to any women who were beginning to recognize the truth in Friedan's analysis of popular culture.

In a November 1964 episode of *My Living Doll*, Dr. McDonald must finish his proposal for a book entitled *How Not To Be Dominated by Females*. He gives Rhoda an order not to let him leave the apartment until the following morning. When the publisher calls to reschedule the meeting for that evening, though, Dr. McDonald learns that Rhoda's "command circuit cannot be reprogrammed." When she defies his subsequent orders to let him depart, Dr. McDonald says of Rhoda, "She's getting too big for her plastic britches."

When the delayed meeting finally takes place at McDonald's apartment, he explains that the thesis of his work—getting a woman to be submissive—"is merely a matter of conditioning." The publisher is much impressed when McDonald demonstrates. The doctor says to Rhoda, "You may press my pants, please." And she responds, "And you may press my buttons."

Those who were feeling anxiety about changes in women's attitudes toward their traditional roles did not welcome the establishment of the National Organization for Women (NOW) in 1966. A group of twenty-eight professional women, including Betty Friedan, founded the organization "to take action to bring American women into full participation into the mainstream of American society now." Their agenda included not only fair pay and equal opportunity but also a new, more equitable form of marriage. Their grievances included as well an attack on "the false image of women" in the mass media.

By the late 1960s, a social and cultural earthquake was taking place in the United States. Many of the assumptions on which conventional marriage and family patterns had been based were being challenged. As the 1970s dawned, American women in real life and on the TV screen were ready to get their consciousness raised.

Hear Me Roar

In the wake of the 1960s struggles for civil rights and protests against the war in Vietnam, a full-fledged movement for women's liberation came into being. On August 26, 1970, the fiftieth anniversary of the ratification of the Woman's Suffrage Amendment, feminists conducted a "Strike for Equality."

Sprinkled with signs like, "Don't Iron While the Strike Is Hot," a huge parade in New York City and smaller demonstrations in numerous other cities put the media spotlight on issues such as equal opportunities for women in jobs and education, the need for child care centers, and feminists' demand for abortion rights.

Just a few weeks later, in mid-September, the debut of *The Mary Tyler Moore Show* brought an unusual concept to prime time. The lead character was an unmarried woman in her thirties. Although she wasn't like real-life female activists who protested the Miss America pageant by tossing bras, girdles, false eyelashes, curlers, hairspray, makeup, and high-heeled shoes into a "Freedom Trash Can," she was a cultural revolutionary nonetheless.

The first episode of the series implies that Mary Richards had lived with her medical-student boyfriend for several years—an unheard-of situation in TV comedy. When she eventually realizes she is being strung along, she moves to Minneapolis to start a new life. Mary applies for a secretarial job at WJM-TV, but the position has been filled. So she applies for an associate producer opening, even though the salary is $10 a week less. "If you can get by on fifteen dollars less a week, I'll make you a producer," news director Lou Grant tells her. "No," Mary says "associate producer is all I can afford."

Americans of that era who might have been thoroughly confused and disgusted by news reports of women forcing their way into male-only bars and clubs were eased into a new way of thinking about women's options in life through the weekly Saturday night ritual of watching *The Mary Tyler Moore Show*. In many respects Mary Richards was timid and self-conscious. She was the only one on the WJM staff who wasn't comfortable calling the boss by his first name. Lou was always "Mr. Grant" to Mary. But despite her sometimes childlike need for approval and conflict avoidance over minor matters, at the essence of her character was a woman who would not compromise her standards just for the sake of a traditional lifestyle.

Mary dated lots of men and would have liked to meet Mr. Right. But she was never desperate the way high school teacher Connie Brooks had been on *Our Miss Brooks* twenty years earlier as she shamelessly pursued the biology teacher, Mr. Boynton. TV's single women of the fifties and sixties were biding their time until matrimony would bring deliverance from the pressures of paid employment. But Mary Richards loved her job and grew in it.

Mary lived alone but wasn't a lonely or sad person. Being childless was a circumstance of her life, not a cause for sorrow. There were many avenues besides procreation for a woman of the 1970s to leave her mark on the world.

During the seven-year run of *The Mary Tyler Moore Show* great changes were occurring in American life. Women were beginning to experience more financial and professional success. Middle-class women in particular were marrying later, having fewer children, and getting more education. Inroads were being made in traditional male bastions. In 1971, the All-American Soap Box Derby admitted a female contestant for the first time. Four years later, Karren Stead became the first girl to win the classic contest. In 1972, women were finally allowed to compete in the Boston Marathon.

Many female TV characters of the decade contributed to a profound shift in how Americans thought about marriage, parenthood, and family life. Maude Findlay, for instance, was one who stirred up the national dialogue. But her voice was not as soft and sweet as Mary Richards's. Maude thundered her liberal political views.

The same year *Maude* debuted, 1972, Congress approved the Equal Rights Amendment and American feminists began an intensive, although ultimately unsuccessful, campaign to secure its ratification by two-thirds of the state legislatures. Opponents could point to Maude as everything that was wrong with women's liberation, and supporters could cheer as she demolished social conventions in each episode.

Maude was first introduced on *All in the Family* as the strong-willed, outspoken cousin of Edith Bunker. In her spin-off series, Maude lives in upper-middle-class Tuckahoe, New York, with her fourth husband. Her first three marriages ended in divorce, not widowhood. Maude's divorced daughter, Carol, in her late twenties, and her young son share the home with Maude and Walter.

In November 1972, viewers were stunned when Maude had an unlikely problem for a lead character in a sitcom. At the age of forty-seven, she was pregnant and unhappy about it. The episode called "Maude's Dilemma" had its genesis in 1971, when the Population Institute held a special luncheon at the Waldorf-Astoria hotel in New York. The organization was hoping to persuade TV executives to focus on population issues in their programs. Norman Lear, the creator of *Maude*, was one of those in attendance. The Population Institute continued efforts to educate Hollywood's creative decision-makers throughout the following year, succeeding in capturing Lear's personal interest. When several late-life pregnancy ideas were pitched to Lear by scriptwriters, he decided to go with the storyline.

"When we were working on the story," Lear said, "it became clear to me that there was no way we could let it be a false pregnancy or have an accident that caused the baby to be aborted. . . . So then I knew we had on our hands the difficult job of dealing with abortion fairly and getting it on the network."

It took Maude two episodes to reach her final decision to terminate her pregnancy. Initially, the distressed character is prepared to accept her fate and begin to raise another child as she approaches menopause. But Maude's daughter suggests that her mother consider an abortion. "We're free," Carol tells her mother. "We finally have the right to decide what we can do with our own bodies. . . . There's no reason to feel guilty and there's no reason to be afraid."

Maude's decision is not made lightly. But when she does finally opt for the abortion, she also convinces her husband to undergo a vasectomy. Although Walter chickens out of having the operation, the audience is led to believe he will eventually muster the courage to go through with it. More than fifty million American families observed the Findlays agonizing over and working through their predicament.

Waves of protest followed. The National Council of Catholic Bishops unsuccessfully demanded equal time from CBS to present the other side of the abortion issue. Church leaders understood and were frightened by the power of entertainment to unfetter long-held canons.

When the *Maude* abortion episodes were first broadcast in November 1972, the Supreme Court had not yet handed down the *Roe* v. *Wade* ruling and abortion was still illegal in some parts of the country. But on January 22, 1973, the landmark decision legalized abortion in every state. So when the episodes were rerun in the summer of 1973, all American women had the same prerogative to choose.

As the series progressed, Maude's advancing age did not lessen her feisty ways. She argued that marijuana should be legalized. She went through the change of life and had a facelift. On her fiftieth birthday she visited a psychotherapist. When the series ended in 1978, Maude was contemplating a career in politics.

Another Lear-created female character who reframed perceptions of women in the seventies was Ann Romano of *One Day At a Time*, played by Bonnie Franklin. A divorced mother in her thirties raising two teen-aged daughters, she retained her own surname after her separation and asked to be referred to as "Ms." Many Americans found these new cultural conventions easier to accept coming from Ann Romano than from Gloria Steinem, the publisher of *Ms.* magazine. "Our divorcee isn't a chicly turned out woman of the world," Norman Lear explained about Romano's wide appeal. "She is vulnerable and scared."

The backstory of the 1975 series was that Ann Romano married at age seventeen and divorced seventeen years later. When her ex-husband has a financial setback, he stops paying child support. She has every reason to despair, but instead she plugs away at making a better life for herself and her kids. Her determination never wavers. When Ann Romano encounters unfairness because she is a woman, viewers who might have easily overlooked biased conditions in their own world shared her frustration.

By the mid-1970s women were assuming higher level positions in government, business, labor, the judiciary, and the military. The character of Billie Newman, played by Linda Kelsey in the 1977 series *Lou Grant*, also helped give viewers a sense of how tough a climb it was to the top. The hour-long drama revolved around the newsroom of the *Los Angeles Tribune*, where Lou Grant landed the job of city editor after being fired from WJM in the final episode of *The Mary Tyler Moore Show.*

Upon Billie's arrival at the paper as a new reporter, she's assigned to write a piece for the "Women's Page" on an art exhibition. When a famous playwright drops dead while attending the event, the story instantly becomes hard news bound for page one. Billie's male colleague from the city desk, Joe Rossi, steps in and says "Look, this is my story." But Billie doesn't let go and Rossi gets a lesson in the folly of underestimating a woman. Her tenacity earns Billie a transfer from the women's feature section to the city desk, where she and Rossi are equals.

Unlike Mary Richards, Billie Newman, who was several years younger, was not deferential to her boss. He was never "Mr. Grant" to Billie, always "Lou." She stood up for her rights and wasn't afraid to spar with those whose judgment she questioned. Billie was an ideal role model for the rapidly increasing number of female university students majoring in journalism in the late-1970s. Like other assertive female characters striving to be heard, Billie Newman sent a cultural message loud and clear in that decade. Barriers to women's professional progress and personal satisfaction would not fall until voices were raised in protest.

Families in Flux

As the 1980s began, the possibilities for women seemed boundless. The number of cities with female mayors, including Chicago, Honolulu,

Houston, and San Francisco, increased with each election. Sandra Day O'Connor's appointment as the first woman Supreme Court Associate Justice in 1981 was an inspiring accomplishment. School girls playing house had many more scenarios than their mothers ever imagined.

"Having it all" was the media buzz phrase for contemporary women. The ideal new American woman excelled at a demanding career, had a loving marriage that was a true partnership, lively, maybe even mischievous, but good kids; the house was never a mess even though she employed no hired help; and she looked better than anyone else at her high school reunion.

One such character was Elyse Keaton, played by Meredith Baxter Birney in *Family Ties*, which debuted in 1982. Ms. Keaton is the exemplary Super Woman of the era. The comic foundation of the series was that the parents were former flower children of the sixties who were still liberal and idealistic as the Reagan years picked up steam. Their oldest son, Alex, age seventeen when the series began, had developed into a true-blue conservative. It was the typical Generation Gap in reverse.

Elyse and husband Steven, manager of a public television station, had served in the Peace Corps before starting a family, which eventually would include four children—after Alex came Mallory, Jennifer, and Andy. Exactly when and how Elyse managed to study architecture and enter the arduous profession was not made clear to viewers. But fans of *Family Ties* happily overlooked the incongruities of the Keaton family history.

Few episodes in the show's six-year run involved Elyse's work. She didn't seem to spend long hours at the office and was never seen at a home drafting table. Being an architect was incidental to her character. While millions of American women in the early 1980s were experiencing the "Divided Life" phenomenon, the conflict between being a mother and a professional, Elyse Keaton was somehow exempt from the epidemic of anxiety.

Show creator Gary David Goldberg explains that the professional lives of the parents were of far less significance to the series than what happened in the home: "The turning point for us was to realize that those small intra-family shows—Jennifer is using Mallory's wardrobe without asking or someone's opened two milks—those moments have tremendous resonance for our audience."

"Three things have to happen for *Family Ties* to be successful," he said. "One is the audience has to want to be a part of that family. Then, the second thing is, they have to see themselves in that family. And the third thing, and a very important thing, is the audience has to begin to want to watch because they think they can learn how to be a better family."

Another series which also premiered in 1982, however, acknowledged head-on that working women with families needed to be skillful jugglers. *Cagney and Lacey*, starring Sharon Gless and Tyne Daley in the title roles, was a police drama like none other on television. Detective Chris Cagney was single, ambitious, and often hot-tempered. Her partner Mary Beth Lacey was a married mother of two boys and eventually went through a third pregnancy and gave birth to a daughter.

Harvey Lacey, Mary Beth's husband, experienced the irregular employment patterns of his construction trade. So, he willingly took on the primary homemaking duties. He was a good cook and an able parent and he went out of his way to please his spouse when she came home from a long shift. Harvey and Mary Beth were a couple who clearly enjoyed each other's company.

But their mutual affection could not eliminate all the stresses in their lives. "Give me a break, Mary Beth," Harvey complained in one episode. "I haven't had a job in three-and-a-half weeks. It gets to a guy." Reassuring her husband that his contributions in the home were equivalent to her paid employment, she says, "Harvey, we both work—even steven."

Despite their professional advances, in the early 1980s real-life working women continued to carry the brunt of household tasks. A family counselor who saw many exhausted women in her practice felt that *Cagney and Lacey* provided a new model for some of her clients. "About two years after I began visiting with the Holts," she recalled, "I began to see their problem in a certain light: as a conflict between their two gender ideologies. Nancy wanted to be the sort of woman who was needed and appreciated both at home and at work—like Lacey, she told me, on the television show *Cagney and Lacey*."

"She wanted Evan to appreciate her for being a caring social worker, a committed wife, and a wonderful mother. But she cared just as much that she be able to appreciate Evan for what he contributed at home, not just how he supported the family. She would feel proud to explain to women friends that she was married to one of these rare 'new men.'"

Cagney and Lacey won kudos for treating women's issues such as date rape, abortion, sexual harassment, and domestic violence. But the series' more subtle and important contribution was in showing that female friendship could be deep and true and that women could be capable workers and effective bosses in the most stressful circumstances.

Another pair of female buddies entered prime time in 1984, the year Geraldine Ferraro became the first woman vice-presidential candidate, running with Walter Mondale on the Democratic ticket. *Kate and Allie* was a reflection of the profound changes the family structure was undergoing. Longtime girlfriends Kate McArdle, played by Susan St. James, and Allie Lowell, played by Jane Curtin, move in together in a New York Greenwich Village apartment after divorces force them into the growing ranks of single mothers. Sharing rent and the responsibilities of raising children helps them make it through the difficulties caused by their diminished resources.

At the time of Ronald Reagan's reelection, the rising divorce rate meant that about a quarter of first marriages ended by the time a woman reached her fortieth birthday. The idea of the American family as a lasting and cohesive unit, economically supported by the father and emotionally nurtured by a mother, was becoming more myth than reality.

Motherhood was no longer perceived as a full-time, lifelong occupation. Stay-at-home Moms disappeared from TV screens. Even television's intact families of the mid-1980s, like the Huxtables of *The Cosby Show* and the Seavers of *Growing Pains*, operated on the assumption Mom had a career and a life separate from the household. But, despite great gains in the work force, women were still primarily gender-segregated in lower paying jobs, earning about two-thirds as much as men.

The unflappable career wives on prime time in the 1980s were an impossible ideal to emulate. "In the real world," a TV critic observed, "women work to keep out of poverty and send their kids to college. They are fatigued and short-tempered." Blue-collar family life, with all its stresses and strains, was rarely depicted on television. But in 1988, with the debut of *Roseanne,* American viewers got an entirely different take on the tribulations of a working mother.

Roseanne is on the slow track, the stagnant track, to success and financial security. Though her real dream was to be a writer, she now works in a plastics factory. When that job evaporates, she is variously employed as a fast-food operative, a bartender, and a telephone salesperson. Roseanne's income is the linchpin in the Conners' fragile economic situation. Husband Dan, a construction worker, is often idle in the recession-hit town of Landford, Illinois.

"When I speak, I'm speaking for all womankind," Roseanne Conner declared—not only polyester-clad, Chee-tos-eating, overweight wives and mothers like her, but all women whose lives seem like a perpetual double shift. Dan and the kids don't cheerfully help out around the house. Dishes, laundry, and garbage pile up. "I wanted to send a message about how much we mothers really do," said the show's star and creative force, Roseanne Barr, during its first season.

Roseanne provided few affirmations of family as refuge from the harsh world outside the front door. When teenage daughter Darlene gets on her nerves, Roseanne doesn't chalk it up to a difficult phase of adolescence as Donna Stone would do. Instead she tells her daughter to get a fork out of the drawer and "stick it through your tongue."

Regular viewers of *Roseanne* learn that Dan has a temper. Mostly he keeps it in check. But in one episode he throws all the furniture in the front yard. His family—and his audience—knows it will probably happen again.

Money problems are constant. Roseanne's method of paying bills is: "You pay the ones marked final notice and throw the rest away." When that strategy failed once and the electricity was shut off because Roseanne chose to pay the water bill, her sister Jackie asked, "Did you tell them you have children?" "No, they don't want 'em," Roseanne cracked.

The series quickly became a blockbuster hit, heralded for its willingness to deal with hard realities. The crassness of the Conners, though, was troubling to many observers. Roseanne's sarcasm toward her children was especially unnerving to viewers who believed in the modeling power of the medium. "Couldn't that just squelch some people, the way Roseanne speaks to her children?" wondered Barbara Billingsley, the actress who portrayed June Cleaver on *Leave It to Beaver*. "I wouldn't want to be treated that way. I wouldn't want to treat kids that way."

Hope was not abundant for the Conners as the 1990s approached. Little had been saved for college educations and Dan's attempt to run his own motorcycle business went bust. The distressed condition of the American family, on TV and off, was seen by many as a dangerous element in the future of the nation. The age-old debate over whether television was as an active shaper of social dynamics or merely a reflector even ignited presidential politics.

Nuclear Family Meltdown

In 1945, 80 percent of American children were raised in a family and lived with two biological parents who were married to each other. When the family unit was broken by the death of a spouse, it was tragic. When it was broken by divorce, it was considered both tragic and shameful and often the children were unjustly stigmatized. Fifty years later, a child therapist observed, "There are already neighborhoods in this country where a child is considered an oddball if he grows up in the same house with both biological parents."

For the sake of pathos and plot, television has always presented non-traditional families. Widowers, just about ready to put their pain in the past and get on with life, such as Steve Douglas on *My Three Sons* or Tom Corbett on *The Courtship of Eddie's Father*, were especially attractive characters. Having cute kids plus the freedom to date provided a wide range of storylines.

Television's happiest blended family, *The Brady Bunch*, was formed when a widow with three daughters marries a widower with three sons. No one could begrudge their union. But most children in the audience who were growing up with step-siblings and stepparents were coping with stickier family dynamics than the Brady kids. Divorce was the reason for the reshuffling of their young lives.

By the end of the 1980s, divorce and remarriage were still less prevalent on television than in real life, but reconstituted families were growing more commonplace on the small screen in series such as *Life Goes On* and *Step By Step*. The ideal was still a family formation in which a mother and a father raised children together.

As the 1990s began, demographic trends were indicating that the standard concept of family was eroding in American society. Childbearing and childrearing were increasingly severed from marriage. Births by single women were skyrocketing. Between 1980 and 1992, the birth rate for unmarrieds rose by 54 percent.

What some saw as increased diversity in families others saw as evidence of moral decay. Regardless of the viewpoint, however, social science was providing ample evidence that children in families headed by unmarried mothers were at far greater risk than children in two-parent families for emotional and behavioral problems, brushes with the law, and dropping out of school.

On television unwed motherhood was being introduced in situation comedies and dramas as an accepted, unscandalous occurrence. Rebecca, the manager of the bar on *Cheers*, for instance, decides to ask Sam Malone to impregnate her and fulfill her maternal instincts before her biological clock reaches midnight. On *Designing Women,* Mary Jo, a divorced mother of two, is artificially inseminated by an unknown donor to a sperm bank. Although she miscarries, she vows to try again. Policy makers and child experts were cautioning that television's portrayal of unmarried women attempting pregnancy as groundbreaking heroines was not in the best interest of American children. The mainstreaming of single motherhood hit a sensitive cultural nerve.

When the forty-year-old-plus title character of *Murphy Brown,* a rich and famous TV journalist, became pregnant, a long-simmering debate about family values came to a full boil. An episode in which real-life anchorwomen attended a baby shower for Murphy prompted reviews questioning the show's "celebration" of single parenthood. A column appearing in *The Washington Post* on Mother's Day called "this new cultural idea" one that was "hostile to the needs of children."

Months before Murphy Brown's protruding tummy reached its utmost, President George H.W. Bush's 1992 reelection campaign had announced that the decline in traditional values would be a major theme of the Republican Party. Vice-president Dan Quayle decided to seize the moment as the hoopla surrounding Murphy's impending delivery on the show's season finale heightened in May 1992. Campaigning in San Francisco, he said that America suffered from "a poverty of values." The Vice-president claimed "the anarchy and lack of structure in our inner cities are testament to how quickly civilization falls apart when the family foundation cracks." "Bearing babies irresponsibly," he said, "is simply wrong." The character of Murphy Brown, he added, "doesn't help matters" by "mocking the importance of fathers, by bearing a child alone and calling it just another 'lifestyle choice.'"

The denunciation of *Murphy Brown* instantly became a consuming issue of national attention. *The New York Times* reported: "Thailand is in turmoil, the Federal deficit is ballooning and hot embers of racial resentment still smolder in the ruins of inner-city Los Angeles. But today the high councils of government were preoccupied with a truly vexing question: Is Murphy Brown really a tramp?"

Caught off-guard by the brouhaha, President Bush, meeting at the White House with Prime Minister Brian Mulroney of Canada, explained to clamoring reporters, "I don't know that much about the show. . . . I've told you I don't want any more questions about it." Exasperated, Bush turned to Mulroney and said, "I told you this was the issue. You thought I was kidding."

The producer of *Murphy Brown*, Diane English, responded to Vice-president Quayle by saying: "If he believes that a woman cannot adequately raise a child without a father, then he'd better make sure abortion remains safe and legal." White House spokesman Marlin Fitzwater, who initially endorsed the Vice-president's remarks heartily, soon praised the series for exhibiting "pro-life values which we think are good." The confusion in public statements reinforced Dan Quayle's unfortunate image as a blunderer, prone to speaking out before measuring his words.

When Murphy Brown finally gave birth to a baby boy whose father was her former husband, thirty-eight million viewers were present in the delivery room. The contentiousness of the family values debate grew more bitter as Campaign '92 progressed. At the Emmy Awards ceremony in Hollywood in late August, *Murphy Brown* was named the winner for Outstanding Comedy Series. Accepting the award, Diane English thanked sponsors who did not back away from the program in the wake of criticism. "I would also like to thank in particular all the single parents out there who, either by choice or necessity, are raising their kids alone. Don't let anybody tell you you're not a family." Then she added, "As Murphy herself said, I couldn't possibly do a worse job raising my kid alone than the Reagans did with theirs."

Because of the partisan nature of the debate in an election year, many Democrats and liberals were loath to say they agreed with Dan Quayle. He might, in their view, have been hypocritical, but he wasn't entirely wrong. It was impossible to deny that culture affects behavior. "It pains me to admit it," wrote an editorialist in the trade journal *Electronic Media*, "but Dan Quayle has a point about Murphy Brown. . . . Producers, writers, actors and network executives often have great difficulty accepting the notion that what they do for a living somehow affects what others do in real life. It's as if they don't want to believe that TV sells ideas and attitudes just as surely and effectively as it sells soap and deodorant."

Some of those who came of age in the "Do Your Own Thing" 1960s were beginning to wonder about the wisdom of non-judgmentalism. Television's perceived promotion of value neutrality was considered to be a genuine contributor to the breakdown of the nuclear family by many of those who worked in the trenches of urban America. "Somebody has got to say this is wrong. We have got to stop being so accepting and get real," said Marie Farrell-Donaldson, an official with the city of

Detroit—where 61 percent of families were headed by singles in the early 1990s. "Murphy Brown doesn't live in Detroit. She's got a high-paying job and lots of options. We've got 13-year-old girls having babies who are destined for a life of poverty. . . . If we have to bring back stigma and shame, so be it."

On the campaign trail, George H.W. Bush urged American families to aspire to be "more like the Waltons," referring to the dramatic TV series of the 1970s about a close-knit extended family from rural Virginia struggling through the Depression and eventually World War II. It was an appealing message to those for whom the women's movement served as the standard scapegoat for the splintering of the family—things were obviously better before mothers routinely worked outside the home.

The role of fathers in the pathology of American families was rarely explored on prime-time television. But the series *Grace Under Fire*, which debuted and became a quick hit in 1993, illustrated that sexual equality was not what hurt the family structure. The most common damage stemmed from irresponsible male dominance. The twin issues of domestic violence and the feminization of poverty were at the heart of the program, in which comedian Brett Butler plays a woman with three young children who refuses to be a victim and finds the wherewithal to leave an abusive husband.

Like Roseanne, Grace is working-class and money is a constant problem. In contrast, though, Grace protects the emotional well-being of her children at all costs. In one episode Grace buys and gift-wraps Christmas presents for the children and puts their father's name on the packages so they won't feel neglected. The oldest child is still upset because his father didn't call or come to visit for the Holidays. Grace assures the boy that his father really loves him very much, reminiscing about how proud his dad was the day he was born. But, like some men, Grace tells her son, his father just wasn't very good at expressing himself.

A reader of the syndicated advice column "Dear Abby" was so touched by the storyline she felt compelled to write a letter acknowledging its important lesson. "Abby, I was emotionally overcome with this episode," the correspondent said. "I'm sure many divorced mothers identified with it, as I did. Grace sacrificed the momentary 'satisfaction' she might have gotten from making a few nasty remarks and pointing out what a heel the father was. Instead she built him up to be more of a loving father than he really was, avoided saying anything negative about him. Let's face it, if the father is really an insensitive slob, the kid will figure it out for himself soon enough. Grace refused to reinforce the boy's feeling that his father didn't love him."

Grace Under Fire promoted family values by conveying the message that kids come first no matter what. It illustrated that television programming about perfect, intact families with minor problems isn't the only route to contribute to a strengthening of American values. Hollywood producers were urged to create programs with characters who, regardless of their circumstances, behaved with dignity and responsibility—portrayed not as suckers but as true champions of American life. "For 30 years, our families have been under assault," President Bill Clinton told an audience of studio executives, producers, directors, and stars in 1993. "We have to have the help of the people who determine our culture."

"If you strip away *Murphy Brown*," reported NBC Washington bureau chief Tim Russert, "you will find that Dan Quayle and Bill Clinton sound remarkably alike." Candice Bergen, the actress who portrayed Murphy Brown, commented that although she wouldn't vote for him, "I don't disagree with Dan Quayle. . . . That's the irony. Once you divorce that comment [regarding *Murphy Brown*] from the text of the speech, it was a very valid speech and absolutely something I believe in. I totally subscribe to the fact fathers are not dispensable."

No one believed that television alone could create a cultural climate in which lasting marriages and two-parent households flourished. But in the 1990s, the potential of popular entertainment to define the meaning of gender and family in the nation's collective consciousness entered the political arena not only because it was considered a hot-button issue to rouse voters, but also because men and women across the political spectrum understood that strong families were essential to a strong country.

At the beginning of the 21st century two TV series about peculiar families were among America's favorites—the longtime hit animated series *The Simpsons* and *Malcolm in the Middle*, which debuted in 2000. Deeply dysfunctional dynamics prevailed in the households of Homer and Marge Simpson, an inept nuclear power plant worker and his homemaker wife, and Lois and Hal Wilkerson, an overworked drugstore clerk and a low-level, cubicle-dwelling systems management worker in a large corporation.

Homer was selfish and lazy while Marge was overprotective and indulgent with Bart, Lisa, and baby Maggie. Lois was a cruel disciplinarian and

Hal an ineffectual wimp in the parenting of four, eventually five, boys. Some family advocates despaired about these high-profile examples of bad parenting and childhood trauma, but defenders of the shows believed the over-the-top satires shared a common theme of resilience and offered a beneficial lesson—despite chaos, confusion, and hard times, good families hang tough, forgive shortcomings, and stay together.

Fig. 4 One of the bloodiest shows on television, *The Untouchables* brings both high ratings and controversy in the early 1960s. (ABC publicity photo.)

CHAPTER 4

The Killing Tube: Violence and Crime

"Last one in, lock the front door," was a common practice in a great many American households in the first half of the 20th century. But if the last one in forgot to turn the latch, no one worried much about it. And locking car doors was done more to deter curious children than thieves.

At the end of World War II, citizens could walk down most streets in the United States of America without great anxiety. Trusting strangers was an unremarkable trait. In a big city, a murder was front-page news; in a small town it was unfathomable. The social contract of "live and let live" was essentially intact.

As television programming expanded in the years after the war, sports was an economical way to fill TV schedules. Broadcast rights to carry sporting events, especially wrestling and boxing, could be had for next to nothing since promoters were interested in hyping the live gate through television exposure. These sports were also perfectly suited to the primitive equipment of TV's formative years. They took place in a small area with only two participants, so a limited number of cameras and crewmembers could cover the action.

Even before the television age, professional wrestling was beginning to transform itself from a genuine sport, in which matches could go on for several hours with two combatants stalemated in mutual hammerlocks, to action-packed morality plays. The changeover was speeded by TV's need for programming.

Aerial moves such as drop kicks, flying head scissors, backward flips, and the ever-popular airplane spin replaced the traditional and less excit-ing arm- and head-locks. Undoubtedly, some naïve viewers believed in the authenticity of the TV bouts. Most, though, understood it was all an act, "as spontaneous and unrehearsed," one wag explained, "as a Balanchine ballet."

The script never varied: One wrestler was the good guy who followed the rules of fair play; the other a villain who defied the laws of the sport and brought chaos to the ring. The evil competitor slammed his opponent's head into the corner posts, pulled his hair, and stomped on him while he was down. But the hero ultimately prevailed. So, fans could redeem their pleasure at witnessing dirty fighting with the satisfaction of seeing some justice in the world.

Theatrics motivated TV wrestling, not athletic achievement or strategy. Gorgeous George was a burlesque-style showman who became TV's biggest wrestling star. He wore his peroxided hair in long ringlets, dressed in flowing robes, and purportedly bathed in Chanel No. 5 perfume. Other wrestlers with names like Nature Boy, The Hooded Phantom, The Zebra Kid, and The Swedish Angel developed their own schticks.

The ringside announcer was also a major contributor to the viewers' experience. Dennis James of WABD, the DuMont network's New York station, was the pioneer and master of a peculiar new form of show business. Seated behind his microphone at Jamaica Arena on Long Island, James was equipped with dog biscuits, walnut shells, and pieces of wood, which he would crack into the mike to accentuate any "bone-crushing hold." By drawing his thumbnail over a balloon, James would send over the air what sounded like a groan of horrific pain. When a wrestler was sent flying across the ring, James would provide a glissando on the harmonica to emphasize the flight and fall. When wrestlers and referees exchanged heated words, James would reproduce the argument for the benefit of the TV audience: "Whassa matter with you?! You wanna lose on a foul?" "Lemme at him, lemme at him. I'll moider him."

By the early 1950s wrestling was generating big profits even for small, non-network TV stations. And the violence levels increased. Ear biting, eye gouging, and choking became more prominent. Some promoters added variety to their tickets by putting on wrestling matches fought by midgets and, where local authorities permitted, matches between women. A *Business Week* article, "It Pays to Sponsor Television Corn," pointed out that because not only men but families watched the broadcasts, "wrestling has become an almost perfect show for retail stores to sponsor on local TV stations."

Boxing was also a staple of television's first decade. Wednesday and Friday were fight nights on the networks, but by 1953 so many local and regional telecasts had sprung up that in some cities prizefighting could be seen in prime time six nights a week. Television brought viewers the great practitioners of what some called "defensive science." But along with the likes of Rocky Marciano, Sugar Ray Robinson, and Archie Moore were new made-for-TV ring heroes, less skilled in the art of fisticuffs and more adept at pugilistic soap opera. Fighters who in the pre-television era would be considered palookas were profiting handsomely from the law of supply and demand.

The sport adapted to television and the audience was apparently punch-hungry. "Skillful defense and subtlety were never less in demand," a knowledgeable observer reported. "TV viewers like their fighting rough, wild and emphatic. . . . The boys are doing their best to cripple one another." An attempt to knock the brains out of an opponent, he sadly opined, "goes down the audience's throat just as easily as pink lemonade."

Along with the change in fighting style and the increased frequency with which viewers were exposed to boxing matches, the fact that women and children could watch freely was troubling for those who believed a nation's culture could be debased by its choice of entertainment. "Brutality right on the family rug," one columnist and boxing aficionado lamented, "the animal instincts of dog-eat-dog and savage-kill-savage paraded for Mother and Grandmother and little Jackie and Betty and Ann and Patricia to see. The fight back of the barn was now the fight in the heart of the family. The illegal battles of my youth were now the recreation of the nation." By mid-decade some viewers could not help but wonder what consequences there might be to a society that accepted as a respectable postime a sport with the objectives of bloodshed and coma.

A Prime Suspect

TV's first cowboy hero, Hopalong Cassidy, who rode onto the small screen in 1949, was a role model beyond reproach. Brave and patriotic, he accompanied the President of the United States in the 1950 "I Am An American" parade in Washington, D.C. Actor William Boyd believed it was his character's duty to "strengthen the fiber of American Youth." Each of the two million young members of his *Hopalong Cassidy* Troopers Club was asked to swear allegiance to an eight-point creed:

To be kind to birds and animals
To always be truthful and fair

To keep yourself neat and clean
To always be courteous
To be careful when crossing streets
To avoid bad habits
To study and learn your lessons
To obey your parents

Early Western TV heroes, created primarily for children, always carried a gun, but they did not shoot to kill. If they had to shoot, they'd shoot to wound. The Lone Ranger, for instance, might go for the wrist of the bad guy's gun hand. Still, the need for a weapon was unquestioned. Hundreds of American manufacturing firms capitalized on *Hopalong Cassidy*'s success in the early 1950s by making toy guns for his fans.

In adult series, though, like *Man Against Crime*, the bad guys were usually not subdued without extreme resistance. A villain making a break for it gave the hero a legitimate reason to engage in forceful combat or gunplay. Justice always seemed to have a violent component in the crime and action teleplays that were multiplying by mid-decade.

Something else besides televised violence was also on the rise in American cities—juvenile delinquency. Could the increasing antisocial behavior of teenagers have some connection to the aggression they watched on TV? It seemed a fair question and one important enough to the future of the country that it should be raised officially. So a Senate subcommittee led by Senator Estes Kefauver was organized to probe the matter.

After several months of hearing testimony including the opinions of psychiatrists and police chiefs, monitoring programs, and examining the relatively small body of academic research that existed at the time, the panel released a report in August 1955. Since radio, motion pictures, and comic books had also been alleged to be harmful to adolescents, the Kefauver subcommittee first emphasized that television was different from the other media—it was potentially much more injurious. The average child's exposure to movies was at most a few hours per week, but television was available at the flick of a knob and children were watching some four hours per day. Stories on TV were considered more realistic by kids than were radio or comic book tales.

The nature of TV crime dramas was characterized by the report as programming in which "Life is cheap; death, suffering, sadism and brutality are subjects of callous indifference and judges, lawyers and law-enforcement officers are too often dishonest, incompetent and stupid."

The senators raised a red flag about the consequences of such television shows. Well-adjusted children, they conceded, could probably tolerate the "added tension that would be acquired through viewing television." But the concern was with the unstable or hostile child for whom televised crime and violence "may provide suggestions and a kind of support . . . leading him to imitate these acts in expression of his own aggression."

The long-term impact on American society was pondered as well. Clearly TV was teaching young people the techniques of crime. Children taken into custody often identified crime dramas as the source of their ideas. But, perhaps, more frightful was the effect on viewers who would never commit a serious crime. The Kefauver report speculated: "Repeated exposures to scenes of crime and violence may well blunt and callous human sensitivity to, and sympathy for, human suffering and distress."

Although the Senate subcommittee urged the Federal Communications Commission (FCC) to become more involved in setting standards for programming that might be "damaging" to children, the issue quickly faded from national attention as the TV industry's growth curve shot off the map. The networks felt no obligation to tone down their offerings. The bloodiest was yet to come.

By the late 1950s adult Westerns—also seen by millions of young viewers—were the hottest trend in prime time. Unlike TV Westerns earlier in the decade, most post-1955 shows allowed their heroes to shoot to kill with impunity. Gun fighting was at the heart of popular series such as *Have Gun Will Travel*, *Wanted: Dead or Alive*, and *The Rifleman*.

It was the introduction of *The Untouchables* in the fall of 1959 that raised television violence to a new high-water mark. Loosely based on the life of Eliot Ness, a Treasury Department agent in Chicago during the Prohibition days of the 1930s, each episode featured multiple shootout scenes in which victims were sprayed with bullets.

An episode called "The White Slavers," which aired in March 1960, contained a scene in which a group of young Mexican women was being imported to Chicago to be forced to work as prostitutes. When the gangsters realize they won't be able to get their chattel across the border, the girls are simply machine-gunned down. So disturbing was the scene that the advertising agency representing the sponsor insisted on a reediting before the program aired.

Such concessions to the queasy were rare, however. Scriptwriters who could contrive novel incidents of sadism were especially prized by the producers of action TV as the 1960s arrived. Defenders of the genre pointed out that the bad guys were always defeated, therefore the shows provided a wholesome lesson for young viewers. But the villains' defeat never proved that brutality was wrong, only that the good guys eventually managed to dish it out in greater force. The real lesson was that violence is the surest solution to conflict and that might makes right.

For some viewers it was the lives of bad guys that appeared exciting and attractive. A devoted fan of action shows who was a third grader in 1960 remembered: "I wanted to be a gangster—be like Al Capone. Have a big corporation . . . buy the lawyers, judges. Have a lot of girls around me . . . party twenty-four hours a day. Never came true." Although the boy had several run-ins with the law before he reached his thirties, his experience fell far short of his gangster fantasy: "I bought a suit. That's all that came true."

By the time John Kennedy assumed the presidency in 1961, television had schooled Americans in a violent vocabulary and was propagating modern myths of justified aggression. Although social science was beginning to develop a body of evidence that would eventually prove that watching TV violence heightens the probability of a viewer engaging in aggressive behavior, the networks rejected this "stimulation theory" in favor of the "catharsis theory." The broadcast industry maintained that watching violent TV shows could actually reduce the aggressiveness of viewers by purging their hostilities. It was the analytical equivalent of the tobacco industry touting the health benefits of smoking as an aid to digestion.

When JFK appointed an activist young regulator named Newton Minow to be chairman of the FCC, the television networks sensed there might be trouble ahead. Minow was close to the president's brother, Attorney General Robert Kennedy, who worried about the effect of television on children and believed government had a legitimate role in guiding broadcasters onto a responsible path. The fears of the industry were realized in full measure.

In his first address to the National Association of Broadcasters, Minow captured headlines when he referred to American television as "a vast wasteland." He warned the industry to clean up its own house or the government might be forced to take action. "There is nothing permanent or sacred about a broadcast license," he reminded his stunned audience.

Even though the television networks regarded Minow's threats as unconstitutional, they could not take the chance of simply defying a popular government official who was most effective in making his case with the public. So, changes came to prime time in the short span of the Kennedy years. Violence did not disappear, but it was considerably reduced. Instead of action-adventure shows dominating the schedule, the number increased for character dramas, such as *East Side/West Side* and *The Nurses*.

The assertive stance of the FCC was making a difference. "The blood on the living room floor isn't as deep as it was a year ago," Minow reported during the 1962–63 TV season. But the murder of President Kennedy in November 1963 quickly changed the direction of the FCC. President Johnson, who came into the Oval Office with millions of dollars in broadcast holdings, put the brakes on the agency's regulatory zeal. The industry breathed a sigh of relief and soon it was back to business as usual.

There were critics who drew a connection between the nation's trauma over the president's death and the culture of television. "A heavy sense of guilt should rest with the gentlemen who determine what's on your TV screen," wrote Harriet Van Horne in the *New York World-Telegram*. Jack Gould in *The New York Times* questioned the medium's "constant and unremitting use of the gun to resolve dramatic situations."

For a few days after President Kennedy's funeral, the television networks made an effort to reschedule programs having murderous themes, such as an episode of *Route 66* unfortunately entitled "I'm Here to Kill a King." But programming executives were not about to be shamed into soul-searching by a few dour columnists. In the mid-1960s the television industry's profits from prime-time programming escalated so dramatically that TV station licenses were likened to a license to print money. The huge success of violent shows, many with espionage themes like *The Man From U.N.C.L.E.*, deflated arguments about their possible consequences. Those who questioned the impact of comedic violence—the "Pows" and "Kabooms" of *Batman*—were dismissed as humorless cranks.

The real-life violence that gripped the country in 1968, though, jolted even the ambivalent into considering the possibility that television might be a contributor. After the murders of Martin Luther King, Jr., and Robert Kennedy, just weeks apart in the spring of 1968, television was on the defensive. A groundswell of commentary was questioning the industry's sense of moral responsibility. The charge that American television was deliberately and cynically exploiting violence for profit was being leveled in every newspaper and public affairs show in the country.

In the raw-nerved days immediately following the assassination of Senator Kennedy, the networks once again postponed and rescheduled especially violent episodes of entertainment offerings. Network executives, ad agencies, and sponsors consulted one another on strategies for dealing with the crisis of public perception. "Come fall," it was reported in *The Nation*, "the networks promise to move toward lighter stories stressing 'more positive aspects of behavior.'"

In television's creative community in Los Angeles, remorse was being felt by many. One of the most prize-winning TV directors, Jerry Paris, took out a full-page ad in the *Hollywood Reporter*:

> I have looked into the mirror. I see myself and the face of our industry. I do not like what I see. In the name of John F. Kennedy, Martin Luther King, Robert F. Kennedy, and my family, I make this solemn pledge: I will no longer lend my talents in any way to add to the creation of a climate for murder. I call upon all who read this to join me in refusing to write, direct, produce, act or participate in any way in the shaping of any "entertainment" that celebrates senseless brutality, aimless cruelty, pointless and violent death. I ask you, too, to look into the mirror. If you agree with me, let me hear from you. None of us knows where this will stop. But we can make a beginning in the stopping. Together we can change the climate. Please, let me hear from you.

More than three hundred TV professionals responded. Taking out their own ad in *Daily Variety*, 119 writers, actors, producers, and directors signed a "pledge of conscience." "We recognize", the advertisement stated, that motion pictures and television "are among the very significant influences in our society feeding a climate for murder. It is our earnest and deep felt desire to do what we can, in good conscience, to change that climate."

In the wake of the horrible events that spring, President Johnson appointed a National Commission on the Causes and Prevention of Violence (NCCPV), headed by Milton Eisenhower, the brother of the former president. The charge of the commission was to review all the available evidence and report on what the United States needed to do to change the downward course it was following.

Before year's end the NCCPV told the country, "We believe it is reasonable to conclude that a constant diet of violent behavior on television has an adverse effect on human character and attitudes." Prime-time aggression, the report concluded, "encourages violent forms of behavior and fosters moral and social values about violence . . . which are unacceptable in a civilized society."

Optimists believed that excessive TV violence was headed for a fade-out. As the 1960s drew to a close, no one wanted or expected that conflict would vanish from TV drama. But surely the people who ran the networks and the ad agencies and the companies that advertised on television cared about their country. Surely, whatever their First Amendment rights, they would re-think programming that implied that violence is fun, violence is manly, violence gets you the girl.

Embracing the Predator

"Hit me, go ahead hit me, I want you to hit me," says a frumpy housewife played by Imogene Coca to her fist-clenched husband played by Sid Caesar. "I wouldn't give you the pleasure," he sneers. Then he walks over to a hanging portrait of his mate and puts his fist through the picture as well as the wall behind it. "Now ya see," he scolds, "if you were a nicer person, you could've gotten that."

It was a typical sketch on a 1950s variety program like *Your Show of Shows*. Most viewers laughed. A few undoubtedly cringed inside when the fist hit its target. But none debated whether or not the gag condoned spouse abuse. Men hitting their partners was unfortunate but hardly considered a crime. It took the women's movement of the 1970s to heighten awareness of the problem enough to register on the national radar screen. By decade's end, objections about billboards that read "Beat Your Wife Tonight—Take Her Bowling" seemed less prickly and more reasonable.

Young women still hoped their futures might include a Prince Charming. But realistic ones were earning college degrees and preparing themselves for self-supporting careers. In the late-1970s, a campus fad, the soap opera break, swept American universities. In student lounges and dorm rooms, college kids congregated daily to watch programs once reserved for stay-at-home housewives.

As mature women entered the workforce in greater numbers and began weaning themselves from the soap opera habit, producers consciously went after a new segment of the audience. Plotlines involved younger characters with steamier problems and skimpier clothes. The most popular of the serial dramas with matriculating viewers was *General Hospital*. Even Harvard celebrated the craze with a *General Hospital* weekend.

A character who became a cult favorite was Luke Spencer, a former errand boy for the Mafia now working as the manager of a disco in the fictional town of Port Charles. Played by actor Anthony Geary, Luke was an odd candidate to attain heartthrob status. Chicken-chinned with unchiseled features and a head of tangled, frizzy orange curls, he was a lowlife with what fans described as "a quirky charisma."

The show took an ominous turn in a 1979 episode. When the dance floor of his disco was deserted one night, Luke assaulted and raped Laura Baldwin. His victim, a Port Charles teenager, was herself no stranger to vice, having already killed an older lover and letting her mother take the rap. Laura, played by Genie Francis, refused to name her rapist and a romance blossomed between the two. As the 1980s dawned, Luke and Laura were being promoted as America's favorite sweethearts.

For $5.50 fans could mail order a Tony Geary Friendship Kit, complete with membership card, color poster, a bio, and a pack of wallet-sized photos. At shopping mall appearances around the country Geary was mobbed and greeted by teeny-boppers with cries of "Rape me, Luke, rape me!" At one appearance in St. Louis, Geary received a mock award naming him "America's Most Beloved Rapist." Criticism over the glorification of a rapist came quickly from feminist groups as well as ordinary citizens who were flabbergasted by *General Hospital*'s cultural message. In response, the soap's creators explained there was no reason for such a brouhaha, it was merely an "acquaintance rape."

When Luke and Laura were married in 1981, the wedding, which spanned two episodes, achieved the highest ratings ever for a daytime drama. Elizabeth Taylor made a guest appearance at the nuptials portraying diamond-studded Helene Cassadine, a mystery bad woman suddenly returning to Port Charles. "She needs *General Hospital* the way she needs another chin," a critic wrote of the movie star. "But it's her favorite show."

By and large the popular press treated the whole affair as harmless fun. But the story of Luke and Laura contributed to television's mainstreaming of a classic theme of pornography—the yoking of violence and eroticism. The presentation of rape on prime-time television was studied by Professor Caryl Rivers for *The New York Times*, who commented in particular on attacks shown in an episode of *Hawaii Five-O*:

> "Titillating" is the word for the way it was presented. Lovingly, the camera stalked the rapist's victims, it peeped at shapely legs in miniskirts, leered at a wiggly walk, watched a swaying bottom. It made rape seem like a subject for a *Playboy* centerfold, an incident without terror and pain. . . .

The camera ogled legs and bottoms, but we got only a glimpse of the victims' bodies. A gorgeous female hitchhiker in tight jeans and a blouse that bared her midriff climbed into the rapist's car. A few minutes later, her body rolled out of the car and down an embankment. For the audience it was a brief glimpse of a cipher, not a human being.

In the early 1980s, MTV was selling the brutal concept of the intertwining of violence and eroticism wholesale to American kids. Music videos that combined violence with sexual imagery were standard fare on the cable network. Michael Jackson's 1982 mega-hit *Thriller* was a rape fantasy joyously saluted as artistry by pop culture critics.

On network television, the prime-time blockbuster of the mid-1980s, *Miami Vice*, was reportedly created after NBC's programming chief, Brandon Tartikoff, invited TV writers to develop a series around the concept he characterized as "MTV cops." The lead characters in the action series, Sonny Crockett and Ricardo Tubbs, were an undercover detective duo. Crockett, played by Don Johnson, wore pastel sports jackets over T-shirts and no socks. His often-scowling face always had a few days of stubbly beard growth. The look was called "macho grubby" and became a fashion sensation.

Female characters typically swooned for Crockett, but usually they were blown up or shot before episode's end. Even the important women in his life were expendable. He was estranged from his first wife, the mother of his son, and a later quickie marriage did little to cramp his style.

One episode of *Miami Vice* in particular highlighted the misogyny of the series. In "By Hooker By Crook," Sonny finds himself making passionate love to a madam—presumably justified as being in the line of duty. This scene of bedroom action is intercut with the graphic murder of a prostitute, linking titillation and horror as natural companions.

By the early 1990s, violence committed against women was so common a theme in American entertainment that a series like *Twin Peaks*, created by filmmaker David Lynch, could air on broadcast television with only minimal concern by ABC about its essentially pornographic content. The story is set in a Northwest lumber town in which two teenaged girls have been tortured and one of them murdered. FBI agent Dale Cooper, trying to solve the mystery of who killed Laura Palmer, uncovers layers of details as the series progresses—how many men she slept with, the drugs she consumed, how she'd been tied up.

"It's as though Lynch tried to think up a series of cruelties that would boggle any imagination," one critic wrote, "and add them on week by week.

That way we wouldn't notice all at once; we'd be gradually seduced, in the way a diabolical wife might addict her husband to a drug by doctoring his food over a period of months."

In the climactic scene of the series, viewers learn that Leland Palmer murdered his own daughter, with whom he'd had an incestuous relationship. The revelation takes place while Mr. Palmer assumes a savage alter ego named Bob and then proceeds to attack Palmer's niece, Madeline. Madeline is dragged screaming into the living room and is beaten. Alternately biting her and kissing her, the beast-like twin drags Madeline about as she bleeds from her nose and face, choking in her own blood. While still semiconscious, she is thrown head-first toward a picture on the wall. In the next shot, lying on the floor with more blood on her head and face, the girl is completely silent. Viewers deduce the head smashing was a fatal blow.

Leaving one's conscience in the elevator has frequently been a requirement for decision-makers in the television industry. With *Twin Peaks*, however, the moral standard went on a permanent vacation. "Lynch had seduced me into his forbidden world," one guilty viewer admitted. "And now it's the morning after and I'm ashamed. . . . If taboo sex and violence with classy background music add up to a vision, I'll pass. . . . I think he's getting away with murder."

The Violence Escalator

One million dollars was earmarked by Congress in 1969 for more study on the impact of TV violence on the mental health of viewers. The Office of the Surgeon General accumulated a large body of new scientific data. More than fifty studies informed the final report, which was released in 1972. Much to the dismay of the broadcast industry, the evidence pointed to a strong link between the viewing of TV violence and subsequent antisocial acts.

While the networks tried to discredit the validity of the Surgeon General's report, Americans continued to hear about terrible crimes that appeared to be direct imitations of television programs. One of the most sensational occurred in 1974. The TV movie *Born Innocent* was set in a teenage girls' reformatory. The drama contained a scene in which one of the juveniles is raped in the shower with the wooden handle of a plumber's plunger by other female inmates. "A few years earlier," an observer of programming trends noted, "the serious topic and brutal setting of

Born Innocent might have sent shock waves through the industry." But by the fall of 1974, even rape scenes were becoming a storytelling standard.

The two-hour movie aired at 8:00 p.m. and several NBC affiliate stations complained to the network that the early scheduling of the program was inappropriate, since they knew there would be a large percentage of children in the viewing audience. Four days after the broadcast of *Born Innocent*, a nine-year-old girl was accosted in a San Francisco park. Three older girls, and a boy who held her down, inflicted a similar violation with a soda bottle. When apprehended, the youngsters said they had seen the movie and emulated the attack in the story.

The parents of the real-life victim sued NBC, claiming the network instigated the crime committed against their daughter. Although NBC was not found to be responsible when the case reached its conclusion four years later, *Born Innocent* served as a rallying point for various groups lobbying against gratuitous TV violence.

The National Citizens Committee for Broadcasting (NCCB) took the lead. With funding from the American Medical Association and other private foundations, the NCCB compiled violence ratings that identified the most action-packed shows on the tube and the sponsors who paid for the most depictions of physical force per hour. No formal product boycott was organized, but the sponsors understood the implied threat.

When the national PTA declared a war against TV violence, the threat of consumer action was used as a negotiating chip to get the networks involved in a dialogue about programming practices. The PTA had more than six million members. In 1976 the organization began a series of hearings that drew considerable press attention in eight major cities. Advertisers realized that those who were protesting TV violence were not persuaded by the claims of network social scientists that a "causal link" between fictional gore and antisocial behavior in real life had never been established. The nuances of the research just didn't matter to those who knew in their hearts there was a real connection—teachers, for instance, who were breaking up TV-themed playground fights with far greater frequency. Their stories, dismissed by network researchers as "anecdotal evidence," were compelling proof to other citizens who shared their fears.

In the bicentennial year of 1976, America's history and America's future were pervasive subjects in popular public discourse. In the thirty years since the advent of television, crime and violent deaths by handguns had risen dramatically. Contemplating the remainder of the century, *U.S. News and World Report* posed a simple question to Erik Barnouw, the country's preeminent historian of the broadcast industry: "Is it fair to blame television for increasing violence and crime?"

"Yes, I think it is," said Barnouw. His response captured the sentiments of reasonable men and women who saw America redefining itself in horrible ways: "Television changes people's hairstyles, clothing, and the words they use—almost everything. I can't imagine that this constant display of violence would not affect them in some way, especially when it's shown as a way of solving problems. We are actually merchandising violence."

The ghastly case of a fifteen-year-old Miami boy, Ronnie Zamora, added fuel to the fire. When his eighty-two-year-old neighbor caught Zamora in the act of burglarizing her home, the youngster murdered her. During the 1977 trial the defense argued that countless hours of viewing television had warped his sense of morality and value of human life. His mother testified about her son's fascination with the show *Kojak* and his pleading to be allowed to shave his head to look like the series' star, Telly Savalas.

Advocacy groups were beginning to see results by the fall of 1977. Fewer hard-action police shows appeared on the network schedules and those that remained, such as *Starsky and Hutch*, which had been deemed the most violent, experienced drastic reductions in body-counts and shootouts. Advertisers were growing wary of violence and the changes in their prime-time buying habits were most encouraging. As the season ended, so too did the expensive monitoring done by the NCCB. "Like the Vietnam War," the director of the organization said, "we declared victory and went home."

But as the 1970s gave way to the 1980s, two critical factors merged and negated whatever progress the media reform groups felt they had accomplished. First was the rise of cable television, which, since it did not use public airwaves for transmission, was unrestrained by public-interest standards. And the new industry had no interest in developing a tradition of self-restraint. Graphically violent feature films shown on premium channels were competing with prime-time network fare and pushing the limits of what was acceptable on the home screen.

The second punch in the double-whammy that hit anti-TV-violence activists was the deregulatory climate that flowered with the Reagan administration in the 1980s. The FCC's *laissez-faire* policies signaled that broadcasters could press the boundaries of public tolerance without fear of government action. It was a different ballgame for citizens' groups as the new decade unfolded. The rules had changed and their clout had been drastically diminished. With consternation they watched American television—and the rest of American culture—step onto a steeply rising violence escalator.

Yet a ten-year follow-up to the Surgeon General's 1972 report concluded unequivocally there was a causal relationship between the TV screen and human behavior. Still, publication of the evidence had no effect on the escalation. The debut of *The A-Team* in January 1983 perfectly represented the new "in your face" climate of TV violence. The show's premise was that a squad of Vietnam veterans had robbed the Bank of Hanoi of one million yen four days after the war ended in Vietnam. Unable to prove they had been given such orders, the men were imprisoned by their own government. But they escaped and were now free-lance mercenaries who were still being pursued as criminals.

The cigar-chomping leader of the team, Col. Hannibal Smith, was a master of disguises. Howling Mad Murdock was a pilot sprung from a mental institution to join the group. Lt. Peck was known as Faceman because of his good looks and ability to hustle what the team needed for their missions. The most flamboyant was Sgt. Bosco Baracus, called "B.A.," as in Bad Attitude. Played by the massive actor known as Mr. T, B.A. was an ebony devastation machine.

In their first year, *The A-Team* vigilantes assumed the top spot of television's most violent. Of the forty-two million viewers who tuned in weekly, it was estimated that seven million were children between the ages of two and eleven. In response to a Maryland grade-school teacher who asked the network on behalf of her students to reduce the violence on the popular show, a letter arrived from Warren J. Ashley of NBC's department of broadcast standards. "Dear boys and girls," it said, "*The A-Team* is a fantasy program. . . . in real life, shooting guns, especially automatic weapons, would result in serious wounds, if not death. In *The A-Team*, despite all the shots that are fired, no one has ever been hurt by a bullet. Because no one is hurt, we feel the fighting, shooting, and car crashes in *The A-Team* are action, not violence."

Criticism that Mr. T. was a bad role model for his young fans didn't stop the White House from inviting him to a Christmas party for children or prevent First Lady Nancy Reagan from being photographed sitting on his lap. "The fact he brandishes weapons and barely speaks a complete sentence on the show doesn't bother him," *People* magazine reported. "When he sees adoring kids off camera, he tells them, 'When I be fightin' or whatever on TV, it all just fun, we don't hurt nobody. But I don't want you to be a fighter. Study to be a scientist, study to be an astronaut. Everybody can't be Mr. T.'" Blessed with a potent gift of denial, Mr. T and his colleagues could divorce themselves with ease from the consequences of their performances.

As the 1980s marched on, no one could deny that violent crime committed by young people was reaching epidemic proportions. When crack cocaine entered the scene in 1983, the statistics grew grislier. At mid-decade, the homicide rate for seventeen-year-olds raced upward and increased more than 120 percent by the early 1990s. During the 1980s, violent television programming became so entrenched in American culture that the country's shock threshold rose to new levels. Violent cartoons created with the intent of selling theme toys became a normal business practice, its beneficiaries considered savvy entrepreneurs rather than morally bankrupt exploiters of children. Phrases like "blowing away" one's opponent entered the everyday lexicon.

One night in 1988, Senator Paul Simon of Illinois was flipping through the channels of his hotel room TV when he happened to come across a gory movie murder scene in which a chainsaw was the weapon of choice. At that moment he realized in a clear vision the dangerous course the country had taken in allowing brutal violence to assume such a casual status. Against the odds, he decided to try once again to put the issue on the table. In 1990, through Simon's efforts, a bill was passed that would exempt the broadcast and cable networks and program producers from antitrust laws if they decided to work together to devise a common set of standards regarding violence. It was the tiniest of baby steps on the road back to a more civilized national environment. But it felt better than pure despair.

Getting a Grip

Shortly after his 1992 victory, President-elect Bill Clinton, who had close and powerful friends in the business of TV entertainment, told *TV Guide* that television networks and program producers should move toward "deglamorizing mindless sex and violence." The industry understood that even though Clinton's popular vote was not an overwhelming mandate, responding with howls of protest would simply not be prudent. Instead the big three networks, under the antitrust protection of Senator Simon's legislation, agreed to adopt voluntary guidelines to reduce violence in their programming for the following season. Among the eleven points they approved was the recommendation that whenever violence is used to advance plot or develop character, the consequences of that violence to the victims as well as the perpetrator be shown. Under the new guidelines, mixing violence with sex or showing violence to be erotic was an unacceptable practice.

Skeptical observers were quick to point out that with no arbiter and no provision for enforcement, a voluntary promise to do better was meaningless. The industry track record on adhering to guidelines, such as the National Association of Broadcasters Code, was plainly poor. Even if the participants kept their pledge, though, the Fox network would continue to broadcast old-fashioned TV violence packaged in slick new ways for young viewers and the cable networks would still telecast feature films like *Die Hard* and *Terminator* without misgivings. The agreement was just another small step, but it was an indicator of a noteworthy change in mood. The broadcast industry was beginning to accept the fact it could not endlessly deny its impact on culture.

Viewers too were more willing to acknowledge a connection between the TV violence and their increasingly dangerous world. Horrible incidents of children copying TV behavior continued to make news, such as a five-year-old boy who was inspired by the MTV cartoon *Beavis and Butthead* to light a fire that killed his younger sister. In March 1993, a startling *Times Mirror* survey indicated that 80 percent of Americans believed violent entertainment was harmful to society. Ten years earlier, the figure was only 64 percent.

Questioning and quibbling about the validity of research that documented harmful effects became less pronounced. Fair-minded people were generally willing to believe that even though watching TV violence rarely prompted instant reactions, over time it could heighten aggressive instincts as well as desensitize viewers to the pain and suffering of others. It was not a long inferential leap to conclude that television was indeed one of many key factors in making the nation a more perilous place.

Critics in the industry were less likely to challenge the damning conclusions of social scientists and more likely to point out that legislators should be working on gun control laws and equitable economic policies instead. Questioning the sincerity of politicians raising the issue, rather than denying a problem existed, was also a frequent tactic. Considering the high percentage of viewers expressing concern, it was better from a public relations angle to characterize politicians as opportunistic rather than citizens as foolish.

By summer 1993, the question was less about whether TV violence contributed to America's dilemma and more about how it should be dealt with in a free society. Those calling for restraint did not want to be perceived as censors and those invoking First Amendment rights did not want to be perceived as callous, especially regarding children.

In July, ABC, CBS, Fox, and NBC unveiled a plan on Capitol Hill to broadcast parental advisories before violent programs and send warnings to newspapers and magazines that carried their program listings. The heads of the networks, with downcast eyes and somber expressions, a newsmagazine reported, "tacitly conceded that violence on television can indeed beget violence in real life."

The following month a summit conference of sorts, sponsored by a group called The National Conference for Families and Television, took place in Los Angeles. Just days before, fifteen cable networks, including HBO, MTV, USA, and Nickelodeon, announced they would join the broadcast networks in putting warning messages on their shows. No one could quarrel with the industry's contention that more parental responsibility was needed in many homes. But in the real, not ideal, world, children of working parents watched TV unsupervised most of the time. Professor George Gerbner of the Annenberg School of Communication argued, "The notion of parental control is an upper-middle-class conceit."

Richard Reeves, like other syndicated columnists then, took up the question of control and the family TV set. "Just turn the thing off. That would seem to make common sense," he wrote. "And I wish it were true. But I don't think it is. You cannot control television with a clicker or an on-off button, because television is not an appliance, or even a 'medium' as we now use that word. It is an environment. Television is more like the weather than it is like this newspaper. . . . For me, common sense dictates that too much television is dangerous to children's health—but it also tells me I do not have the power to deal with it alone."

President Clinton continued to speak out. In December 1993 he told a group of four hundred Hollywood leaders that the expanding violence in the country stemmed from complex social and economic roots, but popular culture was also a critical influence. Their violent programming and movies, he told his audience, were especially hurtful to children of the underclass, those whose lives were not organized around family, work, and community institutions. He asked the decision-makers in the creative community to think differently about what they do. The President granted that violence did have a legitimate role in drama, "But there are different ways to do it." He felt the time was right for a radical change in the way Americans respond to violence, and entertainment, he believed, "can begin to reshape the culture."

Clinton's quixotic rhetoric was unprecedented. Never before had a chief executive applied such direct moral suasion on the industry. Few in the audience, if any, however, were born-again by the President's preaching, but promises were offered to give prayerful thought to his point of view. There was evidence that Clinton's initiative was having some resonance. Handgun control lobbyists, for instance, were finding television producers willing to consult with them on how best to weave anti-gun themes into many programs. In shows like *Blossom*, *Empty Nest*, and *Family Matters*, plots were scripted concerning tragedies involving guns and teenagers.

Cop shows, like *Homicide: Life on the Street*, were showing the consequences of violent acts. Scenes of mothers crying, widows grieving, and hard-boiled detectives displaying emotion at a crime scene led viewers to the inescapable conclusion that the violence was senseless. "Action plays second-fiddle to humanity," a TV critic wrote of *Homicide*. "There are no 70s-style shootouts, where the villains' bodies were never seen again and nobody had to face the acts' impact on family and friends."

In March 1995, fifty-one cable channels teamed up to present seven days of special programming with the theme "Voices Against Violence." "This week", it was reported in *The New York Times*, is part of an effort by the cable industry "to address mounting criticism of violence on television and show that the industry can regulate itself without government regulation." Some observers found the campaign a meaningless stunt, pointing out that a documentary on HBO about children killed by handguns was the height of hypocrisy. But some took heart from a comment made by one of the organizers of the effort, including a senior vice-president of Viacom: "Frankly, if television doesn't have the ability to influence behavior, then a lot of advertisers have been conned. We do have some responsibility."

Less than a month later, a horrible tragedy forced television executives to scrutinize their schedules yet again and rethink their programming. The April 19th bombing of the Murrah Federal Building in Oklahoma City killed 168 people, including several children. Unprecedented mass murder had struck the American heartland. Because of speculation that the 1992 government raid on the Branch Davidian compound in Waco, Texas, may have been a primary motivation for the Oklahoma bombing, HBO pulled the movie *In the Line of Duty: Ambush in Waco*.

At ABC, the soap opera *All My Children* was in the midst of a storyline in which a character was assembling a homemade bomb to send to the father of her baby on the man's wedding day. The actress who played the scorned woman appeared on camera and read an announcement expressing regret at the "unfortunate coincidence" that the bomb plot appeared so soon after the Oklahoma explosion. She assured viewers the plot would be altered.

The Fox network too had to grapple with bomb-related stories. The season's final episode of *Melrose Place*, not yet shot, involved a disturbed woman exploding a bomb in an apartment building. An episode of the animated show *The Critic* was pulled because the show's main character was caught inside a building during a bomb threat.

A CBS made-for-TV movie in which a gunman holds hostages in a maternity ward and threatens to set off a bomb was canceled. The network also had to revisit its planned airing of *Die Hard 2* during the May sweeps weeks. A short postscript program on the making of *Die Hard With a Vengeance* was scheduled. But under the circumstances the comments of one of the actors discussing the film's special effects was haunting: "Everybody likes to see a car wreck or a building blow up."

In the summer of 1995 a new term, "the V-chip," became a household expression. At a July town meeting on the family and the media organized by Vice-president Al Gore, President Clinton endorsed Congressional proposals that would require television makers to install a computer chip that could automatically screen out programs broadcasters had coded as violent. "The question," Clinton said, "is how we get beyond telling parents to do something they physically cannot do for several hours a day unless they literally want to be at home without a television or monitor their kids in some other way. This is not censorship, this is parental responsibility."

Those who hoped the President would lose enthusiasm for cultural concerns were disappointed with his State of the Union address in January 1996. "To the media," Clinton declared, "I say you should create movies, CDs and television shows you would want your own children and grandchildren to enjoy. . . . To make the V-chip work, I challenge the broadcast industry to come to the White House next month to work with us on concrete ways to improve what our children see on television."

Hillary Rodham Clinton too was contributing to the national dialogue on media and culture. "Since the 1950s," the First Lady wrote in her book *It Takes a Village: And Other Lessons Children Teach Us*, "a steady stream of articles, books and studies have documented the harm television does to children." Hundreds of studies have reached the unshakable conclusion, she explained, that "'viewing violence increases violence' and 'prolonged viewing of media violence can lead to emotional desensitization toward violence.'"

The passage of a new Telecommunications Bill in February 1996 included a provision that newly manufactured television sets come equipped with V-chips. Meeting with President Clinton shortly after the bill became law, a coalition of broadcast, cable, and production company representatives agreed they would devise a rating system for their entertainment programming that would guide parents in setting the V-chips on their TV receivers. The logistics were daunting. "We are embarking on the TV equivalent of the Lewis and Clark expedition," said the man who agreed to coordinate the task. "No one knows what's on the other side of the mountain."

Some in the industry saw it as defeat. NBC's West Coast President Don Ohlmeyer felt it was "unfortunate" the networks did not file suit to challenge the V-chip. "Because it's an election year," said NBC's Entertainment President Warren Littlefield, "let's not fool ourselves that labeling product will create a safer society." Even the strongest supporters of the V-chip did not believe it would make an enormous difference by itself. But as the 1990s advanced, the specter of a significantly more violent future made every possible method of prevention important.

Although serious crime rates declined overall in the mid-1990s, America's children were turning to crime at an alarming rate. Teenage violence, particularly with guns, was rising steadily. On April 20, 1999, a massacre at Columbine High School in Littleton, Colorado, stunned the nation and reinvigorated the debate about connections between violent entertainment and criminal behavior. The murderous spree resulted in the deaths of twelve students and a teacher and the wounding of twenty-four others. The two students who staged the shooting rampage committed suicide at the scene. They were young men with mental and social problems that undoubtedly had many contributing causes. But, as the gruesome details of the cold-blooded murders and the life histories of the killers emerged, what generated a flood of public reaction was their obsession with violent video games, movies, and music lyrics.

The day after the horror at Columbine High School, George W. Bush, a candidate for the Republican nomination for the presidency of the United States, blamed popular culture for "romanticizing violence." He acknowledged that he had no problems with Clinton's V-chip initiative and favored parental filtering devices for the Internet as well. But the best solution, he said, was "simply not to watch violent shows."

Both were simplistic solutions to a complex problem. Instead of assigning accountability to gun manufacturers, media conglomerates, and executives who had the power to greenlight violent programming, the people who profited from the culture of violence, the burden was handed to those who had little or no input and responsibility for the content of entertainment. When asked on the campaign trail about the influence of popular culture, Bush replied, "The fundamental question is going to be, can America rededicate itself to parenting as the Number One priority for all of us?" In a TV debate with the Democratic nominee in 2000, Vice-president Al Gore, Bush repeated. "The best weapon is the on-off button and paying attention to your children."

As the new century began, the television industry's nonchalance about violent murder was celebrated in the HBO drama *The Sopranos*, the first cable series to outscore broadcast competition in ratings. The protagonist, New Jersey mafia boss Tony Soprano, grappled with the competing needs of his nuclear family and his crime family, putting suburban life and killing without compunction on the same plane. "If it is truly possible to make a bunch of criminals, thieves, and cold-blooded murders amusing and appealing," conjectured a reviewer, "then the much praised [series] *The Sopranos* did the trick." Critics raved about the sophistication of drama drenched with "moral ambiguity," somehow missing the distinction between right and wrong in a heartless homicide.

By the year 2000, the body of social scientific evidence continued to grow larger and more convincing—there were clear connections between viewing television violence and subsequent aggressive, anti-social behavior. Desensitization to real violence and suffering was another well-documented consequence. At the turn of the century, savage crimes were being committed by children. Somehow, at their tender age, they had learned to define human life as a commodity of little value. "Each time I tried to rule out television," said an epidemiologist studying the probable causes in America's explosion of youth violence, "it just wouldn't rule out."

Fig. 5 Sexual innuendo and suggestive poses were the formula for *Three's Company*, an example of late 1970s "Jigglevision." (ABC publicity photo.)

CHAPTER 5

TV Goes All the Way: Romance and Sexuality

Betty Grable was a bombshell in her swimsuit and high heels, a worthy candidate for pinup girl of World War II. The famous photo of the movie queen, enticingly looking over her shoulder, could easily rouse the fantasies of a young man far from home. By the standards of the day, the picture was a bit racy, not meant for schoolboys to hang in their lockers. But even Sunday school teachers could overlook the presence of Betty Grable's glorious posterior and million-dollar legs in a military barracks.

Whatever their sexual experiences during the war, servicemen and women returned to an American society in which carnal matters were a covert subject. Sex was a private part of life, not openly discussed in polite company. In the mass culture of movies and radio, sexuality was implied— as in the double entendres of Mae West—but never depicted explicitly. The sexual behavior of characters was left entirely up to one's imagination.

In 1948, a professor of zoology at Indiana University, Alfred Kinsey, published a book that cracked open the door to sex becoming a mentionable topic in daily conversation. *Sexual Behavior in the Human Male* was a graph- and chart-laden tome not intended for popular reading. But within ten days of the volume's release, the publisher of the 804-page scholarly book ordered a sixth printing.

Kinsey's report, based on twelve thousand personal histories, concluded that half the husbands in America had engaged in extramarital affairs. He also extrapolated that 10 percent of American men could be considered homosexuals. They were shocking—and fascinating—revelations. Some critics questioned the validity of the sample. Others were angered that the data were presented clinically and that Kinsey did not condemn what he had found. Viewers of the infant medium of television, though, found no evidence that the picture Kinsey offered was believable. The entertainment in their living rooms remained grounded in traditional social mores.

One of television's first controversies revolved around the neckline of the off-the-shoulder evening gowns worn by a talk show hostess, whose program debuted in 1949. Even though *The Faye Emerson Show* aired at 11:00 at night, some viewers complained that her low-cut, revealing designer dresses were too much. But the sophisticated Emerson, who would soon be named to the International Best Dressed List, held her ground.

Another late-night TV star of a different ilk arrived on the scene in 1950 and raised eyebrows. Dagmar, a tall, buxom blonde who played dumb, was a regular on *Broadway Open House*, an informal talk show starring Jerry Lester. Her tightly fitted evening wear was definitely eye-popping, but the network assumed the audience at that time of day consisted only of adults.

The dress code in prime time was a little more rigid. A costumer of early 1950s variety shows recalled: "The costume department was called the Department of Cleavages and Crotches. The network didn't seem to care what anyone wore as long as there was no cleavage. The slightest shadow on bare skin could cause a panic. We always had flowers and bits of lace standing by to add to the fronts of lady performers."

Professor Kinsey's second investigation, published in 1953, was even more explosive. *Sexual Behavior in the Human Female*, which outsold its companion study, concluded that half the American women who married after World War I were not virgins on their wedding day. In some cases, Kinsey reported, women's infidelity helped those wives to make sexual adjustments with their husbands. It was hard to imagine these scenarios applying to the average American sister, wife, daughter, or mother. Fearful the content of Kinsey's study might dampen the morale of soldiers, Army brass banned *Sexual Behavior in the Human Female* from service libraries in Europe. Upset members of Congress felt it was unpatriotic, considering there were fighting men in Korea, for Kinsey to make the statement that a quarter of all women had extramarital sex.

The same year Kinsey's exploration of American females hit bookstores, so did another publication that pushed the door open much wider. Hugh Hefner, a twenty-seven-year-old man with Calvinist family roots, published the first issue of *Playboy* with the express intention of bringing sex out into the open. He wanted a magazine different from the crude girly magazines men bought surreptitiously. "It was Hefner's particular genius," author David Halberstam writes, "to know that it was now going to be permissible to have an upscale, far more sophisticated magazine of male sexual fantasies that customers might not be embarrassed to be seen buying—or even leaving out on their coffee table."

The *Playboy* ethic, albeit a watered-down version, came to television in 1954 with *Love That Bob*. The series starred Bob Cummings as a bachelor photographer surrounded by a never-ending parade of curvaceous models. Winks and leers were his calling card. His romances, however, were usually foiled by his widowed sister with whom he lived, or by his assistant and secretary, Schultzy, a scrawny, plain-looking gal with an unrequited crush on the boss.

By the mid-1950s, the subject of sex was growing more prominent in American culture. Because of competition from television, motion pictures were exploring more mature themes, such as adultery, in more explicit ways. Seductive images like the love scene on the beach in *From Here to Eternity* and Marilyn Monroe's white dress fluttering in an updraft in *The Seven Year Itch* were filling neighborhood movie screens.

Another force was shaking up the traditional value system and loosening long-held sanctions against suggestive movements in public. The social implications of rock 'n' roll music were giving parents a scare. Even the term "rock 'n' roll" was trouble. Coined by disc jockey Alan Freed, it was borrowed from rhythm and blues lyrics in which "rockin' and rollin'" was a euphemism for sexual intercourse.

Because of improvements in health standards and nutrition in the years after World War II, American kids were maturing physically at an earlier age. Yet, the same abundance that was fortifying them was exempting them from economic responsibilities, such as working on the farm or in a factory. Families could afford to keep teenagers in a nonproductive status for longer periods of time. Going to high school was their job, hormonal frustration was their condition, and rock 'n' roll music was their elixir.

In 1956, a twenty-one-year-old guitar-playing singer posed a problem for television's biggest variety shows. Music was only part of his act; his uninhibited body movements were the other. Even if adolescents didn't fully understand why Elvis Presley elicited their own desires to twitch and thrust, parents could see he was a sexual persona. When Elvis appeared on *The Milton Berle Show* in June of 1956, an audience of forty million saw him grind out "Shake, Rattle, and Roll." Critics were appalled at "Elvis the Pelvis." *Time* magazine referred to him as a "sexhibitionist."

Steve Allen wanted Elvis to appear on his show to boost ratings but didn't want to be accused of corrupting American youth. So Elvis, dressed in a white tuxedo, sans guitar, sang "Hound Dog" to a droopy basset hound wearing a top hat and bow tie. Elvis stood virtually still while serenading the pooch. The odd stationary performance, a news magazine observed, was like "trying to embalm a firecracker."

Despite Ed Sullivan's public vow never to let Elvis Presley on his stage, the stone-faced impresario could not ignore the size of the audiences the rock 'n' roller had garnered on the shows of his competitors. Sullivan relented and signed Presley for three Sundays. After the first two shows, critics, including Jack Gould of *The New York Times*, attacked Elvis's suggestive body language and distasteful "movements of the tongue." For the third performance in January 1957, Sullivan gave cameramen what proved to be the legendary order to shoot Presley strictly from the waist up.

Television couldn't ignore rock 'n' roll, but it could do its best to put a more wholesome spin on it. While Elvis was confounding the standards of the medium, Ricky Nelson was playing rock 'n' roll by the rules of respectability. The teenager, whom viewers watched grow up on *The Adventures of Ozzie and Harriet*, formed a rock 'n' roll band with high school friends in one 1956 episode. A few months later he picked up a guitar on the show and sang "I'm Walkin'"—a Fats Domino hit at the time—and Ricky's real-life recording career was launched. Soon his performances became a regular feature at the close of the family series.

Playing rock 'n' roll music for his friends in the living room with mom and dad proudly looking on was a curious TV convention, but Ricky Nelson became a bona fide idol and star of the rock era. He looked clean-cut, like the kid next door—no slick hair or flashy clothes. Most important, he didn't gyrate like Elvis. Ricky's sensuality was understated. If Elvis was about getting to third base in the back seat of a car, Ricky was about holding hands and pecks on the cheek.

By the end of the 1950s, for better or worse, several factors coalesced to make sexuality a more conspicuous component of mainstream American culture. Movies, music, magazines, and books were redefining the boundaries of appropriateness. Television, though, resisted the push. Unmarried characters on the tube merely flirted toward oblivion and married ones slept in twin beds.

Sea Change

In so many ways, 1960 was a pivotal year in American history. Some transformations were easy to see. Presidential politics, for instance, would never be the same after television assumed a central role in the contest between Kennedy and Nixon. But another change, ultimately more penetrating in everyday lives, was not immediately discerned as an earthquake that would rearrange America's traditional moral foundations. In May 1960, the Food and Drug Administration approved an oral contraceptive called Enovid. For married women who wanted to avoid pregnancy, "the pill" was a modern miracle. There was a catch, though. It worked for unmarried women too.

As the New Frontier unfolded, no TV series captured the contemporary chic of the era better than *The Dick Van Dyke Show*. Rob and Laura Petrie, young and attractive like the couple in the White House, had more spark than any of the other married couples of prime time. But television was still a discreet medium in 1961. Precautions were taken to ensure that the spark didn't ignite into a little flame in the imaginations of viewers.

Actress Mary Tyler Moore suggested that her character, Laura, wear Capri pants around the house instead of the full-skirted, floral-print dresses that were more typical of TV wives. Moore writes in her memoir that her request received the blessing of the show's producer, Carl Reiner, "after he promised the sponsors that my trousers wouldn't 'cup under'. . . . I wasn't sure [what it meant], but we figured it must be a rear-end issue. So we were careful about fit and camera angles for the first season."

Like Lucy and Ricky Ricardo before them, Rob and Laura's obligatory twin beds were separated by a nightstand. And in flashback episodes of their son's birth, the word "pregnant" was still considered too indelicate to use in dialogue. There was an undeniable chemistry, though, between the two. When little Ritchie was tucked in for the night and when the last dinner guest had said good-bye, Rob and Laura looked at each other with a glint in their eyes. "The reviewers were enamored," Moore recalls, "of these two nearly, actually, sexual beings who inhabited the television screen."

As prime time was inching toward an acknowledgment of sex as a part of life, the rest of the culture was galloping full speed ahead. In 1962, Helen Gurley Brown's provocatively titled *Sex and the Single Girl* shot to the top of the bestseller list. By 1965, the singles-bar concept was introduced in New York City and the commercialization of sexual freedom seemed to be a surefire investment in the future.

Television dramas of the early 1960s were met with fearful resistance from advertisers and affiliate stations when they attempted to deal with sexual issues in a serious manner, such as a storyline on *Mr. Novak* about venereal disease among teenagers or a *Defenders* episode concerning abortion. But, abstinence from overtly sexual content could not last indefinitely.

In the fall of 1964, ABC brought *Peyton Place* to the small screen. Based on the 1956 novel by Grace Metalious, the serial drama was set in a little New England town bubbling with extramarital and premarital sex. The central intrigue revolved around the dark secret of bookstore proprietress Constance Mackenzie, who eighteen years earlier had "made a terrible mistake" and nine months later had given birth to an illegitimate daughter.

The spicy subject matter of *Peyton Place*—the idea that good people, especially good women, had sexual feelings and appetites—was unexplored territory for prime-time episodic television. But the morality was conventional. Consequences would be paid for straying from the established codes of social conduct.

As the mid-1960s were giving way to the late 1960s, all the conditions were in place for a rapid acceleration of sexual permissiveness in the United States. Still, television refrained from discarding traditional values. In the 1966 TV series *That Girl*, lead character Ann Marie, played by Marlo Thomas, was an aspiring young actress living in New York City. Although she lived alone, her fiancé, Donald, went back to his apartment every evening after the two exchanged a chaste kiss at the door. Ann Marie's virginal state was reinforced in an episode in which the sweethearts face the crisis of only one room being available when they're snowed in after a lovely dinner at a cozy inn. The resolution is to avoid temptation.

In 1967 the Rolling Stones were scheduled to appear on *The Ed Sullivan Show*. The group were allowed to perform only after the network extracted a promise that the lyrics to "Let's Spend the Night Together" be changed to "Let's Spend Some Time Together." He might be able to control what happened on his stage, but Sullivan, the master of family entertainment, had his finger in a dike that was about to rupture.

The social movements of the 1960s, urging freedom and reform in other realms, influenced the general thinking of young Americans about sexual matters. "A loose amalgam of youthful socialists, feminists, gay liberationists, black activists, drug enthusiasts, Eastern religionists, human potentialists and other assorted idealists and rebels comprised the counterculture," observed the author of *The Americanization of Sex*, Edwin Schur. "Youthful activists invariably called for sexual freedom. But they did not always think through carefully the details and implications of such freedom."

Counterculture ideals included noncompetitive and nonpossessive human relations. The dominant culture, the thinking went, oppressed people by demanding that they defer gratifications when, in fact, free-wheeling sensual exploration was an avenue to "self-actualization." Sex without guilt was a statement of personal liberation.

However repellent these ideas might have been to old-fashioned television executives and sponsors, the selling of the counterculture was clearly a bonanza for other mass media. Network TV was the last—and most important—domino standing. With television's endorsement in average homes across America, the sexual revolution would be truly consummated.

The teasing began in January 1968, a watershed year in the history of the republic. *Rowan and Martin's Laugh-In* was an overnight sensation. The show had a frenetic pace unlike anything seen before on television. The format was called a "comedy happening." Sight gags, blackouts, mini-sketches, one-liners, and catchphrases were delivered by a large cast of regulars and lots of celebrity guest stars.

Sexual innuendo was the core of the formula. Ostensibly innocent lines like "You bet your bippy" and "How about a Walnetto?" were delivered in suggestive tones. The shapely bodies of bikini-clad Judy Carne and Goldie Hawn were covered with gag graffiti to be read by viewers as the dancers undulated freely. The virtues of maximizing free choice and expanding pleasure was a message *Laugh-In* delivered loud and clear as the decade of the 1970s unfolded.

In shows like *Love, American Style*, an anthology of comic vignettes, a new risqué image was apparent. Although the Puritan ethic was always maintained in the end, the dialogue was predominantly about affairs, sleeping together, and premarital sex. The novelty of mentioning the once unmentionables was akin to a junior high school student sneaking out past curfew.

A few series of the early 1970s used the new freedom to deal with sexuality in a mature way. *The Mary Tyler Moore Show*, for instance, allowed viewers to assume that its thirty-ish lead character had a sex life that was nobody's business but her own. In one episode when her parents come to visit, Mary's mother tells her father, "Don't forget to take your pill. Inadvertently Mary responds, "I won't,"

Sex was a recurring theme in the sophisticated sitcom *M*A*S*H*. Hawkeye Pierce and Trapper John were skillful surgeons but absolute cads with the nurses in the operating room. Major Margaret "Hot Lips" Houlihan carried on a not-so-clandestine affair with the married Major Frank Burns. Lieutenant Colonel Henry Blake cheated on his wife with a woman half his age. And Corporal Radar O'Reilly was anxious to lose his virginity. But sex was not woven through the storylines just to titillate viewers. The humanity of the characters was explored through their weaknesses and their desires.

The biggest TV hit of 1976 did not treat sex with dignity or compassion, however. *Charlie's Angels* celebrated women as sexual *objects*, not as human beings. It was a landmark series because it pushed the envelope of acceptable prurience on the home screen. The premise was that a trio of gorgeous young women were taken from their routine work on the police force and assigned to undercover detective duty. Their boss, Charlie, called the women his "angels." Charlie was never seen; he appeared only as a distant voice on a speaker phone used to call in their orders. Their dangerous missions, critics observed, were nothing more than "an excuse to show sixty minutes of suggestive poses by walking, talking pinup girls."

Viewers ignored the torrents of lambasting *Charlie's Angels* received in the press. It might have been "schlock," "stupid," and "dreadful," but the wardrobes of the heroines were just too seductive—bra-less outfits, bikinis, and baby-doll nighties. CBS newsman Morley Safer's characterization of *Charlie's Angels* as "a massage parlor in the living room" did nothing to hurt the show's success.

As the campaign against TV violence by various citizens groups intensified in 1976 and 1977, the networks felt compelled to reduce the amount of "hard-action" in prime-time series or risk the consequences of consumer boycotts. The trade-off, a PTA leader was reportedly told by a network executive, would be sex: "If violence goes down, sex will go up." The prediction was right on the money.

The "T & A Season" was the way critics described 1977. *TV Guide* translated the gutter term of "tits and ass" to "bosoms and buttocks." "Jigglevision" was another way to express the phenomenon of *Three's Company*: Two young women, with a penchant for not wearing undergarments, need a roommate. They agree to take in a male roomie who tells them he is a homosexual and has no interest in sleeping with either of them, when in fact heterosexual sex was his constant preoccupation. An impotent landlord with a sexually aggressive wife added to the opportunities for the characters to deliver risqué lines and strike suggestive poses. Reviews of

Three's Company such as "Quite simply, the worst piece of sitcom trash that's ever been on television" seemed only to embolden the creators. The jejune humor of *Three's Company* was defended by some as "all-talk-no-action," so the dirty thoughts were really in the minds of viewers.

Soap, however, was a sitcom of breathtaking sexual explicitness for 1977 America. The show was about the internecine affairs of two families, the wealthy Tates and the lower-middle-class Campbells. The ABC network called it "a breakthrough in TV comedy." Concerned church groups, who mounted a vigorous protest against the series, called it an ongoing dirty joke. In one episode a recurring character, Danny, a young man involved in organized crime, breaks into the home of a gangster. When he crawls through the window of the gangster's daughter, she turns on the light, grabs a bedside gun and points it at the intruder:

SHE: Are you a rapist?
HE: No.
SHE: Oh. (Disappointment. Pause.) Are you absolutely sure you're not a rapist?
HE: I don't know what you want.
SHE: Get your clothes off.
HE: What? Are you serious? (She cocks the gun.) I mean, under this kind of pressure, don't expect much.

Later, during the show's closing credits, Danny is seen in his underwear and the gun is still cocked.

In the late 1970s, as cable TV was displaying more eagerness to tantalize viewers with sexual material, there was an explosion of sexual content on traditional broadcast television. Sexual innuendo became ubiquitous, and direct references to intercourse, prostitution, and rape—often in a humorous context—increased dramatically. The overwhelming number of sexual acts on television involved unmarried partners.

The America that was heading into the 1980s was a radically different country than the one heading into a new decade twenty years before. Because of television, sexuality was an ever-present subject. "Television tells the child viewer over and over," a reviewer wrote as the 1970s waned, "that human sexuality equals sexiness and that sexiness is an acceptable subject if it is cloaked in humor or ridicule or viewed as a harsh, hurtful, criminal part of life." Television used its expanded freedom to present sex primarily as an exciting activity when illicit but rarely as an integrated, fulfilling dimension of a well-adjusted adult life.

Invisibility Fade-Out

Percy Dovetonsils was a homosexual, but nobody said it in that many words. A recurring character featured in comedy sketches on *The Ernie Kovacs* Show in the 1950s, Percy spoke with a lilting lisp, loved poetry, wore an elegant smoking jacket, and was a gentle man with impeccable manners. Everyone knew the type and many despised it. During the communist witch hunts of the Cold War, those accused of being Reds were regarded with contempt, but a special venom was reserved for those identified as "commie-queers."

Other than ridicule, prime-time television had little interest in the concerns or tribulations of homosexuals. In the late 1950s, when Paddy Chayefsky, the superlative scriptwriter of the Golden Age of television, submitted a story idea about a homosexual character, the network nixed it in a heartbeat.

By the early 1960s, in large cities like New York, some daring homosexuals were beginning to live their lives more openly. But bars and restaurants that catered to them risked revocation of their liquor licenses. Even though there was a growing belief among psychiatrists that homosexuality was not a mental illness to be cured, it was considered by society at large to be a perversion and a crime.

In 1964, a rare episode of *The Nurses* dealt sympathetically with a victim of what, in later years, would come to be called gay-baiting. A burly middle-aged military veteran, Elihu Kaminsky, was a wartime medic. As a civilian he becomes a nurse and is hired to work in the obstetrics department of Alden General Hospital. Whether or not the character is actually homosexual is unrevealed and immaterial to the story. The plot revolves around the mockery he is forced to endure. A male intern refers to Kaminsky as "sister" and taunts him with comments like "I bet the girls tell you things they don't even tell their hairdresser." Leeringly the young doctor adds, "I used to know a male nurse once in Chicago. Awfully sweet fellow! Of course, he had one or two little quirks that got him into trouble. For instance, he liked to dress up in the other nurses' clothes."

At the close of the episode, a black nurse apologizes to Kaminsky for not defending him and for harboring her own prejudices. "To be a little unsubtle," she says, "I've been keeping you on the back of the bus." It was a powerful statement of solidarity. But in 1964, many Americans sickened by racial bigotry did not place the rights of sexual preference on the same moral plane.

In 1969, though, an incipient gay liberation movement took inspiration from the struggles of civil rights activists. When the police raided a gay bar in Greenwich Village, called the Stonewall, in June of that year, it sparked several days of rioting by gay and lesbian people unwilling to yield to what they perceived to be oppression as grievous as anything that other minority groups had experienced.

News media attention of gay issues increased as the 1970s began, the same time Norman Lear was pioneering the infusion of social relevance into situation comedy with *All in the Family*. An early episode of the series, entitled "Judging Books By Covers," dealt with Archie Bunker's discovery that a much-admired football player friend was a homosexual.

The show didn't generate a great deal of feedback, perhaps because *All in the Family* was not yet enjoying the massive audiences it soon would. But one important viewer who watched the show because a baseball game was rained out had some thoughts on the matter. President Nixon's aide, H.R. Haldeman, recorded his boss's response to the broadcast: "The President wants a study done for his own knowledge. . . . This show was total glorification of homosex. Made Arch look bad—homo look good. Is this common on TV?"

It wasn't yet common for homosexuals—whether they looked bad or good—to be part of the television mix. There were the occasional affected characters, like Dr. Smith on *Lost in Space* or Samantha's effeminate Uncle Arthur on *Bewitched*, who behaved in stereotypically homosexual ways. But their sexuality was just comical subtext—an in-joke for those worldly enough to get it.

A 1972 made-for-TV movie, though, was considered a breakthrough for the visibility of homosexual characters. *That Certain Summer* starred Hal Holbrook as a divorced father whose son comes to stay with him during his school vacation. The boy is stunned to learn his father is homosexual and lives with a lover, played by Martin Sheen.

It was a high-quality production and a sensitive script. The characters struggled with issues of honesty, personal choice, and acceptance. Although some militant gay activists criticized the TV movie for not going far enough—"Why did the two male lovers never touch or kiss?"—*That Certain Summer* was seen by most supporters of the cause as an encouraging sign that TV was ready to incorporate positive portrayals of homosexuals in the vast amount of programming produced each season.

In 1973, the Gay Activist Alliance, a New York-based organization that had hoped to work with the networks on realistic and constructive storylines about homosexual characters, was horrified by an episode of *Marcus Welby, M.D.* In "The Other Martin Loring," a married man asks Dr. Welby to help him with his homosexual desires. The wise and kind physician assures his patient that if Martin suppresses his tendencies, he could still be successful as a husband and a father. The following year, *Marcus Welby, M.D.* aired another episode that was deeply troubling to the gay community. It revolved around a male teacher who molested a teenage boy. Tying homosexuality to child molestation was exactly the kind of depiction activists knew would reinforce fears and hatreds.

In the wake of the *Welby* shows, the National Gay Task Force redoubled its efforts to serve as an educational lobby in the television production industry. When a 1974 episode of *Police Woman* centered on three lesbians who ran a rest home and systematically murdered residents, the Task Force prevailed upon NBC executives to drop the program.

By the mid-1970s, the advocacy of homosexuals in helping the networks shape portrayals of gay and lesbian issues was evident in prime-time programming. "The year of the gay" is how one TV critic dubbed 1976. But syndicated columnist Nicholas Von Hoffman referred to it as "The year of the Fag." At least seven situation comedies and several made-for-TV movies included homosexual characters.

"Many of the shows that featured gays that season," writes media historian Kathryn Montgomery, "appeared to be conscious efforts at public education. In virtually every one, the heterosexual characters learn to accept gay people and their life-styles." In the sitcom *Phyllis*, for instance, the title character encourages a gay friend to tell his parents. "These are the 1970s," she preaches. "Being gay isn't something you have to hide anymore." The gag at the story's ending is that he discloses his secret at a family gathering by saying, "I want everyone to know that I'm gay and I have this woman to thank for it."

Gay activists saw 1977's *Soap* as a big disappointment, however. Jodie Dallas, played by Billy Crystal, was the first continuing gay character in prime time. Dallas held promise for a layered and strong characterization, but that hope didn't materialize. When the show premiered, Jodie was stereotypically swishy. An advertisement was taken out in *Variety* to protest the show: "We of the National Gay Task Force are particularly angered by a gay character on *Soap* who is portrayed as a limp-wristed, simpering boy who wears his mother's clothes, wants a sex change operation, and allows everyone to insult him without a word of response."

The real progress gay activists were achieving in the late 1970s and early 1980s was in made-for-TV movies. Stories like *A Question of Love* offered textured drama based on actual events. The 1978 movie recounted a lesbian mother's child-custody case. Although the women lovers are never shown kissing, a scene in which one is tenderly drying the hair of the other conveyed an intimacy between women that television had never before been willing to offer.

It was a slipperier slope for sitcoms and episodic dramas to introduce recurring, sympathetic homosexual characters. Viewers did not form attachments to made-for-TV movie characters or one-time guest stars, but the lead characters in weekly series became friends. They had more potential to influence, or indoctrinate, depending on one's point of view.

In 1981, NBC planned to run a sitcom called *Love, Sidney*, based on the TV movie *Sidney Shorr*, about a homosexual commercial artist who becomes the surrogate father to the child of an aspiring actress. But the bold concept was diluted considerably before the series appeared on the air. The homosexuality of Shorr, played by Tony Randall, was not acknowledged. "The very idea of a gay man coming into our homes so close," a reviewer wrote, "offended so many people that NBC relented." Shorr became "just a strange, sad little man who doesn't date much."

A year later, the first stirrings of the AIDS crisis were reported by television news—"a rare cancer" had reached an epidemic level among male homosexuals. The revelation in 1985 that movie star Rock Hudson was dying from the disease was a turning point in the public consciousness about the magnitude of the problem. The amount of news coverage devoted to AIDS-related stories jumped sharply in 1985. That same year, the made-for-TV movie *An Early Frost*, about a young lawyer forced out of the closet by AIDS, christened a sad chapter in entertainment television's role as an agenda setter of social concerns.

Of course, cultural and political battle-lines over homosexuality did not dissolve as gay TV characters became commonplace in the late-1980s and 1990s. But because of the advocacy of homosexual groups in shaping their own images on television, the social landscape changed. "Openly lesbian and gay people are more visible throughout society," communication scholar Larry Gross observed, "and the movement has accomplished the goal of being taken for granted as a fact of our social life even by those who oppose us."

The contentious debates over President Clinton's "Don't Ask; Don't Tell" policy on gays in the military, the legality of same-sex marriages, and the constitutionality of laws discriminating against homosexuals were taking place as American viewers were meeting a multitude of gay characters of every stripe on television weekly. The 1994 wedding on *Northern Exposure* of two gay men, bed-and-breakfast owners Ron and Erik, was a formal ceremony in the fictional town of Cicely, Alaska, which, according to the series' legend, was founded by lesbian lovers. A short-lived, acclaimed series, *My So-Called Life*, included a storyline concerning a gay teenage boy. Rickie Vasquez, who is half-black and half-Puerto Rican is shunned and forced out of his home by his parents. The 1995 made-for-TV movie *Serving in Silence: The Margarethe Cammermeyer Story*, a project shepherded by executive producer Barbra Streisand, told the true story of a highly decorated career officer discharged from the Washington State National Guard because she would not lie about her sexual preference when asked during an interview for a security clearance.

In some particularly controversial cases, such as an episode of *Roseanne* in which the title character receives a surprise kiss from a lesbian, advertisers walked away. Kraft General Foods, for instance, refused to allow its commercials to appear on that broadcast. Other sponsors, though, such as American Express and Apple Computers, were attracted by the high education levels and relative affluence of gay consumers. Their demographic desirability outweighed the risk of offending viewers opposed to the inclusive stories.

By the mid-1990s, not only external gay activists, but increasing numbers of openly gay writers were putting their mark on prime time and prodding the culture. "Virtually every beloved series from *Frasier* to *Seinfeld* to *Friends*," an industry analyst reported in 1996, "is fashioned in some part—and sometimes large part—by uncloseted homosexuals."

In 1997, speculation fueled months of media debate about whether bookstore manager Ellen Morgan, the lead character in the ABC sitcom *Ellen*, would acknowledge her lesbianism in a sweeps-weeks episode. Shortly before the episode aired, the series star, Ellen DeGeneres, openly discussed her lesbianism on *Oprah* and *20/20*. She was also the subject of a *Time* magazine cover story with the headline, "Yep, She's Gay." While some regarded the "coming out" as a historic TV event, others wondered, in light of the high visibility of homosexual characters in the nineties, "What's the big deal?"

It was the mega-success of the NBC sitcom *Will and Grace*, which debuted in 1998, that cleared the decks for homosexuality to be treated matter-of-factly on television. The series was about a handsome, successful gay lawyer named Will who lived with his best friend Grace, a heterosexual interior decorator. Grace's hard-drinking assistant Karen and her flamboyant, but childlike, gay pal Jack were the comic foils. During its eight-year run, the series gave unprecedented visibility to gay characters. Neil Giuliano, president of the Gay & Lesbian Alliance Against Defamation, believed, "This is a comedy that created an emotional connection between millions of viewers and its characters. Audiences laughed along with characters like Will and Jack, and a door opened for viewers to have a greater understanding of our lives."

Men and women who hoped for a full integration of gay people into American life could find no more effective vehicle than entertainment television—an illusory form of human interaction—in redefining the spectrum of acceptable loving partnerships.

Horizontal Hold

Sam Malone's promiscuity was a source of pride to the owner of the Boston bar. His friends and patrons at Cheers held Sam in high esteem for his ability to procure sex from beautiful women at will. "I haven't had much experience saying 'no' to a woman," the former big-league baseball pitcher and recovering alcoholic boasted. "The closest I've ever come is, 'Not now, we're landing.'"

When *Cheers* premiered in 1982, most Americans assumed that white middle-class heterosexuals had nothing to fear from the immune deficiency disease that was spreading among homosexuals and Haitians. Sam's lifestyle of sexual consumption—treating women like fun-offering products to be used and discarded—resulted in no adverse consequences, either physical or emotional. But, the message that recreational fornication was a legitimate pursuit among decent men and women worried sex educators. Television, they knew from their work with young people, was an important factor in the development of behavioral repertoires in regard to sex.

In the 1985 hit series *Moonlighting*, the amorous tension and suggestive repartee between Maddie Hayes and David Addison were the key ingredients. Would the beautiful, upper-class former fashion model-turned-detective agency owner and her earthy male associate "get horizontal"? It was the show's propelling issue.

"What's happened to all the rules—love, marriage, romance?" Maddie wonders in one episode. "What's happened?" David replies, "This is the 1980s. Take your romance where you can get it." Eventually Maddie gets pregnant, after having slept with two men. "She is not treated as a wicked woman for this situation," a critic observed, "but rather a confused person in a confusing world. . . . Appropriately for the age of narcissism, the characters experience no problems with desire or sexual pleasure, only with commitment."

In the mid-1980s, frank sexual dialogue suggesting there was no such thing as bad intercourse met little interference at the networks. On *The Golden Girls*, for instance, the lusty Southern belle Blanche Devereaux offered her senior citizen housemates bawdy descriptions of her many dalliances past and present. The co-producer of *The Golden Girls*, Terry Grossman, explained, "I do think that competition from cable and VCRs has prompted more liberal attitudes at the networks toward adult themes and dialogue. Viewers have more choices."

By the late 1980s, another factor was accelerating the relaxation of television standards—the emergence of the Fox network and its appeal to young viewers with raunchy, no-holds-barred comedy. The success of *Married...With Children* signaled a new low. The humor in the show about the dysfunctional Bundy family centered on mom's frustrated attempts to coerce sex from unwilling dad. Neither Peg nor Al seemed too concerned that their scantily dressed teenage daughter was perilously close to being a prostitute.

With the AIDS crisis escalating, television's exaltation of casual sex seemed irresponsible, especially considering the medium's reluctance to carry advertisements for contraception. In 1988 the Planned Parenthood Federation of America purchased full-page newspaper and magazine ads pointing out, "They did it 20,000 times on television last year, but nobody used a condom."

"It used to be that potential partners, while perhaps not married, were at least comfortably beyond their teens," wrote *New York Times* columnist John J. O'Connor in assessing the popular prime-time themes of the early 1990s. "Virginity is decidedly unfashionable."

Beverly Hills, 90210, a rage among pre-teens, gave the clear impression that the cool kids in high school were having sex. The series exhibited what one critic aptly called a "made-for-TV morality," meaning the show essentially glamorized what it professed to caution kids against. The only member of the crowd who wanted to hang on to her virginity, Donna Martin, was presented as an odd duck with low SAT scores whose old-fashioned ideas caused complications in her social life. Brenda Walsh, on the other hand, the star of the show, has sex with her boyfriend Dylan McKay after the prom without fear or remorse.

In the 1990s, good kids, attractive kids, on TV were having sex. When Becky asked for birth-control pills on an episode of *Roseanne*, the teen confided to her mother that she and her boyfriend had already engaged in intercourse. A common theme on sitcoms of the time, such as *The Fresh Prince of Bel Air*, was the acute embarrassment teenagers feel about being virgins and the need to rectify the situation as quickly as possible.

Defenders claimed the shows were just reflecting the reality of teen sexuality in America. But, how could anyone deny they were shaping ideas as well? When third graders began sending each other notes about "getting into bed together," teachers could only infer that television was the instigator.

In the autumn of 1991, the Senate hearings on the nomination of Clarence Thomas to the U.S. Supreme Court brought the issue of sexual harassment to the forefront of news coverage for several weeks. The country was riveted by the charges of law professor Anita Hill that she was a victim of Thomas's lewd remarks and unwelcome requests for dates.

Some citizens were perplexed as to why the nominee's alleged behavior was considered so serious a transgression. He didn't, after all, physically hurt the young woman and she always had the option of leaving her employment. Not surprisingly, perhaps, the very type of behavior that was the focus of the investigation was routinely shown on television series, usually accompanied by a laugh track.

Researchers at the University of Dayton found that in the 1990 television season, 40 percent of the sexual behaviors presented in prime-time situation comedies on ABC, CBS, Fox, and NBC amounted to sexual harassment by legal definition. "We were really amazed to find that nobody was ever sanctioned or told that they were out of line," said one of the professors conducting the study.

When Bud Bundy of *Married...With Children*, approached a model at an auto show, for instance, and said: "Excuse me, I couldn't help but notice you undressing me with your eyes. How would you like to hear my recipe for a love cocktail—one of you, two cups of me, put it to a boil and serve while hot," the come-on was presented as a nothing-ventured-nothing-gained attempt to win her interest.

Tempestuous bed-hopping and dirty talk continued to be the hallmark of the Fox network in the 1990s with series like *Melrose Place* and *Martin*. The other networks kept up the pace of the race and broke new ground.

Seinfeld mined the previously taboo topic of masturbation in a 1992 episode in which Jerry challenges his friends to see who can go the longest without self-stimulation.

The traditional notion that the 8:00–9:00 p.m. hour was a family viewing time fell by the wayside. Programmers no longer felt any need to refrain from sexual content or harsh language in the early prime hour. "Producers and network executives are seemingly in denial about their impact on and responsibility toward younger viewers," a critic wrote about the 8:00 p.m. network shows during the 1995 season. "There are cheap references to sex, extramarital one-night stands—often without a mention of contraception—and, in some series, a real knack for casual profanity."

An overriding concern of the young adults who comprised the ensemble of characters on *Friends*, which aired in the former family viewing hour, was satisfying their sex drive. In one episode Chandler has intercourse with a woman he just met that afternoon in the Central Perk coffee shop. In another storyline, Phoebe is disheartened because a young man she's just started dating has not yet attempted to be intimate with her. Frequent sex is viewed as central to one's self-esteem.

In 1997, the TV networks began to display a self-assigned ratings code before each show, not unlike the designations familiar to moviegoers. Some observers quickly realized, however, that a TV-PG rating, presumably indicating the programming should be fit for ten-year-olds, was no guarantee against raunchy sexual references. The ABC family comedy *Life's Work* was rated PG and included an episode in which the mother, who worked as a prosecutor, discussed a man arrested for masturbating against a tree. "You haven't lived," she joked, "until you've gotten yourself some oak."

Along with the expanding permissiveness of network prime-time TV in the 1990s, syndicated talk shows were growing dramatically more lurid. Graphic discussions of sex and highly abusive language were routine on programs like *Jenny Jones*, *Jerry Springer*, and *The Ricki Lake Show*. The trend was called "the sleazing of America." Nielsen ratings indicated that millions of children under the age of seventeen were part of the viewing audience for the daytime talk shows on which basic standards of decency were utterly abandoned.

However perplexing to individuals with even a modicum of self-respect, when adult guests subjected themselves to the demeaning and exploitive questioning of talk show hosts, it was their prerogative to do so. When teenagers and children were drawn into the depravity, however, the boundary line into amorality was crossed. "Like pornographers and pimps," a columnist observed in 1996, "the talk show hosts and their producers found a gold mine in the sexuality of troubled children. There is no mystery involved. Viewers get turned on, the ratings go up, and the cash rolls in."

On *The Sally Jessy Raphael Show*, a thirteen-year-old girl was urged to talk about her sexual experiences, which began at age ten. Although those responsible would claim the show was meant to be a warning about the dangers of early, unprotected, and unloving sex, a professor of psychiatry at Harvard Medical School, Dr. Alvin Poussaint, believes such programs "belong on the same sordid continuum as child pornography." "They often dress the young girls very provocatively," he said, "with miniskirts and lots of makeup, trying to make them look highly sexual." Children and teens, urged by adults who ought to know better, were revealing the most intimate and often traumatic aspects of their lives as studio audiences whooped and cheered.

In 1995 the Kaiser Family Foundation released a report entitled *Sex and the Mass Media*. It concluded that teenagers themselves believed that television was contributing to "irresponsible sexual behavior, including unwanted pregnancies, among young people." "In terms of modeling behavior," said Dr. George Comerci, president of the American Academy of Pediatrics, "the older child particularly will repeat what he or she sees on TV, while the adolescent develops a personal attitude about life and the world he or she lives in as a result of what they're seeing on television."

More than two-thirds of the ten- to sixteen-year-olds surveyed in a nationwide poll in 1995 agreed that television shapes their values. "I think it pressures people my age," said fourteen-year-old Rayelyn Rodriguez; "they think if they see it on TV, they want to go do it, too."

As a result of a stunning political development in early 1998, the most sexually explicit discussions on television would soon be on the 24-hour news channels. The story began in summer 1995. Twenty-two-year-old Monica Lewinsky of Beverly Hills, California, had come to the White House in July as an unpaid intern in the office of President Bill Clinton's chief of-staff, Leon Panetta. On November 15, 1995, there was a temporary federal government shutdown because Congress refused to pass the Clinton budget. Paid staffers stayed home that day, so it was not business as usual at the White House. Clinton happened to walk in to Panetta's office amidst an informal birthday party. Lewinsky brazenly flirted with the President and he invited her back to his private study. Their affair continued for eighteen months, during which time they had ten sexual encounters in the Oval Office suite.

The rumor that President Clinton had had an affair with a White House intern was posted in the Internet gossip column "The Drudge Report" on January 17, 1998, and carried later on broadcast and cable news programs. On January 26, the President delivered a public statement, emphatically declaring "I did not have sexual relations with that woman, Miss Lewinsky."

While the President maintained his denial, the investigation of the Clinton–Lewinsky affair by Independent Counsel Kenneth W. Starr garnered a tremendous amount of media coverage. It was the top TV news story throughout the summer of 1998, receiving more airtime than all the other major stories of the time combined. On August 17, after testifying before a grand jury, President Clinton acknowledged that he had had an inappropriate relationship with Lewinsky: "It constituted a critical lapse of judgment and a personal failure on my part for which I am solely and completely responsible."

The sordid details were contained in the 453-page report and thirty-six boxes of evidence that Starr delivered to the House of Representatives in September 1998. The Republican-controlled House Judiciary Committee began releasing near-pornographic descriptions of the sexual encounters between the President and the young woman, who was not much older than his daughter.

The discussion of sexually graphic evidence, including the photograph of Lewinsky's blue dress from the Gap visibly stained with the semen of the chief executive, was unrelenting throughout the Clinton Impeachment Hearings and subsequent Senate trial. Late-night comedians had a field day with gags about the peculiarities of the presidential penis, the use of cigars as sex toys, and whether or not oral sex really counted as an infidelity.

A follow-up study to the 1995 report by the Kaiser Family Foundation found that between the 1997–98 TV season and the 1999–2000 TV season, sexual content on the small screen had nearly doubled. Television critic Tom Shales discussed the findings for his *Electronic Media* readers, "At some point the floodgates broke and in a twinkling, television became not just sex saturated but sexually explicit to a degree some of us thought would never be reached."

As the 21st century arrived, the period of childhood innocence about sexual matters was in steep decline. Television programming, especially sitcoms and talk shows, continued to define promiscuity as a standard feature of American life. Young television viewers were told in countless ways that being sexually attractive and sexually active is the yardstick by which to measure personal worth. Communications professor

Dale Kunkel of the University of California at Santa Barbara, one of the researchers for the Kaiser study, explained: "Across all the programs with sexual messages, only one in 10 had any mention of risk or responsibility. One in four of the sexual portrayals on TV involve people with no established relationship. In those situations, there's no mention of unplanned pregnancy or risk of AIDS or any other sexually transmitted disease. If more of the sex happened in loving, responsible relationships, the prevalence of sex wouldn't be as troublesome. But that's not today's TV reality."

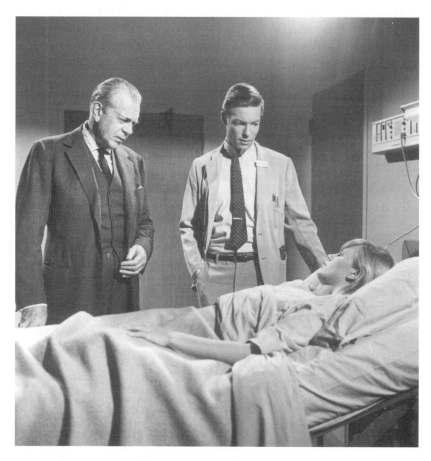

Fig. 6 The American Medical Association offered free consultation services to medical series such as the 1961 hit *Dr. Kildare* to enhance the image of the profession. (*Broadcasting and Cable* collection, Library of American Broadcasting.)

CHAPTER 6

The Boxed-In Workplace: Jobs and Professions

"Hard work always pays off." It was a lesson learned well in World War II and Americans took it on faith as the postwar era began. A returning veteran, despite a background of meager means before the war, had the opportunity to move into the middle class and provide his family with a standard of living his parents could never achieve. The GI Bill made it possible for new civilians to go to college or to pursue technical training. They received tuition as well as subsistence pay while they prepared themselves for careers. Those who wanted to establish their own businesses could get loans from the Veterans Administration.

In the burgeoning postwar economy there was no shortage of work. Low birth rates during the Depression created a labor scarcity just as U.S. companies needed to staff up for a boom. Home construction soared and growing families were anxious to fill their new houses with electrical appliances and their new driveways with cars.

Modern assembly line techniques brought prices down and ordinary workers could, for the first time, expect to own a home and a car and to enjoy leisure time as well. By the 1950s, an American family could sustain itself quite decently on the income of a single breadwinner, even one who lacked higher education.

On television, Chester A. Riley was an example of what was possible in this land of plenty. The lead character in the 1952 series *The Life of Riley* was not the brightest of the lunch-bucket brigade, but he made $110 a week as a riveter at Stevenson Aircraft and Associates in Los Angeles. Wife Peg stayed home to take care of Babs, Junior, and the dog named Rex. Their domicile was modest, but the Rileys had everything they needed. Before the series ended in 1958, Babs got married and Junior went off to college.

Unlike Chester Riley, though, his blue-collar prime-time contemporary Ralph Kramden of *The Honeymooners* was unwilling to invest honest sweat and patience in the American Dream. A driver for the Gotham Bus Company, Kramden was a get-rich-quick schemer who resented every rush hour behind the wheel on the Madison Avenue line. Instead of cultivating safe long-term investments, Ralph buys into a uranium mine in Asbury Park, markets glow-in-the-dark shoe polish, buys a formula for phony hair restorer, and sells beef stew that turns out to be dog food. All, of course, are failures. Ralph never learns that big ideas alone won't amount to anything. Imaginative enterprise for some lucky risk-takers is a shortcut to financial independence, but it requires knowledge and homework that Ralph can't be bothered with.

In one episode Ralph finds a suitcase stuffed with a million dollars in the back of his bus. After buying new furniture and appliances and having a telephone installed in his apartment, he is finally able to experience true joy when he calls his boss: "Hello, Mr. Marshall? You may or may not remember me, but this is Ralph Kramden, one of your bus drivers. For the past fifteen years I've worked for you, never missing a single day, never getting a raise or promotion. I just called to tell you that I have decided to terminate my employment at the company. (Pause) Oh yes, and just one other thing, Mr. Marshall, YOU ARE A BUMMMM." Ralph's dishonesty is punished when the money turns out to be counterfeit and he has to eat his words and return to his regular route.

Like a child who wants a bigger piece of pie, Ralph pouts about his lot in life, while his buddy Norton, a sewer worker, can't believe his good fortune that there's a sliver of pie on his plate. Norton regards himself as an "underground engineer" and believes there is an essential dignity in his labor.

In the 1950s, most Americans believed that if you got up in the morning and went to work, life improved. They believed it because they experienced upward mobility. They also believed that a rising tide lifted all ships. When a former head of General Motors, Charles E. Wilson, testified before a Senate committee considering his nomination to be Secretary of Defense in 1953, he told the committee that what's "good for our country is good for General Motors and vice versa." His remark evolved into the familiar sentiment, "What's good for General Motors is good for the country."

The nature of American work was changing in the postwar years. Labor-saving automation was increasing productivity in factories. More inventory was being made by fewer blue-collar workers. But white-collar jobs were increasing. Although fewer people were needed to build each car, more people were needed to sell them in the showrooms, advertise them, insure them, finance them, and issue licenses to drive them.

The emergence of a managerial class of salaried workers was the result of America's shifting from an industrial to a service-oriented, information-based economy. In 1956, the crossover was official—white-collar workers, for the first time, outnumbered blue-collar laborers. That same year the book *The Organization Man*, by William H. Whyte, Jr., offered advice to the swelling ranks of large corporations: "Be loyal to the company and the company will be loyal to you." Implicit in the deal was lifetime employment, steady promotions, and generous benefits.

The life of the Organization Man as presented on television wasn't humdrum but rewarding. Jim Anderson on *Father Knows Best* was the manager of the General Insurance Company in Springfield. He left for work in the morning with enthusiasm. He knew the hours he spent at the office allowed his family to be comfortable and secure. On the weekends there would be time for yard work and picnics. It was a fair trade.

Even on the rare occasion when television presented an unflattering picture of corporate culture, as in Rod Serling's play *Patterns*, which aired on the *Kraft Television Theatre* in 1955, the problems rested not with a system inherently flawed but with individuals so preoccupied with success that their morality withered.

Patterns was a story about a dynamic young executive, Fred Staples, hired by the Ramsey Corporation. Unbeknownst to Fred, he was brought in to replace Andy Sloane, a vice-president in his late sixties whose concern for the "human factor" of business decisions had long been a thorn in the side of the big boss. Lacking the guts to fire an employee who had been with the company so many years and someone who was a close friend of his father, CEO Ramsey hopes Sloane will quit if his work life is made unbearable. A campaign of humiliation results not in Sloane's resignation, however, but his death from a heart attack.

Staples, realizing what Ramsey was trying to accomplish, confronts the boss: "You're a genius, a production, organizational marvel with no compassion for human weakness! You drive and fight and tear your people into peak efficiency if they can make it, or a grave, like Andy, if they can't."

Assuming he'll be fired for his outburst, Fred is surprised when Ramsey asks him to stay: "Be a conscience for me if you want. Be anything you like. And what I don't like you'll surely know about. But if you stay you're going to have to fight for every idea and principle that's holy to you.

I think you're strong enough to take it. If not, I'm sure you're strong enough to get out."

His play, Rod Serling said, was "no indictment of big business." Viewers could interpret Staple's final decision to stay with the Ramsey Corporation in different ways. It could be regarded as a sad ending in which a talented young man sells out for a cushy vice-presidency. More likely, though, a viewer in 1955 would regard Fred as the moral winner. He decides to stay and fight on his own terms. He believes it's possible for decency and justice to coexist with growth and profits.

In the 1950s, television reinforced the American work ethic, its stories showing that prosperity was within the reach of every citizen willing to make the effort to succeed. Each week Dinah Shore closed her musical variety show singing the words "America's the greatest land of all!" Few could argue; most nodded in agreement and simply said "Amen."

Professional Fine Tuning

By the 1960s, television's influence on viewer perceptions of various occupations was a growing concern among professional organizations. They wanted greater input in their fictional imagery. "Dental groups howl when a TV character expresses dread of the dentist's chair," the head of NBC's standards and practices department remarked in 1961. "Bankers and securities dealers don't like it when one is depicted as a crook or embezzler. . . . Librarians' organizations write bitter little notes about the stereotypes of the librarian."

The practice of using technical consultants on prime-time series helped not only in the accuracy of scripting, but in public relations as well. No organization was better prepared to assist producers and scriptwriters—or had more at stake—than the American Medical Association (AMA). Since 1955 the AMA had maintained an advisory committee to work on radio, film, and television projects. But with the terrific success of two medical shows in 1961, *Ben Casey* and *Dr. Kildare*, "our workload has gone up one thousand percent," said the chairman of the committee, Dr. Eugene Hoffman, a urologist as well as medical director of Blue Cross insurance in Southern California.

The AMA media committee of the early 1960s consisted of thirteen doctors. Four resided in New York and nine were on the West Coast. Without charge, scriptwriters could get questions answered about the dosage of medicines, the equipment needed in an operating room, and proper medical procedures. In one story, for instance, a doctor reviewing the script advised that a scene in which a physician administered an anti-tetanus shot without first testing for allergies was a blatant error. Small corrections were often made in scriptwriters' dialogue. If a TV surgeon referred to "making a cut," the word "incision" would be substituted. Instead of "break," the word "fracture" was preferred.

Besides insuring that a diagnosis was properly made or that a scalpel was held correctly, the committee concerned itself with the image of the doctor that was being conveyed to a huge audience. "The efforts of the AMA physicians advisory committee are particularly significant now," the *Wall Street Journal* reported, "because the 190,000 member AMA is seeking public support of the profession in the profitable showdown ahead over medical care for the aged under Social Security." To the AMA, Social Security was "the entering wedge to socialized medicine."

Each week, about 30 percent of all television sets in the country—fifteen million households—were tuned into both *Ben Casey* and *Dr. Kildare*. It was a remarkable opportunity for shaping and enhancing the image of the medical profession. The programs were, according to a committee spokesman, "the best public relations the AMA ever had."

Among the viewers were twin sisters Judith and Julie Swain, growing up in the small Southern California town of Cypress. Almost thirty years later, *The New York Times* profiled their remarkable careers. Judith became the director of the division of cardiology at the University of Pennsylvania School of Medicine and Julie became the chief of cardiovascular surgery at the University of Nevada School of Medicine. The *Times* noted the influence of the TV doctors: "Both [sisters], after watching *Ben Casey* and *Dr. Kildare* wanted to be doctors and save lives."

Although the AMA was quick to point out it had no power to censor the content of the programs, the advisory committee did "admit to an occasional successful attempt to squelch unfavorable shows." On one proposed episode of *Ben Casey*, a colleague of the title character, also a neurosurgeon, turns out to be a quack. The AMA protested saying that such a charlatan would never have been able to become a doctor in the first place and rise to such a level before his incompetence was discovered. The script was scrapped.

The producers of medical series often wanted to show doctors with character flaws or problems such as alcoholism or drug addiction, for the sake of drama. It's hard to create an interesting story, they argued, if all the principals are perfect. The AMA had to make allowances. But it was always made very clear that these were rare cases. And, of course, it was never the lead characters who had serious problems. Beating disease and death was their challenge—and they hated to lose. No resource would be spared in the fight. Doctors helped everyone, rich and poor alike. No questions about insurance or ability to pay ever stood in the way. On shows that displayed the AMA seal in the closing credits, doctors' work was shown as sacred. Those who questioned their medical judgment—like malpractice attorneys—were villains standing in the way of progress.

By comparison, one rare medical show that chose not to use the AMA advisory committee was the 1962 series *The Nurses*. Even the offer of help from the American Nursing Association was turned down. Instead, three nurses were hired as independent consultants. The result was scripts that were far more controversial, including one on euthanasia and one episode that dealt with a nurse who was being harassed by doctors because of her public support of Medicare.

In the early 1960s, several prime-time courtroom series, including *Perry Mason*, *The Defenders*, and *Arrest and Trial*, were generating images of the American justice system to millions of viewers—the great majority of whom never had occasion to consult a lawyer and even fewer of whom had ever participated in a trial. The scriptwriters were offered technical advice through an appointed committee of the American Bar Association. The shows also retained lawyers on staff to guide the productions.

The image of lawyers was a little trickier to protect than that of doctors, though, since their adversaries were not disease and death, but other lawyers. Attorney Edward Bennett Williams, evaluating the impact of legal shows on public perceptions, wrote in a 1964 article in *Television Quarterly*: "Television has taught the public through endless repetition that trial lawyers are a scheming tricky lot. This has actually produced repercussions in real life. The least significant witness now comes to court expecting to be tricked, ridiculed and harassed by inquisitorial gimmicks."

The disproportionate number of courtroom triumphs by TV lawyers was also seen as a problem in raising expectations for the performance of real-life lawyers. "Perry Mason has only lost one case in the past eight years," Williams wrote. "One might expect that his services would be in great demand, that his waiting room would be overflowing with clients and that, in preparing his cases, he would be working some long days. Yet he is free—day or night—to speed to the scene of a crime and beat the police to the

discovery of a murderer. He practices law, as far as any viewer can determine, with one secretary, one investigator and one legal assistant."

Reginald Rose, the creator and executive producer of *The Defenders*,
responded to Mr. Williams's criticisms of the genre: "The realistic drama
is obliged to provide verisimilitude but it cannot offer literal adherence to
actuality. . . . The fact that the legal details which might occupy a full day
of courtroom procedure are related in five minutes on *The Defenders* is
quite irrelevant. If what results is a fuller understanding of the meaning
of law and justice among multitudes of human beings, then the charge of
'unrealistic' is pointless. . . . I am convinced that we are doing good."

Teachers were another group of professionals concerned with their
television portrayals. So, when E. Jack Neuman, the executive producer
of *Mr. Novak*, a series about a rookie high school English teacher, asked
the National Education Association (NEA) for help, the organization
didn't hesitate. It agreed to set up a rotating panel of educators to work as
ongoing consultants, reviewing scripts and suggesting themes. Yet, in spite
of the effort to involve the NEA, "there are teachers who pick and pull and
pout about the damnedest things," wrote Neuman. "For instance, they say
Mr. Novak is too handsome. What do they want me to do cast a gnome?"

John Novak's occasional alcoholic drink after work was troubling to
some teachers, who felt it sent the wrong message of approval. In one
episode Mr. Novak urged a beautiful young remedial-reading teacher in
whom he was romantically interested to have another glass of wine.
Letters of protest arrived from many teachers worried that students would
get the wrong idea. "He is not a perfect man," Neuman responded, "he is
certainly not the perfect image of a teacher. I didn't want him to be perfect
and I didn't want him surrounded by perfection. But I wanted him to try
for perfection and to keep trying, week in and week out."

Some of the input that networks and producers received was less than
useful. In 1966 a prominent group of sales executives offered advice on
how the CBS production of Arthur Miller's *Death of a Salesman* could be
improved. The play, they felt, could use some trimming of "needless anti-
selling, anti-business" lines that added "nothing to either plot, mood, or
characterization." It was also suggested that a brief prologue called "Life
of a Salesman" could be added pointing out that "with modern customer-
oriented selling methods, Willy Lomans are ghosts of the past."

Of all the ways in which Americans learned about and formed opinions
about professions and their practitioners in the postwar era, the most

persuasive messenger was television. In the 1960s, organized attempts to influence the medium's storytelling—some successful and some ignored—became routine as it became obvious that in the real world, familiar images mattered.

Declining Fortunes

Richard Nixon correctly perceived that white, middle-aged, hardworking, blue-collar Americans who paid their taxes and kept their houses tidy were feeling neglected as the 1960s came to a close. He dubbed them the "silent majority" and validated their resentments over a decade in which they were made to feel unimportant. Women, blacks, Hispanics, gays, and college students seemed to be getting all of society's attention. Even on television, working stiffs had virtually vanished

Norman Lear had his own instincts about the social divisions that were beginning to take hold. When *All in the Family* was introduced in January 1971, Archie Bunker, a loading dock laborer who occasionally drove a cab, articulated—however ungrammatically—the frustration of many working-class Americans as the good economy of the 1950s and sixties began to be eroded away by inflation.

Archie's fears about losing ground were a welcome TV subject for organized labor—itself losing ground quickly. But his racism and pigheadedness became part of a troubling prototype. In the 1972 presidential election the term "the Archie Bunker vote" began finding its way into the press. The reference was understood to mean "the stupid worker vote." A Teamster Union newsletter took issue with the stereotype: "Some Teamsters are thin, intelligent, compassionate, and truly believe everyone deserves an equal opportunity."

In the early 1970s the growth that had followed World War II began to slow down and middle-class incomes began to sag. "The American example of the good life became a beacon for the rest of the world," said author David Halberstam. "But we took our affluence for granted. We took a historical fluke and began to think it was a permanent condition."

The Organization of the Petroleum Exporting Countries (OPEC) oil embargo in 1973 and 1974 harshly ended the assumption of unlimited prosperity. As unemployment swelled and productivity declined, American workers were no longer filled with the faith and optimism of the previous two decades. With inflation and the soaring cost of heating fuel, the dream of suburdon home ownrship grew more elusive. The gap between the incomes of the well-to-do and those of the poor and working class began to widen into what would eventually become the Grand Canyon.

On television, "the great American class struggle" became a popular theme. "Working people," critic Robert Sklar wrote about the 1970s, "are popping up on prime-time television like mushrooms on the forest floor." And when working-class characters confronted wealthy characters, the rich were typically shown to be morally bankrupt.

On *Happy Days*, set in the 1950s, Arthur Fonzarelli, better known as Fonzie, is a leather-jacketed teenager from the wrong side of the tracks whose father deserted his family when his boy was three. Working as a garage mechanic, Fonzie meets a beautiful and rich young woman named Adrienna Prescott. The Uptown Girl invites the Fonz to join her for a game of tennis at her club. Despite coming from different worlds, romance blossoms. At the high school prom, Fonzie hears the rumor that Adrienna is a married woman. She doesn't deny it and tells Fonzie that she and her husband have "an understanding." But the Downtown Boy won't have any part of it. "I got some rules I live by," he says. "And one is I don't take what ain't mine, understand?"

Class antagonisms, infrequently exhibited on TV in the 1950s, erupted in the 1970s. On *Laverne and Shirley*, the title characters work the assembly line in the bottle-cap division of Shotz brewery. In one episode, they wander into an exclusive dress boutique to browse and daydream. When the haughty manager insinuates they're in the wrong place, Laverne shoots back: "We wouldn't buy dresses here if we were rich and naked."

Workplace comedies of the mid- and late-1970s featured low-status workers who had more brains and dignity than their bosses. *Alice* was a series about a young widow and mother who takes a job as a waitress at Mel's Diner as a pit stop on her way to a singing career. She's too smart for the room and everyone knows it, but she's stuck serving chili because she just can't get a break. Ambition and hard work no longer guarantee a comfortable station in life.

On *Taxi*, the tyrannical dispatcher and manager of the Sunshine Cab Company, Louie De Palma, has the power to make his drivers miserable. Alex Rieger, a middle-aged career cabbie is the senior member of the crew. The younger drivers have not yet had their aspirations drained, and so they continue to pursue bigger and better things while hacking part-time. Elaine hopes to run her own art gallery, Bobby is an actor, and Tony is a prizefighter. But Alex—a man with all the potential needed to climb the ladder of success, but not the stomach for it—has made peace with his dead-end job.

The workaday existence of the Organization Man presented on television in the 1950s and sixties in such attractive terms took on a different complexion as the 1970s advanced. When sitcom episodes had working-class folks dealing with white-collar, mid-management folks, such as insurance claims adjusters or department store managers, the white-collar workers were revealed to be powerless cogs in a boring and slow-moving bureaucracy. Since they produced nothing, their value was nebulous. Success for the pen-pushers depended on how well they pleased and flattered those on a higher rung.

Businessmen became stock villains. On the final episode of *The Mary Tyler Moore Show* in 1977, new management took over the television station to boost weak ratings. A cold-hearted executive fired the entire news staff of WJM, except for Ted Baxter, the shallow anchorman who depended on the efforts of the others to get through a broadcast.

On action-adventure shows, a character wearing a three-piece pinstripe suit was most likely to be the bad guy. Businessmen as criminals became a standard formula. "On almost every episode of *Columbo*," wrote critic Ben Stein, "a rich businessman has killed someone and seeks to bully Columbo into leaving him alone because of his high status. . . . Not even the smallest of businessmen is exempt from the mark of Cain. In a recent episode of *Kojak*, a local candy store owner in New York was, in reality, fencing stolen goods and giving teenage suppliers heroin."

The loss of confidence Americans were feeling about their economic future in the 1970s was both reflected and bolstered by television. It was no longer a certainty that good, smart, hardworking people would come out on top. There was an odd comfort in stories that suggested the deck might be stacked against working men and women—that their financial stagnancy was due to factors beyond their control.

TV on TV

Characters who made their livings by making television programs were naturally intriguing to viewers. In 1950 two popular series involved a show within a show. The great radio comedian Jack Benny migrated to the new medium, and a frequent premise of *The Jack Benny Show* became the star's preparation for his weekly television program. *The George Burns and Gracie Allen Show* also making the shift from radio, portrayed the super comedy duo as performers in a fictional weekly comedy show on television. Little of the nuts and bolts of show biz, however, were really featured in either show since they focused primarily on the home life of the characters.

The first TV series that gave a feel for the behind-the-scenes work involved in putting on a television program was *The Dick Van Dyke Show*, which premiered in 1961. Rob Petrie was the head writer for *The Alan Brady Show*, a live comedy-variety program akin to Milton Berle's or Sid Caesar's show. Rob and his co-writers, Buddy Sorrell and Sally Rogers, were always under deadline pressure to come up with great scripts that would meet the approval of the show's producer, Mel Cooley, the sycophantic brother-in-law of the neurotic star Alan Brady.

Despite the difficult egos of Cooley and Brady, the writers always managed to rise to the occasion and give the viewers of *The Alan Brady Show* a great hour of entertainment. Working in television was shown as an occupation that contributed to the national life in an upbeat way. Rob, Buddy, and Sally were held in high esteem by friends and strangers. Their principles were never compromised by what they did to achieve success.

When a sneaky game show host gets Laura Petrie to reveal a secret about Alan Brady on live television, he's made out to be an unethical bad apple in a bushel full of well-intentioned professionals. "Have you ever been to Alan Brady's house?" the host asks Laura. "Oh yes, many times," she replies. "Does he wear his toupee at home?" he prods. "Oh, yes, he wears it all the time," the innocent Laura answers before she realizes she's been tricked. "You mean Alan Brady is bald!" "Well, no," Laura hesitates. "Then why does he wear a toupee?" the host laughs. "Well, well..." his victim squirms. "Well gals, the secret is out. She said it and she knows. Alan Brady is bald and you learned it here! How about that folks? Aren't we devils?!"

By the early 1970s, characters who were honest and competent television professionals were having a harder time. In the WJM newsroom in Minneapolis, Mary Richards, Lou Grant, and Murray Slaughter try their best to produce a newscast of integrity, only to have it bollixed by Ted Baxter, the self-absorbed newscaster who believes the capital of New York State is Albania. *The Mary Tyler Moore Show*'s model of a TV anchorman who was all style over substance coincided with the real-life trend of "Happy Talk" in local newscasts around the country. News consultants were urging local stations into more sensational story presentation and the physical attractiveness of newscasters was becoming more critical than their journalistic skills.

Capitalizing on the public's growing perception of television as an industry with a shrinking commitment to public service, several series in the late 1970s made fun of the excesses of the medium. *America 2-Night*, a parody of TV talk shows, which began as *Fernwood 2-Night*, featured a week-long build-up for "Electrocution Night '78" in which a convict would be executed on live television while his wife negotiated book, movie, and T-shirt deals. Viewers were encouraged to submit entries to a contest that required they complete the sentence "I would like to throw the switch because...."

Second City TV was a collection of sketches that all revolved around the mythical SCTV studios of channel 109 in Melonville. Each episode took viewers through an entire broadcast day with every imaginable TV format parodied in wickedly accurate send-ups. The show was for people who had grown up with television, viewers who knew the conventions and had the same memory bank of TV images.

SCTV offered an entirely different view of television as an institution than *The Dick Van Dyke Show*. Rob and his writers strived for excellence each week. But Guy Caballero, the sleazy station owner of channel 109, is just in it for the money; he doesn't have a greater calling to inform or entertain. The optimism of the early sixties that TV was a benefit of modern life had given way to a dubious outlook. Television's schlockiness made it ripe for ridicule.

In one episode station manager Guy Caballero is on the phone discussing a new series with producer Grant Tinker. The show has some similarities to the hit series *Diff'rent Strokes*. "No, it's not exactly a spin-off," explains Cabellero. "It's more of a rip-off."

The propensity of television to imitate rather than innovate was displayed in full measure with a short-lived 1978 dramatic series called *W.E.B.* The idea of a show about an ambitious female television executive was inspired by the successful 1976 film *Network*, written by Paddy Chayefsky and starring Faye Dunaway, which questioned the responsibility of ratings-hungry programmers. The TV series depicted a television network as a workplace full of ruthless and unsavory characters, where backstabbing was standard operating procedure.

In the early 1980s, dramatic series about professional ethics included *Hill Street Blues*, which was about police work, and *Lou Grant*, set at a major Los Angeles newspaper. Though not nearly as successful, the 1981 series *Fitz and Bones* was in the same genre and dealt with television journalism. Ryan Fitzpatrick is an aggressive investigative reporter for a San Francisco TV station and Bones Howard is his cameraman. Neither is burdened by self-modesty.

Fitz and Bones took some intentional and well-placed jabs at the people who produce local news. In one episode involving police misconduct in the shooting death of a fourteen-year-old inner-city kid, a policewoman questions the team about a series of sensational reports they're doing with a disgruntled cop who's blowing the whistle on his colleagues. "Do you know what it's like being a cop on the street?" she asks emotionally. "Yeah, I do," Bones says. "We did a mini-doc on it—won an Emmy, too." In another scene Fitz introduces himself to a stranger by saying, "You probably know me. I'm Ryan Fitzpatrick, news reporter for Channel 3." "No," the confused man replies, "but maybe you know me, I'm a plumber."

Arrogance was also a quality that Bill Bittinger, the lead character of the 1983 sitcom *Buffalo Bill*, had in full supply. As the host of a local talk show in Buffalo, New York, he managed to deceive his viewers into thinking he was a decent and charming man. But off-camera he was an insensitive boor.

In 1984 the lead character of *Newhart*, author Dick Loudon, became the host of a local TV talk show, *Vermont Today*. The producer of the modest program, Michael Harris, a pretentious yuppie, had an inflated sense of his importance in the broadcast industry. His New Year's resolution was "Get chummy with Sinatra." Zealous as he was in self-promotion, the young producer was spineless in doing the right thing if it involved any jeopardy of his status.

As public opinion polls were revealing that Americans were losing confidence in television as an institution, television programs about TV were reflecting the duplicity that viewers perceived. The 1988 series *Murphy Brown* introduced many situations that highlighted the struggle between solid journalistic values and the quest for higher ratings. Murphy is a reporter on a network news magazine show called *FYI*, broadcast live from Washington, D.C., each week. Her specialty is doing hard-hitting interviews with important newsmakers.

In the show's first episode, Murphy is just returning from the Betty Ford Clinic, where she's undergone treatment for alcoholism and cigarette addiction. She meets *FYI*'s new executive producer for the first time and is unnerved when he turns out to be a twenty-five-year-old kid, Miles Silverberg, instead of a seasoned pro with war stories to tell. Another new colleague, Corky Sherwood, is even more appalling to Murphy's sense of professionalism. The perky Corky is a Southern belle and former Miss America with no experience under her belt. Her function on *FYI* appears to be strictly ornamental.

The blurring line between news and entertainment was a frequent issue that surfaced in the plots of *Murphy Brown*. The episode "It's How You Play the Game" opens with Miles lamenting, "If the ratings get any lower, I'll be hosing down the produce at Food World." *FYI* is being clobbered by a tabloid news show that features subjects like "the tragic plight of sex-crazed registered nurses." For the upcoming *FYI*, reporter Frank Fontana has prepared a poignant segment on the plight of the homeless. But he knows his important work will only get a fraction of the audience that schlockmeister Jerry Gold will pull in with his trashy topics.

Murphy and colleague Jim Dial, an erudite newsman whose hero is Edward R. Murrow, decide that if a sleazy opening segment will get people to tune in to *FYI* and stay tuned for Frank's report, then it's a tactic they're willing to employ. Ideas are pitched: "The Secret Sex Life of Cable Installers"; "Nuns Who Mud Wrestle for Charity"; even fetishes and bestiality are considered. They finally come up with a panel of three members of the Hookers Organization for American Rights (HOAR) debating three members of Homemakers Against Gratuitous Sex (HAGS). The confrontation gets out of control and a brawl erupts. When Jim intervenes, he gets decked.

The next morning the *FYI* team is ashamed of what they've done. But there is good news when the overnight ratings come in. They beat Jerry Gold and kept a huge audience for the entire hour. Millions of viewers saw Frank's piece. The gang starts to wonder if maybe they shouldn't fight fire with fire if that's what it takes to get people to watch the show. "Yeah, people watching the show," Murphy tells them. "The way they slow down on the highway to see an accident."

Murphy Brown boldly acknowledged a diminishing of quality in television news as the 1980s drew to a close. But the sitcom did not place the responsibility solely with the network brass or the men and women who created the programming. Television's self-critique could be much more piercing if viewers had to share the blame. Broadcast workplaces were depicted as ethical battlegrounds where all that was needed for evil to triumph was for good audiences to be indifferent to excellence.

Downsizing Blues

Murphy Brown and *Roseanne* both arrived on prime time in 1988 and became hit series. Other than that, the two women had little in common. Murphy's troubles didn't include having her electricity shut off for non-payment. And Roseanne never fretted about a lost-in-the-mail invitation to President George H.W. Bush's inaugural ball.

"My work is just about the most important thing in my life," Murphy tells her young boss after a few days of an unwanted two-week vacation. "And not being here practically killed me. I missed the studio. I missed that incessant noise the Teletype makes. I missed my office."

Roseanne isn't nearly as attached to her job as an hourly worker in the plastics factory—which was a good thing since she lost it soon enough. So, she found new work. She shampooed heads in a beauty parlor. She worked behind the counter at Chicken Divine and reported to a supervisor who had not yet graduated from high school. During her stint in the fast-food industry she moonlighted as a barmaid at the Lobo Lounge. She tried phone sales, but wasn't very good at it. And when the coffee shop of Rodbell's Department store closed its doors, she lost her waitressing job.

"Roseanne's resume, such as it is," wrote media critic Roseanne Freed, "stands as a legacy of the birth of disposable McJobs and a contingency workforce that marks the permanent transition to a post-industrial economy."

The man of the house, Dan Conner, a construction worker by trade, is also frequently unemployed. When Roseanne's sister Jackie gets on his nerves, she asks her brother-in-law what's bothering him. "What's bothering me, Jackie," Dan shouts, "is that you're over here all the time!" "Well, Dan," she retorts, "if you had a job, you wouldn't notice so much!"

As the 1990s dawned, large segments of America's middle class were slipping out of the comfort zone. Working harder and earning less were givens—a fact of life as sure as the entitlements of the Eisenhower era. "So commonplace has the news of corporate downsizing become," *The New York Times* reported, "that the notion of lifetime employment has come to seem as dated as soda jerks or tail fins. And a growing number of Americans have come to doubt one of the basic precepts of the national faith—that their children will have a higher standard of living than they did."

The lead character in *Grace Under Fire* was a crew chief at an oil refinery, a tough but well-paying job. Before long, though, she was bumped back to being a regular crew member in a wave of job cuts. Grace's boyfriend Rick, a member of management, has the unpleasant task of telling long-time employees their association with the company has been terminated. He's not cold-hearted but professional and brief in his dismissals. He believes he's doing the right thing for the company. Eventually Rick too is on the receiving end of a pink slip.

Job insecurity and elusive promotions also dogged many white-collar television characters. The protagonist of *The Drew Carey Show* has worked faithfully for years as the assistant director of personnel in a Cleveland department store. Middle-age is just around the corner and he's stuck in a partitioned cubicle with little hope of moving up. He lives in the house he bought from his parents when they retired, but the neighborhood isn't what it used to be. Exceeding his parents' standard of living just isn't in the cards for Drew—or any of his old high school friends—unless, somehow, the deck gets reshuffled.

The premiere episode of a sitcom with the punning title *Good Company*, set in an advertising agency, dealt with the panic among employees when downsizing is imminent. The head of the creative team is told he has to fire one of his team-members immediately. When he protests that his colleague deserves better, his boss is unmoved. "I'll expect his outplacement papers on my desk at nine tomorrow morning," she insists. The heroine of another mid-nineties series, *Can't Hurry Love*, works in an employment agency and is surrounded by men and women who are casualties of corporate retrenchment.

Comedian Bill Cosby gave voice to this frustration as sixty-year-old Hilton Lucas in the 1996 series *Cosby*. After being downsized, the miserable Lucas resents any references to losing his job. "My job was taken away from me," he insists to anyone willing to listen. In real life, Americans were recognizing the company was family no more. "I'm not going to be like my dad and work 'til 10 o'clock at night and never see the kids," a young worker said in reaction to widespread layoffs. "What for? So I'll be thanked with a pink slip?"

Baby boomers who grew up expecting rosy employment opportunities were rocked by the realities of the stripped-down American workplace of the 1990s. But younger people, the group of Americans labeled Generation X, assumed diminished prospects. "Twentysomethings" knew they inherited a bum deal. In 1955, college fees at UCLA were $200 per semester for an out-of-state student and $50 for a Californian. Well into the 1960s a student could work his or her way through school without substantial help from parents and begin a career without major debts.

By the 1990s, the cost of higher education was breaking middle-class families. On *Roseanne*, high school senior Becky Conner decides to elope with her mechanic boyfriend when she learns the money in her college fund had been lost because her father invested it in a motorcycle shop that went under. When Becky accuses her parents of blowing her chance to have a better life than theirs, Roseanne and Dan are heartbroken because they know she's right. They had gambled away her future.

But even more privileged young people whose families had the where-withal to put them through school were still having a harder time plunging into careers. "There is a tremendous amount of floundering around," observed Nancy K. Schlossberg, professor of counseling at the University of Maryland, who studied the life patterns of eighteen- to twenty-four-year-olds in the early 1990s. "They take longer getting through college and postpone choosing major fields of study. So they often switch jobs and delay marriage and generally proceed at what might seem to middle-age parents as half-speed."

"The reason why we're slower," a twenty-three–year-old college student responded, "is that the opportunities are not out there." Low-pay, low-prestige, low-benefit jobs were what were waiting. Brand new grown-ups in the 1990s were feeling cheated and television tapped into their cynicism about work endowing their lives with purpose and self-respect.

Sipping a cup of wake-up coffee in the kitchen of the *Friends* apartment, Chandler suddenly looks at his wristwatch. "Oh wow, it's late. I've gotta get to work," the entry-level computer programmer says as he reaches for his sports coat. "If I don't get to the office and punch those numbers into the computer..." He stops in mid-sentence and then realizes his mistaken sense of significance. "Actually, it won't make any difference if I don't punch those numbers into the computer, will it? My job is totally meaningless. I hate it."

*Under*employment is the problem for Chandler's friend Rachel, who works as a coffee shop waitress. A college education got her nowhere. Young viewers with college loans to repay and no decent job in sight could identify with her situation (although probably not with her wardrobe and spacious apartment). The overarching theme of *Friends* that so resonated with its young adult audience was that meaning in life comes from relationships, not work. For baby busters, jobs will come and go. Success is better defined by the quality and loyalty of your pals.

Top Jobs

Starting in 1999, the seven-year run of the dramatic series *The West Wing* gave TV viewers a vivid sense of the inner workings of the Executive branch of government. Until then, most fictional presidents had been comic roles. For instance, in the 1987 series *Mr. President*, veteran actor George C. Scott played President Samuel Arthur Tresch. The grouchy former governor of Wisconsin and his family have a hard time adjusting to the lack of privacy in the White House. When his wife walks out on him, her flaky sister—who has designs on her brother-in-law—assumes the role of First Lady with grandiose flair.

President Josiah "Jed" Bartlet, though, was no caricature; he was a complex individual whose great intellect and passion co-existed with his flaws and blind spots. And his coterie of able, dedicated professionals on *The West Wing* respected the office of the presidency as much as they did President Bartlet.

The West Wing creator, Aaron Sorkin, who wrote the 1995 feature film *The American President*, again turned to people who had worked in the White House to assure a level of authenticity to the scripts. Dee Dee Myers, who served as the press secretary during the first two years of the Clinton administration, recalled her invitation to work on the series: "It was early 1998, and the Monica Lewinsky scandal was the talk of the country. I just didn't see how a show about a slightly romanticized White House could succeed in the era of Impeachment. But I told Aaron I liked the pilot and would be happy to serve as a consultant if and when the show got made. I didn't think it would."

A year later, NBC picked up the series and Myers spent several months working with Sorkin, staff writers, directors, producers, and prop people. They asked her questions like: "What happens when the President walks through a door? Where are his secret service agents? What's it like to brief the press?" Consultants came from both parties, including Peggy Noonan, speechwriter for the first President Bush; Gene Sperling, an economic advisor for the Clinton administration; Marlin Fitzwater, a press secretary

Plate 1 The work of independent inventor Philo Farnsworth, who dreamed of "capturing light in a bottle" as a schoolboy, laid the foundation for the development of electronic television. (*Broadcasting and Cable* collection, Library of American Broadcasting.)

Plate 2 Fran Harris was one of eight women selected to become the Women's Auxiliary Television Technical Staff (WATTS) and run a Chicago television station during World War II. (Library of American Broadcasting.)

Plate 3 Watching *Howdy Doody*, a show that celebrated unbridled fun, became an after-school ritual for the first TV generation of American kids. (NBC publicity photo.)

Plate 4   The 1953 drama *Marty* was an example of what scriptwriter Paddy Chayefsky called "the marvelous world of the ordinary." (NBC publicity photo.)

Plate 5   *Life Is Worth Living* catapulted Bishop Fulton J. Sheen to TV stardom in the early 1950s. (*Broadcasting and Cable* collection, Library of American Broadcasting.)

Plate 6   The TV series *Amos 'n' Andy* had both critics and defenders in the black community. (*Broadcasting and Cable* collection, Library of American Broadcasting.)

Plate 7 Contestants on *Queen for a Day* vied to tell the saddest story of need in order to win copious prizes. (NBC publicity photo.)

Plate 8 Lucy Ricardo's schemes to get into show business on *I Love Lucy* only got her into trouble. (*Broadcasting and Cable* collection, Library of American Broadcasting.)

Plate 9 On *The Honeymooners*, bus driver Ralph Kramden's ideas to get rich quick never panned out. (CBS publicity photo.)

Plate 10   The 1964 appearances of the Beatles on the *Ed Sullivan Show* influenced American music, culture, and fashion. (CBS publicity photo.)

Plate 11   In the mid-1960s, women with supernatural powers, such as the title character in *I Dream of Jeannie*, caused trouble for men who didn't want the old order upset. (NBC publicity photo.)

Plate 12   The landmark series *The Mary Tyler Moore Show* redefined the image of single working women in the 1970s. (CBS publicity photo.)

Plate 13   Archie Bunker of *All in the Family* captured the frustrations of many working-class Americans who had been dubbed "the silent majority" in the early 1970s. (CBS publicity photo.)

Plate 14   Chevy Chase cemented the image of President Gerald Ford as a clumsy bumbler with his over-the-top portrayal in *Saturday Night Live* skits. (NBC publicity photo.)

Plate 15 The squad room in the police comedy *Barney Miller* was an ethnic and racial blend. (ABC publicity photo.)

Plate 16 Luke's rape of Laura on *General Hospital* in 1979 did not prevent their romance from blossoming.
(ABC publicity photo.)

Plate 17 NBC's department of broadcast standards defended the fighting, shooting, and car crashes in *The A-Team* as "action" rather than "violence" because no one was ever seriously wounded. (NBC publicity photo.)

Plate 18 On *Cheers*, bar owner Sam Malone was a recovering alcoholic. (*Broadcasting and Cable* collection, Library of American Broadcasting.)

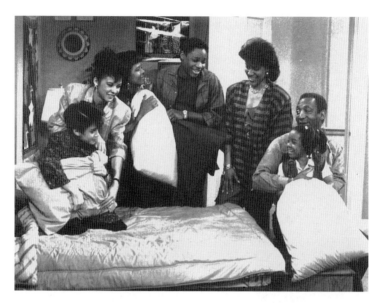

Plate 19 *The Cosby Show,* the top-rated series of the 1980s, presented an intact family with professional parents who emphasized the importance of education. (NBC publicity photo.)

Plate 20 The O.J. Simpson murder trial paved the way for "feeding frenzy" TV coverage of other sensational stories with little genuine extended news value. (*Broadcasting and Cable* collection, Library of American Broadcasting.)

for Presidents Reagan and George H.W. Bush; and Patrick Caddell, a Democratic pollster and advisor to Jimmy Carter.

It wasn't only the logistics and physical trappings of federal workplaces that were captured by *The West Wing*, though, it was the nature of governance that was conveyed. *Time* magazine correspondent Jay Branegan referred to the series as "a national civics lesson." Among the real-world issues tackled on the series were school vouchers, the "Don't Ask, Don't Tell" policy on gays in the military, and the legitimacy of statistical sampling in the national census.

Social studies teachers and college professors found ways to use the series as an educational resource. Dr. Staci Beavers, a professor of political science, wrote, "*The West Wing* presents great pedagogical potential." Students who viewed the series, she believed, would have a deeper understanding of the political process than those whose information came from panel shows such as *Meet the Press* or *Face the Nation*.

Patrick Caddell recalled being a guest at a White House correspondents' dinner in 2000, where the actors of the TV series mingled with their real-life counterparts and discussed plotlines of *The West Wing*. Secretary of State Madeleine Albright sought out Caddell and told him how much she liked "the India–Pakistan episode." "She said it was one of the best expositions on foreign policy on TV that she'd seen."

The veracity of the series was applauded by Gerald Ford, Jimmy Carter, and Bill Clinton, as well as others who were intimately acquainted with the Oval Office, including Secretary of State Henry Kissinger, Clinton Chief of Staff Leon Panetta, and Karl Rove, Deputy Chief of Staff for Political Affairs in the George W. Bush White House. Dee Dee Myers reflected, "The show didn't get everything right, but it got the big things right." Jennifer Palmieri, who worked in the White House for eight years and was the Deputy Press Secretary from 1998 to 2001, was also an admirer of *The West Wing*. "The show depicted the truth—that most public servants are in government for the right reasons, work hard, and make a lot of personal sacrifices, and try to do right thing," she explained. "Sometimes doing the 'right thing' isn't as easy or clear as it looks."

Whether the idealism of *The West Wing* inspired viewers to consider careers in public service may be difficult to measure. But the smash hit police drama, *CSI* (Crime Scene Investigation), which began in 2000, triggered a startling increase in admission applications to forensic science programs at colleges and universities across the country. The director of the program in multidisciplinary studies at the University of Nevada, Las Vegas, Dr. Jennifer Thompson, noted, "*CSI* is getting more people interested in science, which is fantastic." Her colleague, Professor Dan Holstein of the UNLV's forensic science program, was the real-life inspiration for *CSI*'s lead character, Gil Grissom. *Scientific American* reported, "Through *CSI* and its siblings, the public has developed a fascination and respect for science as an exciting an important profession unseen since the Apollo space program."

The importance of female characters in *CSI*—such as Catherine Willows, whose specialty is blood-splatter analysis—has also been credited as a contributing factor in a demographic shift in the male-dominated field. In the early years of the new century, women became the majority in forensic science programs in the country, which were increasing in size and number.

What was called the "*CSI* effect" was having an impact on the workaday lives of trial lawyers and those in law enforcement. John Marquis, Oregon district attorney and vice-president of the National District Attorneys Association, told CBS News: "Jurors now expect us to have a DNA test for just about every case. They expect us to have the most advanced technology possible, and they expect it to look like it does on television." Commenting on the *CSI* effect, a Knoxville, Tennessee, police officer said: "I had a victim of a car robbery, and he saw a red fiber in the back of his car. He said he wanted me to run tests to find out what it was from, what retail store that object was purchased at, and what credit card was used."

CSI, along with other prime-time series dealing with the professions of crime solving, crime fighting, health care, and the law, offered idealized versions of their fields. "People on TV are never doing the minute-by-minute work that they have to do in real life," said Robert Thompson, director of the Center for the Study of Popular Television at Syracuse University. The ordinariness and the mundane tasks of every occupation are not the stuff of riveting scripts. Typically, a police officer on duty spends between 30 and 50 per cent of his or her time writing reports. Countless hours are spent in legal research before a case comes to a head in a dramatic courtroom scene. And crime-scene analysis is painstakingly slow.

The occupations of television characters throughout the history of the medium have never reflected real-life proportions. The percentage of police officers, detectives, doctors, and lawyers appearing on prime-time series far exceeded their actual numbers because the life-and-death nature of their work offers storytellers limitless opportunities for developing compelling plots. But even in this unbalanced picture, television provided an index of perceptions about work in 20th-century America.

From television, viewers have learned about occupations for which they lack firsthand knowledge. Recognizing that TV images contribute to the formation of lasting impressions about their work and motivations, the members of various professions and crafts have taken steps to ensure that their jobs are represented in a way that enhances their standing. But viewers also see in TV characters surrogates who experience job circumstances similar to their own. And although the conventions of entertainment TV don't allow faithful depictions of real-life workplaces, TV programs do convey realistic attitudes and opinions. The spirit of American workers since mid-century is embedded in the television record.

Fig. 7 Cigarettes were among the most widely advertised products on television as American consumer culture grew in the 1950s and 1960s. The Lucky Strike Sportsmen pitched their brand. (*Broadcasting and Cable* collection, Library of American Broadcasting.)

CHAPTER 7

Tuning Out Restraint:
Indulgence and Advertising

"Who Will Pay for Broadcasting?" asked a headline in the December 1922 issue of *Popular Radio*. The obvious answer was *not* advertising. In the first blush of radio mania, the manufacturers of radio sets assumed responsibility for programming in order to sell their product. Newspapers and department stores operated radio stations as a promotional strategy, and educational institutions experimented with a new way of disseminating information. On-air talent, lecturers, and studio staff were mostly eager volunteers. "But the time is rapidly approaching," predicted the publication, "when the novelty of singing for nothing into a transmitter will wear off. . . . Broadcasting is bound to become more and more expensive as the public demand for better and better programs becomes more and more insistent."

Some of the methods suggested to pay for an undertaking that generated no revenue included a government tax levied on radio receivers with the proceeds going to support radio stations, an endowment created by philanthropists, and a subsidy program funded by taxpayers. There were grave doubts about the appropriateness of commercialism in a medium that came directly into the household. Opponents of radio advertising considered it untoward, as if an unannounced huckster had walked in the front door. Secretary of Commerce Herbert Hoover was among those who doubted the American public would tolerate such a system.

In the early 1920s, instead of direct advertising messages, many sponsors provided musical programs that incorporated their names in various elements of the show. *The Eveready Hour* was presented by the battery company. The Ipana Troubadours were brought to listeners by the toothpaste company, so too the Lucky Strike Orchestra for the tobacco company, the A&P Gypsies for the food store chain, the Cliquot Club Eskimos for a ginger ale, and the Gold Dust Twins for a powdered cleanser. Advertisers were selling products and listeners were getting accustomed to high-level professional entertainment free of charge.

By the 1930s, commercialism emerged triumphant as the primary means of funding radio programming. Any resistance Americans might have had to broadcast adverting had been completely eroded. Radio became a tremendously profitable industry.

When television was in its developmental stages, there were no great debates about who was to pay for TV programming. which was exponentially more expensive to produce than radio programming and the answer was obvious.

More than a year before the Allied victory, while Americans were still using ration coupons to purchase limited amounts of meat, butter, and gasoline, broadcasters and advertising agencies were already making plans for the postwar economy of abundance. Radio advertisers were being encouraged by the networks to experiment with the visual medium to be ready to go once the war ended.

In October 1944, the NBC station in Schenectady hosted a television demonstration for more than one hundred department store executives. The assembled guests viewed a one-hour program that showed an American family watching television and various commercials. In June 1945, CBS began offering its regular radio clients free airtime on television as a special promotion. Sponsors who wanted to dip their toes in the TV water could rent a studio and production crew from CBS for just $150 per hour.

Unlike any other medium, television had the remarkable ability to show and tell. "The mass producer's dream, which was to send a salesman to every household in America at the cost of only a few cents per sales call, had come true," wrote author Earl Shorris in A Nation of Salesmen.

Americans who had struggled during the Great Depression and sacrificed during World War II were ready to enjoy prosperity. Because consumer goods were largely unavailable during the war due to the concentrated production of weaponry, many families had accumulated savings. Television advertisers were gearing up to convince them that in postwar America restraint was no longer a virtue, indulgence no longer a vice.

Motivational research was dedicated to uncovering new and more sophisticated ways of persuading people to buy. Within a few short years, television's ability to convey the spirit of consumption was well-established. Any sponsor's decision to invest in national TV promotion usually brought sensational results. In 1950, for instance, when the Hazel Bishop company began to advertise its products on television, it had annual revenues of approximately $50,000 from the sale of lipstick. In two years, Hazel Bishop saw its business grow to ninety times that size, with annual revenues of $4.5 million in 1952.

American manufacturers understood that long-lasting products of basic utility were not what were needed to sustain consumer spending. The more quickly an item became unfashionable, the more quickly a replacement could be sold. Planned obsolescence became a fundamental concept not only in the garment industry but in the sale of automobiles as well.

Henry Ford might have believed that one kind of car in one color—a black Model T—was right for every American driver. But his Spartan conviction was completely overthrown in the postwar marketplace as the auto industry expanded dramatically. Two million cars were made in 1946. Four times that many were manufactured in 1955 and customers chose from a wide array of colors, optional accessories, fancy grilles, and tail fins.

Each fall, the annual model changes in the auto industry coincided with the new television season. In the 1950s, the Growth Decade for both cars and television, auto makers sponsored many lavish TV specials as well as the weekly programs of their star sales people, such as Pat Boone, Dinah Shore, and Lawrence Welk. Individual transportation rather than mass transit was defined as the American way of life, and the choice of car was presented as a way of defining oneself. "Sleek, smooth, and sassy," the announcer exclaimed. "This is Chevrolet's new Bel-Air two-door hardtop with a daring departure in design."

In 1956, when TV viewers were being introduced to "new high-fashion fenders," President Eisenhower signed the Interstate Highway Act, which provided $26 million to build 40,000 miles of federal highways that would link all parts of the country.

Although an automobile was a significant purchase in a consumer's budget, as was a new refrigerator or automatic clothes dryer, most of what was advertised on television were consumable household products— shampoos, toothpastes, detergents, cosmetics, aspirin, canned foods, soft drinks, and the like. But the differences among competing brands were marginal. So, successful TV advertising campaigns didn't focus solely on product claims. Rather, they strove to associate a brand name with a deep human need or satisfaction—prestige, security, lovability. The question was not how well the product would work, but how the sale could affect the individual's image of him- or herself.

A can of soup might be nourishing and tasty, but the psychological benefit that the advertising campaign sold was that it made a homemaker feel like a good, nurturing mother when serving it. A hair dressing might keep a man's cowlick under control, but the promise that women would have the overpowering desire to run their fingers through it was the real selling point.

As the decade progressed, so did the American appetite for the good life. "The reason we have such a high standard of living," explained NBC president Robert Sarnoff in 1956, "is because advertising has created an American frame of mind that makes people want more things, better things, and newer things."

One of the things television urged Americans to want in a big way in the 1950s was cigarettes. The habit of cigarette smoking among Americans, which began to grow widespread during World War I, was given a tremendous boost during World War II. Cigarettes were sold at military post exchanges and ship's stores for a nickel a pack. Often they came free of charge, packaged in K-rations and sent to veterans' hospitals. The stigma of smoking for women also diminished during the war years.

Although the suspicion that the tars in cigarettes could be blamed for the formation of cancer in the lungs had emerged by the early 1930s, the first major study to make the connection between smoking and lung cancer appeared in the *Journal of the American Medical Association* in 1950. In 1952, a *Reader's Digest* article entitled "Cancer by the Carton" gave the general public an overview of the findings of the medical experts. As more studies began suggesting close links, cigarette companies, which had long been implying that smoking was actually beneficial, toned down their claims that cigarettes were healthful and instead maintained that no connection with disease had been proven conclusively.

The golden age of cigarette advertising on television in the 1950s corresponded to a steep climb in the American death rate from lung cancer. One of TV's biggest stars of the era opened and closed his variety show, sponsored by Chesterfield cigarettes, by saying, "This is Arthur 'Buy-'em-by-the-carton' Godfrey." In 1959, when Godfrey himself was found to have lung cancer, the message was dropped.

Viewers of the *Camel News Caravan* were instructed to "Sit back, light up a Camel and be an eyewitness to the happenings that made history in the last 24 hours." The sponsor of the newscast required that anchorman John Cameron Swayze have a burning cigarette visible whenever he was on camera. Another mandate was that newsfilm should never show a "No Smoking" sign.

Catchy jingles from TV ads could be repeated by every schoolchild. "Smoke 'Em, Smoke 'Em, Then you'll see, that L.S. L.S./M.F.T." was sung by a square dance caller as animated cigarettes dosey-doed around a barnyard. Most Americans knew that L.S./M.F.T. stood for "Lucky Strike Means Fine Tobacco."

Of all American businesses in the 1950s, the tobacco companies devoted the largest percentage of their earnings to advertising. The marriage of television and cigarettes was as successful and profitable as the union of Lucille Ball and Desi Arnaz. Their hit series, *I Love Lucy*, was sponsored by Philip Morris. The couple was often shown in a moment of togetherness smoking "America's most enjoyable cigarette."

The tobacco industry was unrelenting through its TV commercials in defining smoking as a social norm. The vignettes of cigarette ads persuasively associated smoking with being popular, attractive, and energetic. In 1950, *TV Guide* selected Lucky Strike's "Be Happy, Go Lucky" spot as the commercial of the year. In it, vivacious cheerleaders sing, "Yes, Luckies get our loudest cheers on campus and on dates. With college gals and college guys, a Lucky really rates."

In the decade after World War II, television advertising developed into the most effective means of encouraging acquisitive desires. The medium arrived at an especially opportune moment in American history. The war led the United States out of its worst economic depression and set the stage for unparalleled expansion. An increasingly prosperous middle class grew in size during the postwar years, just as the capability for high productivity in manufacturing was being realized. Americans were anxious to learn about new products and television was anxious to teach them.

By the mid-1950s, gratification through consumerism was well on its way to becoming the cornerstone of American culture. Some worried that the country was not adjusting wisely to its privilege. They pointed to embarrassing facts, such as the United States earning the dubious distinction of being the only nation in the world in which overeating was a major problem.

As the late-1950s arrived, a debate about American materialism and its glorification on television emerged among scholars and social critics. Defenders of TV advertising regarded it as a legitimate exploitation of healthy human desires. They argued that a large number of useful products would not be generally available if it were not for the stimulus of TV commercials. And besides promoting economic growth, advertising partisans believed, TV commercials had become a lively and diverting aspect of American life.

But two best-selling books warned of the dangers of advertising's increasing influence. In 1957, *The Hidden Persuaders*, by Vance Packard, was a protest against social scientists and psychiatrists who worked with advertisers to pinpoint subconscious motives in consumers that could be tapped by sales campaigns. "Marketers are being admonished to reassure consumers that the hedonistic approach to life is the moral one," wrote Packard, "and that frugality and personal austerity are outdated hangovers of Puritanism."

Economist John Kenneth Galbraith felt that advertising created synthetic needs and damaging desires in citizens. His 1958 book, *The Affluent Society*, claimed that while Americans enjoyed private prosperity, the public sector was becoming impoverished. A family could go out for a drive in a new "mauve and cerise, air-conditioned, power-steered and power-braked automobile," he wrote, but they would pass through decaying cities. When they arrived at their picnic destinations in the country, they would dine on "exquisitely packaged foods from a portable icebox," but find the nearby stream polluted.

Increasing consumption at the level set in the 1950s could only be accomplished by taking America's natural resources for granted, Galbraith cautioned. "The more goods people procure," he wrote, "the more packages they discard and the more trash that must be carried away." Only a country that foolishly defined itself as rich beyond measure would deliberately devise products meant to be abandoned before their usefulness elapsed.

If producing goods for profit became the dominant value of the nation, maintained Galbraith, then public services that met social needs, such as schools, parks, and police departments, would be downgraded. He advocated higher taxes to deflect wealth from personal consumption and restore a balance between the private and public sectors.

Although many intellectual Americans found *The Affluent Society* to be provocative reading, the anti-growth message was far from being embraced as a blueprint for the next decade. With the skillful prompting of TV advertising, the material desires of the nation's citizens had already fully blossomed into a consumption ethic—yearning, buying, and wanting more.

The Selling Sixties

Products that American consumers didn't even know they wanted or needed in the 1950s, because they hadn't yet been invented, were being introduced via television advertising in the early 1960s. The development of new ideas in consuming, like the disposable ballpoint pen, became a top priority in American manufacturing.

An avalanche of new products, especially foods, drugs, and cosmetics, relied on television to prime the shopper before she entered the supermarket. An unheard-of item like Baggies, ready-to-tear-off-the-roll plastic bags for sandwiches and leftovers, was defined as a kitchen essential, far superior to old-fashioned wax paper. Commercials on soap operas and daytime game shows depicted new products such as air fresheners, push-button floor-cleaning foam, individual-serving pouches of dog food, and pre-measured dissolvable packets of laundry bleach as imperatives in the modern household.

"Consider the humble potato, that used to sell by the bag," said the president of the Young and Rubicam advertising agency as he discussed the changing marketplace of the early 1960s. "Today you buy it as a potato puff, a potato pancake, potato au gratin, instant mashed, French fried, flaked, frozen, and heaven knows what else."

The proliferation of electric- and battery-operated gadgets promising to make life more comfortable and pleasant was also a hallmark of the sixties. Before the decade ended, more than two hundred different kinds of household appliances were available. The ordinary family owned somewhere between twenty and fifty, counting hair dryers, shavers, clock radios, electric frying pans, automatic toothbrushes, and power tools.

The Sunbeam Corporation learned how effective TV advertising was in convincing American consumers to plug in. When the company switched the bulk of its advertising budget from magazines to television in the early 1960s, it experienced such a buying rush that it was forced to use planes and helicopters to speed distribution of its products.

The goal of TV advertising in the new decade was to raise consumer craving to the level of America's productive capacity, which was enormous. Sales and marketing executives believed that mobilizing the growth ambitions of individual businesses supported the goals of the country. So, urging a family to replace a perfectly serviceable refrigerator was not an ethical dilemma. "People aren't going to buy another," a salesman advised his colleagues, "unless someone, somehow, punches their 'buy' button."

The auto industry expanded its market by introducing lower-priced compact cars and making the concept of a two-car family seem routine. At the same time, petroleum companies increased their TV advertising budgets for what the trade press called "an all-out assault on the under-consuming motorist." The campaign to increase passenger car driving and gas consumption in the early 1960s was informed by motivation studies that showed company image, not information on octane, influenced purchases.

Tidewater Oil credited a TV campaign that used sex appeal for its strong sales of Flying A Gasoline. The "Man with Drive" spot featured a rugged-looking male with a good-looking girl at his side pulling up in a convertible to a Flying A pump. "The attempt has been for a strong masculine image of a man who knows what he wants and who wants the best," the ad agency's representative explained. "The male consumer presumably can identify with 'the man with drive' and emulate him by buying the product."

In the quest for strategies that would successfully push the buy button, the 1960s became the "Image Era" of TV advertising. Brand names became mythologized so that consumers purchased not only a product, but an attitude. The Marlboro Man became a cultural icon. The appeal of the solitary cowboy to male consumers was explained this way by a veteran of the advertising industry: "Such a hero is a loner, a saddle tramp, unattached with no home, no sense of community, and no commitments. He will never grow old and paunchy or have to listen to his wife nag him for not taking out the garbage. He is wedded to his Colt .45 and his horse. He will go out in a blaze of glory, with his six-shooter still smoking in his hand and his boots on. He glories not in life but in death—in the orgasmic ecstasy of his exploding gun."

On the other hand, the attitude women smokers were buying in the 1960s was "You've Come a Long Way Baby." Virginia Slims cigarettes created a feminist mythology that resonated with the times, correlating smoking with liberation. By associating the product with a sense of progress and accomplishment, the decision to light up was transformed from an act of weakness into a statement of rosy defiance.

The irony of the Virginia Slims campaign was that in the world created by advertising, women had not come very far at all. In TV commercials they were either preoccupied with the ring around the collar of their husbands' shirts or they were simply sex objects. One of the most famous TV spots of the decade was for Noxema shaving cream. The former Miss Sweden, Gunilla Knutson, cooed the double-entendre, "Take it off, take it all off," to the theme music from *The Stripper*.

In the 1960s, television ads perfected the art of wrapping products in fantasies. Viewers were encouraged to indulge themselves, which completely reversed the frugality honored during World War II. Even though sitcoms and dramas occasionally presented storylines that ostensibly cautioned against excessive materialism, success and happiness in commercials were always equated with buying the product. America's abundant assembly lines kept moving because American television led the world in manufacturing demand.

Candy-Coated Pitches

Howdy Doody proved that even though kids had no earning power, they had plenty of buying power. In 1954, the debut of another merchandising triumph, the show *Disneyland*, reemphasized to advertisers that the children's market had an enormous profit potential. The ABC show, which aired on Wednesday evenings from 7:30 to 8:30, was an entertaining mix of kiddie adventure tales, travelogues, real-life nature stories, and classic Disney animation. The audience also learned all about the new amusement park in Anaheim, California, which soon topped the list of dream vacation destinations for kids around the country.

But the most visible testament to the power of television's influence over kids was the nationwide fad of wearing "genuine imitation" coonskin caps. The *Disneyland* feature about pioneer Davy Crockett, called "King of the Wild Frontier," touched off the kiddie fashion sensation. Even U.S. Senator Estes Kefauver sported one of the furry caps during his 1956 campaign for the presidency.

By the early 1960s, commercials urging kids to "be the first on your block" to have a certain toy or box-top premium had become a TV standard. But, even though kids' shows effectively moved warehouses of products, the networks realized that the afterschool and early evening hours of their schedules were more lucrative when adult programming was aired.

Saturday mornings, not an attractive time for grown-up viewers, became the "children's ghetto." For sponsors it was ideal. Airtime was much cheaper since the size of the viewing audience was smaller. But because the audience was all children—what was called a "pure demographic"—there was no "waste circulation." Everyone in the audience was a candidate for persuasion. Toy, cereal, candy, soft-drink, and snack-food commercials flooded Saturday morning TV. Advertisers learned they could sell to and through American kids. A successful ad influenced children to be "salesmen within the home."

A 1970 handbook for advertisers entitled *The Youth Market: Its Dimensions, Influence and Opportunities for You*, explained why children had become so prized as targets of advertising: "When you sell a woman a product she goes into the store and finds your brand isn't in stock, she'll probably forget about it. But when you sell a kid a product, if he can't get it he will throw himself on the floor, stamp his feet and cry. You can't get a reaction like that out of an adult."

Since the stakes were so high in creating commercials that could inspire such fierce desire in preschoolers, any information that could enhance the effectiveness of the ads was sought out by advertisers. In the 1970s, companies that specialized in motivation research and children were a growth industry. Many child psychologists found work at testing facilities that explored the reactions of young viewers to TV commercials.

A typical research session was described by the editor of *Human Behavior* magazine: "A group of ten preschoolers is clustered together on the floor in a cozy, shag-carpeted living room. . . . As an adult enters, the tots are enthusiastically playing with toys, coloring with crayons in fat books and chatting with each other. They're part of a group of 150 who will be tested today for their reactions to a commercial pushing a new type of toy, and all have just seen this commercial in an auditorium, sandwiched between cartoons and other familiar ads."

In small groups the children are asked to tell their reactions to the TV ad. The shy ones can register their opinions on a Smiley Scale. The kids are also asked to use the crayons to draw their "feelings" about what they've just seen. The editor explained, the pictures are "analyzed by specialists who link the content of the drawing with how a youngster feels about the commercial, and, ultimately, how much money can be made off his emotions and vulnerabilities." The children are later organized into improvisational teams, the editor continues, and "the tiny guinea pigs then act out how their parents are likely to react to their request for the product, what 'pitches' they themselves would use on adults, and how playmates would feel about the product."

Enlightening the public about the unequal contest between children and advertisers became the mission in the early 1970s of an advocacy group called Action for Children's Television, which petitioned the Federal Communications Commission to eliminate all commercials from children's TV. The morality of advertising any products to children became an issue of public debate. "Selling to children on TV is like shooting fish in a barrel," said Joan Ganz Cooney, the president of the Children's Television Workshop. "It is grotesquely unfair."

For some, it seemed an extreme position in a society based on free enterprise. But if advertising practices aimed at children were abusive or deceptive, then restrictions were warranted. Various citizens and consumer groups set out to expose the deplorable state of kidvid commercials.

The most obvious criticism was that so much of what was advertised to kids was nutritionally unwise. From 1965 to 1975, approximately 50 percent of the ads on Saturday morning TV were for highly sugared cereals, cookies, candies, sodas, snacks, and fast food. In the short term, tooth decay was a concern. But in the larger picture, health professionals worried about encouraging eating habits in children that could lead to heart disease and cancer later in life. Television was teaching children that food was best when it was sweet or deep-fried. The absence of fresh fruits and vegetables in TV depictions of desirable meals, a nutritionist observed, "makes it impossible for a child not to go wrong."

Burger King ads, with the slogan "Where Kids are King," featured the animated monarch pulling up to the fast-food restaurant on a motorcycle and ordering the ideal meal—a burger, french fries, and a chocolate shake. In another spot of the early seventies, Ronald McDonald, an American advertising icon, says to a group of youngsters, "'Bet you kids know a lot of ways to eat McDonald French fries? C'mon show me."

The children then proceed to show Ronald just how clever they are at inventing ways to eat the fries. "Eat 'em with a smile, eat 'em single file . . . eat 'em upside down, eat 'em with a clown." And on and on until one of the little girls says, "Hey Ronald, we're almost out of fries." Instead of letting the kids know that they've consumed a reasonable portion and now they were finished—as any responsible adult would do—Ronald says, "Don't worry. Just wave the magic wand." More fries magically appear. The message is that one order of french fries might not be enough and there's nothing wrong with eating until you're simply too full to continue.

Another McDonald's ad of the era featured the character the Hamburgler on trial for stealing a bag of cheeseburgers. "I sentence you to one week without McDonald's cheeseburgers," the judge orders. Even the prosecuting attorney, who happens to be Ronald McDonald, is shocked at the harshness of the punishment. "Isn't that rather severe?" he asks the magistrate. "Well, all right then," the judge agrees, "one week without rutabagas. Let's all adjourn to McDonald's for a cheeseburger." The idea of fast food as an occasional treat for children was undermined by such an ad. A McDonald's meal was defined for very young boys and girls as a several-times-a-week event.

"Can't get enough of those Sugar Crisps," sang Sugar Bear in TV commercials all through the 1960s. By the 1970s, he and his fellow sugared-cereal spokesmen, including the Lucky Charms leprechaun and Cap'n Crunch, had plenty of company on the supermarket shelf. Count Chocula, for instance, had a standing feud with the monster Franken Berry over whose cereal was more "super sweet." New gimmicks in breakfast food even included a cereal that looked and tasted like little chocolate chip cookies.

The sale of sweet and colorful vitamin pills to children was also worrisome. Some of the vitamins came in the shape of popular cartoon characters such as Spiderman and the Flintstones. The TV ads could, it was argued, give the impression to small children that the vitamins should be consumed freely. "Yabba Dabba Do, Yabba Dabba Do," sang Fred and Barney, "Flintstone vitamins are good to chew." Physicians agreed that the pills could pose an overdose threat for some children. Another issue that critics raised was the danger in promoting pill-popping as a means of feeling good and having power.

Aside from the blatant problems stemming from the nature of the products being pitched, psychologists and consumer groups also looked beneath the surface at the values conveyed in the kidvid ads. "Many children's commercials I've seen emphasize the importance of physical force," said Dr. Robert Liebert, a professor of psychology at the State University of New York. "They show in a variety of ways that force can be used to a make a person successful."

Offering the example of an ad for the fruit drink Hawaiian Punch, in which one animated character asks another "How would you like a nice Hawaiian Punch?" and then gives him a quick smash, Dr. Liebert explained, "It puts that kind of action into an acceptable funny context, teasing and tormenting other people so as to get a laugh out of it."

Toy ads often defined personal success in terms of acquisition. "The most important things about you are what you look like and what you own," Dr. Liebert observed. His statement was especially apropos to TV advertisements for Barbie dolls and accessories. The commercial for Barbie's Glamorous Townhouse featured two little girls getting "Superstar" Barbie ready for a dinner party. "Wow! Three floors," one of the children exclaims as she admires the home. The voice-over announcer adds, "The Barbie Townhouse has a play elevator, six rooms, and all this furniture." Malibu Barbie's Country Camper was a recreational vehicle with a pop-out tent. Barbie's Pool Party came with a swimming pool, slide, and floating chair.

At the same time that credit cards were teaching adult Americans they didn't have to wait to get what they wanted, TV ads were schooling kids in conspicuous consumption. Delayed gratification and living within one's means were defined as un-fun.

The proposed ban against TV advertising to children never came close to being realized, but the advocacy groups gained some victories by the mid-1970s. In response to pressure the networks agreed to reduce commercials in children's television from sixteen to ten minutes per hour. The Federal Trade Commission restricted the advertising of vitamins to children. The Federal Communications Commission (FCC) issued a policy statement acknowledging that children should be treated as "special members of the viewing audience." Cereal commercials began to include phrases like "as part of a balanced diet" and show an orange or glass of juice in the picture. The National Association of Broadcasters (NAB) revised its code to do away with the use of program hosts or cartoon characters from the shows to pitch products.

The raised consciousness about advertising to children and the mild reforms that were taking place in the late 1970s, though, lost ground in the 1980s. After the Department of Justice brought an antitrust suit against the NAB code, the voluntary guidelines ceased to exist in 1983. Most important, however, was the growing deregulatory climate in Washington. The Reagan-era FCC, according to media historian Les Brown, "signaled that the reins were off."

The trend in children's television in the 1980s was program-length commercials. Instead of advertisers buying time on independently produced shows, the sponsors essentially took over the creation of the programs, which were designed to promote products. So, instead of a TV character inspiring a fad, such as Davy Crockett and the coonskin cap, whole product lines, which might include dolls, toys, greeting cards, bed sheets, towels, pajamas, underwear, jewelry, posters, school supplies, soap, and many other items, were devised first.

Strawberry Shortcake, for instance, was not a storybook character who was turned into a TV star. "She was a corporate creation," *Channels* magazine reported in 1984, "developed expressly for the purpose of licensing, and so far the licensing has brought in more than a billion dollars."

The growing number of independent, UHF television stations in the 1980s employed the strategy of airing large blocks of animated children's programming in the afternoons and on Saturday mornings. Product-driven series were offered to them on a barter basis, meaning they didn't pay cash but gave up some commercial minutes during the show. The stations filled their schedules cheaply and the syndicators secured an undiscriminating audience—children who didn't realize that *He-Man* and the *Masters of the Universe* cartoons were meant only to sell action figures and the Attak Trak car.

Approximately forty shows based on toys, dolls, games, cereals, and other products ultimately appeared on the air, including *Care Bears*, *GI Joe*, *Thundercats*, *Voltron*, and *Transformers*. "The multibillion-dollar-a-year toy industry," a media analyst explained, "had become so tied to children's television that toy makers would not even consider introducing a new product unless it was tied directly to a children's television program."

Blurring the distinction between program content and commercial speech, critics charged, was unfair to kids even if the products being pitched were innocuous. But, all too often, the cartoons were being used to instill a craving for toys that celebrated deadly force and other antisocial values.

In the 1970s and 1980s, commercial television's exploitation of children was intensive. Although many societies around the world, including in Great Britain and Canada, regarded children as a precious population in need of protection and limited the ability of advertisers to reach them through television, the United States chose instead to allow the marketplace the freedom to manipulate their gullibility.

Blowing Past the Limits

A tidal wave of commercialism washed over the United States in the 1980s. The amount spent on mass media advertising virtually doubled from 1982 to 1990, from $66 billion to more than $130 billion. Advertising began to permeate every corner of American culture.

To fans of the Rolling Stones since the 1960s, it seemed downright weird that their 1981 tour was "sponsored" by Jovan fragrances. In the eighties, illusions about hard-core rock 'n' roll, or rap, or any other type of music being about a social message faded away. Concert tour sponsorship became the norm. And before the decade ended, music that was once associated with youthful rebellion and the counterculture became the soundtrack for TV commercials celebrating middle-class suburban life. "Let the Sunshine In," from the musical *Hair*, for instance, was transformed from a hippie anthem to a tune that played in a mustard commercial.

Americans became acclimated to the notion that cashing-in was always justifiable. Fame, however it was earned, was a commodity to be parlayed. The appearance of Geraldine Ferraro, the former Democratic vice-presidential nominee from 1984, in a Diet Pepsi ad on TV confirmed the trend.

What at first appeared unseemly became, before decade's end, par for the course. Former Speaker of the House Tip O'Neill popped out of a suitcase in a motel ad and asked, "Who says a politician can't save you money?" Former President Gerald Ford promoted a series of presidential coins sold by the Franklin Mint. "America turns every achievement into a hustle," lamented columnist Ellen Goodman, "and every achiever into a hustler."

Even those whose celebrity derived from shameful circumstances rather than achievement cashed-in as stars of TV commercials. Donna Rice had an extramarital dalliance with presidential candidate Gary Hart, which torpedoed his chances for the Democratic nomination in 1984. Then she starred in a TV ad for "No Excuses" blue jeans. Seductively posed to show off the product, Rice purred, "I have no excuses. I just wear them." The "anything goes" message to young viewers was distasteful. But in the commercial climate of the 1980s, it was foolish to worry about propriety.

As the 1980s advanced, sports fans were being conditioned into a new tradition, to link post-season college football games on TV with the names of their corporate sponsors: the *Federal Express Orange Bowl*, the *Sunkist Fiesta Bowl*, and the *Poulan/Weed Eater Independence Bowl*. Viewers came to expect that all venues for sporting events shown on TV would be laden with advertising. Scoreboards became billboards and many athletes did too, displaying the names and logos of high-paying companies.

In the same way one becomes inured to a dripping faucet, Americans got used to the constant presence of advertising. Few places were safe havens from commercialization. As the 1980s gave way to the 1990s, many school systems around the country even allowed a company named Channel One to provide video equipment in their junior and senior high school classrooms in exchange for requiring students to watch a daily twelve-minute newscast replete with advertisements for candy, snack foods, soda pops, fast foods, clothes, and cosmetics.

Television advertising entered the nineties with the boldness to ignore any perceived limits on acceptable content. In 1991, the Stroh Brewery Company hoped to draw younger men to its Old Milwaukee brand by introducing a quintet of blonde-wigged, wriggling, busty women, the so-called Swedish bikini team.

In an earlier commercial for Old Milwaukee, four flannel-shirted buddies are relaxing in a country setting listening to the birds and enjoying their beer under an open sky. One says to his pals, "Guys it just doesn't get any better than this." In the new spot, the narrator breaks in and says, "Walt Smith was wrong." Things presumably got much better when the girls showed up.

"After the bikini ladies first appear," an advertising columnist pointed out, "the camera rarely concentrates on their faces again. Instead it spends most of its time in lingering looks at deep cleavage, the mound of a breast or the curve of a fanny." "The women never speak," the review continues. "Sometimes they are quietly serving food and drinks to the men. Sometimes they are wrestling with phallic symbols, as does the woman who bends over nearly backwards with a saxophone in her mouth or the one who fights a fishing rod planted between her legs."

The advertising agency defended the brazen sexism of the ads by calling it satire. The creators claimed to be spoofing a stereotype, not celebrating it. But when the girls of the Swedish bikini team appeared in a pictorial feature in *Playboy*, the defense lost its credibility.

Precision-marketing based on "lifestyle segmentation clusters" became even more sophisticated in the 1990s. Advertising to black consumers was a priority as their economic clout grew. In many cases, the ads that resulted were appreciated for their positive messages about black families. But a controversy was aroused by the fact that one product, malt liquor, was marketed seemingly exclusively to black men.

A 1993 campaign for Schlitz malt liquor featured actors in kente cloth hats and vests. One of the young men places a kente cloth sash around the neck of an admiring female. In the background is an African drum. "The notion of Afrocentricism is very high in the target audience," the spokesman for the black-owned ad agency explained. "Kente cloth was just one of the things we identified that tells the black consumer that we are speaking to them."

A columnist covering the issue informed her readers, "The term kente means woven. Different countries in Africa have their own patterns and colors. African families would wear a particular cloth so they could be easily identified." Considering that the death rate for black Americans from cirrhosis of the liver was twice the rate for whites, and considering there was a connection between alcohol and several other devastating problems in the black community, the business reporter concluded: "It is highly inappropriate to link the rich history of kente cloth with the selling of malt liquor. One celebrates a culture of a people while the other leads to destruction."

Another commercial of the era was of even greater cause for despair, though. The rap singer Ice Cube urged young black men, in a flashy TV advertisement, to "Get your girl in the mood quicker . . . with St. Ides Malt Liquor."

The underlying lesson of much TV advertising throughout the history of the medium was that there was no need to exercise restraint. In the

1990s, the sentiment became grossly inflated. "I Can't Believe I Ate the Whole Thing" was a slogan from a popular Alka-Seltzer commercial of the 1970s. Even though the product gave fast relief, there was still a touch of remorse for overindulgence. In the nineties, antacids were promoted as a product to be taken before overeating.

In the 1970s and eighties, the potato-chip challenge, "Betcha can't eat just one," always resulted in the loser eating many more than a single chip. But in the 1990s, snack-food eaters were shown proudly scarfing down bagfuls. The slogan for a product called Air Crisps Chips was actually "Inhale 'Em."

Fast-food chains competed with each other by making their sandwiches bigger—more cheese, more bacon, more beef. The goal of the TV advertising was not only to introduce the new products, but also to weaken any reservations about such large portions. A young man in a Burger King ad tells his female companion, "It's the American way—big houses, big cars, big food!" "And what about moderation?" the young lady asks with a scolding touch in her voice. "Moderation's OK," he says as he picks up his burger with two hands, "if there's a whole lot of it." His good humor trumps her common sense.

A TV commercial for White Castle promoting their Sack of 10 Burgers echoed the celebration of self-indulgence. Two prizefighters appear in a ring—one identified as "The Crave," the other as "Will Power." The crowd roots for The Crave and cheers wildly when he knocks Will Power out cold. The message? Go ahead and eat the whole sack of hamburgers despite your better judgment.

In so many TV advertisements of the 1990s, the concept of limits was challenged. A commercial for a rich ice cream dessert cake used the slogan, "One slice is never enough." Excess was routinely presented as the American way of life. In a TV ad for Rubbermaid storage boxes, a typical American family is shown being squeezed out of its home by all its belongings. Rubbermaid to the rescue. With everything neatly stowed, there's lots of room. "Hey!," Mom exclaims, "We need more stuff!"

The belittling of temperance was especially troubling in car ads geared to younger drivers. Saab automobiles invited potential owners to "Peel off your inhibitions." An ad for Plymouth Neon showed the car apparently speeding down a country road. "It's a pretty hot little number," viewers were told. In a Buick Riviera spot, the auto is shown zipping along a wet highway, while the young driver's hair billows in the wind. The voiceover says, "Go ahead, express yourself."

"There's an implicit encouragement in this kind of advertising for motorists to speed and drive aggressively," said Brian O'Neill, director of the Insurance Institute for Highway Safety, an industry research group. "It is contributing to a general disregard for speed limits."

"There isn't a teenager in America who isn't constantly submitted to this barrage," said Joan Claybrook, former head of the National Highway Transportation Safety Administration and president of the consumer group Public Citizen. "I just think it's unethical for the manufacturers to behave this way. They don't tell their kids at the dinner table to go out and drive 75 mph."

By the early 1990s, a new form of commercialism via television was well-established in American culture—infomercials. The half-hour advertisements for products like juicers, steamers, rhinestone setters, car wax, stain removers, makeup, hair conditioners, or cream to reduce the cellulite on thighs were produced to look like "real" TV talk shows. Celebrities, well-compensated for their appearances, gave the impression their testimonials were unsolicited, that they were just sitting and chatting with friends about a product that made such a difference in their lives.

Although some state legislators and attorneys general tried to introduce laws to drive the infomercials off the air, on the theory they were duping consumers, the genre flourished and prospered wildly. In 1985, the FCC dropped its guidelines for licensees on how much advertising could be carried, which media analysts credited as the primary factor in the explosion of infomercials. "The top has been blown off," wrote a TV reporter for the *Baltimore Sun*. "Television has become a free-wheeling bazaar of goods and services, the denizen of get-rich, lose-fat infomercials."

"Let the buyer beware" was the guiding principle. Television stations that sold time for "paid programming" accepted no responsibility for the rampant charlatanism that was broadcast over their airwaves. Disclaimers scrolled across the bottom of the screen that read: "All claims and representations made in this program-length advertisement are the sole responsibility of the sponsor." If viewers wanted to buy a can of spray paint to cover bald spots or buy a real-estate investment course at two in the morning from a man on a powerboat with two bikini-clad women at his side, so be it.

One of the most profitable and controversial infomercials was for a service called "The Psychic Friends Network." In the mid-1990s, the half-hour pitch ran three hundred times a week on TV stations across the country. Singer Dionne Warwick and co-host Linda Georgian encouraged viewers to call a 900 number to get advance notice on the outcome of their love life, career, or general fate. Warwick reminded skeptics that nothing more was required than "a telephone and an open mind." A TV critic added, "Not to mention the four-bucks-per-minute cost of her hotline."

A fifty-seven-year-old court reporter named Betty Jean Jeffreys, worried about her finances, called the 900 number after seeing the Psychic Friends infomercial. "They had a woman come on the line. Her conversation was very slow," Jeffreys said, "to hold me on the line and tell me nothing, just stuff that would fit anybody." When the exasperated caller asked specific questions about her future, she was told, "I'm not a mind reader." When the bill for $43.89 arrived, Jeffreys filed a complaint with the Maryland attorney general's office, which intervened and helped get her money back.

"It is nothing less than a national shame," said Bob Garfield of *Advertising Age* magazine about The Psychic Friends Network. "It angers me, it frustrates me. At the very minimum, it's grossly exploitive of those probably least capable of defending themselves against naked ignorance and superstition." The producers of the infomercial argued they were only giving people what they wanted and none of the callers who collectively racked up an average of 2.5 million minutes of phone time per month had a gun put to their head.

Along with infomercials in the 1990s, shopping channels were a glorification of impulse purchasing. Already having an item was no reason not to buy another. "You can't have enough white slacks," viewers were told. Why not buy a "second vacuum" to be kept upstairs? Can't decide if you want the handbag in tan or navy blue? Go ahead and order both—but hurry, the minutes on the deadline clock are ticking away.

"Are you bugged by something?" a studio host for the QVC (Quality, Value, Convenience) shopping channel asked the audience. "Well, it just might be that your finger needs a diamond ring." The status the purchase would bring was illuminated by another hostess: "You're wearing the ring on your finger, and driving in your car and kind of gazing at the ring, enjoying your drive, enjoying your ring. And then you go to the store, and maybe you're writing a check, and you just kind of put your hand down to write the check, and the girl behind the counter says 'Whoa, beautiful jewelry.' And you say 'Oh, yes, thank you. It's from QVC; it's for me!'"

But aside from the status or self-respect the item might offer, viewers of shopping channels were encouraged to buy simply because the act of buying would make them feel good. There was satisfaction to be derived from being included on the tote board that showed thirty-five hundred other people ordered the smokeless stovetop grill within ten minutes.

Shopaholics were defined as normal; shopping to relieve boredom or depression was presented as a reasonable therapy. A lady from Long Island called the Home Shopping Spree and expressed her gratitude for the opportunity to "get up at four-thirty in the morning and order something really nice."

Yet another form of commercialization that flourished in the 1990s was the practice called "product placement." By putting brand name, identifiable products in the lives of the characters in TV sitcoms and dramas, an "unzappable commercial" was created. "Every major TV show has a KitchenAid appliance," said Rick Keppler, whose company, Keppler Entertainment, was paid a commission for placing products in television shows and movies. KitchenAid blenders were seen on the counters in *Seinfeld*, *Frasier*, *The Nanny*, *Mad About You*, and many other series.

The premise of product placement was that consumers would want to emulate the characters they watched on television by purchasing the same products they used—from the cereal boxes and snack foods visible in their cupboards to the computers on their desks. The marketing manager for Apple Computers explained that the company only purchased actual TV ad time in the quarter year before Christmas, but through product placement Apple computers had a presence on prime-time television all year long. Apple computers, a TV critic noticed, were on "half the desk tops on television."

When FBI Agent Dana Scully checked her e-mail on *The X-Files*, she was using a Powerbook laptop computer made by Apple. When the middle son on *Home Improvement* did his homework it was also on a Powerbook, while a desktop Macintosh could be found downstairs. "This season," a columnist wrote in 1995, "the cast of *Hearts Afire* appears to be putting out an entire newspaper on Powerbooks."

Opponents of product placement urged the Federal Trade Commission to declare it an unfair business practice and require that an on-screen credit disclose that certain props appeared for a fee. The co-founder of the Center for the Study of Commercialism, Michael Johnson, complained "audiences aren't being told they're being advertised to," which he considered plain deception. But the cause was unable to muster much popular support. By the 1990s, most citizens just assumed that advertising was part and parcel of life in the United States. To rail against it would be as futile as cursing gravity.

On *Seinfeld*, product placement became a signature feature. Brand names such as Snapple, Ovaltine, Tupperware, Arby's, *TV Guide*, Rold Gold pretzels, Calvin Klein, Twix, Saab, and many others were interspersed throughout the action and conversation. The March 1993 "Junior Mint" episode is considered a landmark in the evolution of product placement into product integration. Lead characters Jerry and Kramer are watching a live operation being performed from an overhead viewing gallery. Kramer behaves as if he's watching a movie and snacks on the candy—one of which falls from his vantage point directly into the incision of the patient. The morning after the episode aired, the preposterously comic scene was being talked about on morning drive radio and in schools and workplaces everywhere.

As the 21st century approached, television advertisers were brainstorming new ways of securing the "mindshare" of consumers. Younger audiences especially were divorced from the model of sitting through commercial blocks during their favorite shows. Digital video recorders had the capability to eliminate the ads within a program altogether. Product integration was becoming the norm. Instead of products simply appearing in TV programs, they would be woven into the storylines, actually discussed by characters, and become critical elements of the plot.

In the 20th century, the Great Depression and World War II were important factors in the increasing material desires of Americans. In times of scarcity, the ownership of property naturally enhanced feelings of security. In the postwar era, though, a time of abundance, the role of TV advertising was to stimulate wants far beyond a baseline of security and comfort. "Our tastes and desires as consumers are always being 'upgraded,'" wrote cultural historian Christopher Lasch. "That is at the heart of mass merchandising. . . . What we have is never enough and the mass media feed this addiction."

Television commercials altered the American perception in the second half of the twentieth century to believe it was normal to forever expect more. What advertising sold most effectively was the notion that living with limits was unnecessary. In the postwar period, television advertising enveloped the American spirit by its willingness to supply easy answers to the perennial existential questions—Who am I? Why am I here? What is important?

Fig. 8 CBS newsman Edward R. Murrow in a promotional photo for his April 1955 interview with Marilyn Monroe on *Person to Person*, a series that contributed to the contemporary celebrity culture. (CBS publicity photo.)

CHAPTER 8

Taking the Cue: Television and the American Personality

It was a story of love, war, and heroism that infused more lines of dialogue into the American lexicon than any other movie. *Casablanca* won the Academy Award for Best Picture in 1943. Since then, sweethearts have toasted each other with, "Here's looking at you, kid," and wistfully reminded themselves, "We'll always have Paris" (or Las Vegas, or Grand Rapids or whatever city applied). A fist pounded on the table followed by, "Of all the gin joints in all the towns in all the world, she walks into mine," became a cliché of the brokenhearted. And cynics have made frequent use of "Round up the usual suspects"; "I was misinformed"; and "I think this is the beginning of a beautiful friendship."

Americans have always emulated their stars in fashion, behavior, and attitude. During the Golden Era of Hollywood movie-making, fan magazines like *Photoplay* and *Screenland* fed the curiosity of the public. Reports on the private lives of celebrities—their tastes, their personal habits, their beauty secrets—were published under the control of the studios.

The pages of general interest periodicals like *Life* and *Look* also showcased celebrities. Narratives that provided an inside view of the everyday lives of movie stars were especially popular. Pictures of matinee idols and glamour girls enjoying their rumpus rooms and barbecue pits or playing blind-man's bluff with a group of children on a suburban lawn were common features. "Such ordinariness," wrote Josuah Gamson in *Claims to Fame*, his study of celebrity in contemporary America, "promoted a greater sense of connection and intimacy between the famous and their admirers."

With the coming of television, ordinary people's fascination with the private lives of the famous could be indulged even more intensely. In 1952 the radio show *This Is Your Life* was retooled into a prime-time TV success. Each week an unsuspecting guest of honor, often a show business celebrity, was stunned to hear host Ralph Edwards recite his or her name and say emphatically "...This is your life."

Edwards would present in chronological order the life story of the honoree. Periodically the voice of an off-stage guest would punctuate the host's narration. The star would try to identify the childhood playmate, relative, friend, or teacher behind the curtain. Then the person would be brought on stage for a reunion and some reminiscing. The viewer was an authorized eavesdropper on the most treasured and often very personal memories of the celebrity. And genuine emotion was frequently apparent.

Tears and tissues were a standard element in the format. *This Is Your Life*, observed a reviewer in the *Saturday Evening Post*, seemed to invalidate the immortal line "Laugh and the world laughs with you; weep and you weep alone." Ralph Edwards had the power, posited the critic, to "start some 30,000,000 Americans weeping in unison once a week."

Some detractors felt the calculated sentimentality was unethical. "It becomes cruelty," wrote critic Dwight Newton in the *San Francisco Examiner*, "when all the country is permitted to peer and peek into the private emotions of a private life." But viewers loved the show, and playing the game in churches, schools, and clubs became a national fad. Retirement parties particularly lent themselves to a duplication of the formula.

A prominent West Coast lawyer, being honored with a surprise *"This Is Your Life"* party at a hotel ballroom filled with three hundred distinguished citizens, worried that Ralph Edwards, the owner and producer of the show, could sue the instigators for plagiarism. Edwards wouldn't dream of it, though. He believed all the imitations and parodies brought more viewers to the real thing. He even offered a tip sheet to those interested in producing homemade versions. Sheet music for the theme song and sample scripts were free of charge. An official scrapbook like the one used on the program could be purchased for less than ten dollars and Edwards supplied a list of stationery stores that carried the item.

In 1953, a new TV series, *Person to Person*, captured the fancy of the American audience and further accelerated the cult of celebrity. Each week host Edward R. Murrow "electronically visited" the homes of two famous people. It was a logistical *tour de force*. There were four cameras and twenty-six crew members in the CBS studio in New York, from where Murrow conducted the live interviews. At each of the two locations, there were three cameras and from twelve to fifteen crew members.

For days in advance of the broadcast, the interviewees' homes were taken over by an army of technicians—setting up, mapping out, and choreographing every movement that would take place in the show. If Murrow wasn't able to personally visit the home of the guest prior to the telecast, a photographer was dispatched to provide a complete picture lay-out to the host. A new device, the wireless microphone, was put to use on *Person to Person*. A gentleman could carry it in the breast pocket of a jacket; a lady could hide it in her scarf or bodice.

Thanks to synchronizing generators, the pictures from the studio and the remote locations could be locked together, enabling cuts, dissolves, split screens, and superimpositions. On the home screen, viewers saw the host sitting in an armchair with his ubiquitous cigarette and the inter-viewee at home in the same frame. "May we come in?" Murrow would ask on behalf of the home viewers.

At the outset, Murrow hoped to include non-celebrities in the series. But when visits were conducted to the homes of ordinary Americans— a mailman, a clerk at Macy's department store, a porter at Grand Central Station—viewers did not respond well. Murrow reported that the letters he received after such a broadcast essentially said, "If I want to see how the average guy lives, I can visit my relatives."

Soon *Person to Person* dropped the notion of visiting regular folks and became primarily a celebrity parade, a video version of a fan magazine. Murrow, the premier newsman of broadcast journalism, was criticized for his willingness to engage in non-demanding celebrity interviews. He explained, "I always act like a guest in the house. I wouldn't dream of throwing anyone a curved question."

Famous people around the country were delighted to receive a letter from Ed Murrow inviting them to appear on his show. "I have an old-fash-ioned belief," the journalist wrote to those he was soliciting, "that all of us are curious to see how others live—particularly those we've read about or heard about, but seldom, if ever, had an opportunity to meet."

Barbara Walters, who in the following decades would build an impres-sive career out of interviewing celebrities and providing a view of their private surroundings, was a fan of *Person to Person* in the 1950s. "A camera in someone's house—Wow!" is how she remembers reacting to the pro-gram's concept. "That was innovative, that was something we didn't have." Walters vividly recalled Murrow's TV visit with Sophie Tucker in which the singer opened her linen closet to give viewers a look. Showing unordinary people doing ordinary things was a compelling device.

There was always the possibility that the famous would somehow be unmasked.

Armchair voyeurs watching *Person to Person*, though, rarely witnessed any true spontaneity. "But to its millions of addicted viewers," wrote Murrow biographer Joseph Persico, "the program did create the illusion, however contrivedly, that they were stealing a glimpse into private life at the top, seeing their icons at their ease, and confirming what they needed to know all along, that the celebrated were just like them and nothing like them."

Among the fraternity of famous people, appearing on *Person to Person* brought a special cachet of super celebrity. But movie stars who were conditioned to the luxury of retaking scenes that were flubbed found live television intimidating. Actress Lauren Bacall was nervous about her visit with Murrow, but his questions were not a surprise. "That looks like an interesting bracelet you're wearing," the host said. "Is it special for a television visitor—or just a little thing you picked up somewhere?"

Sitting with two pet bulldogs, Bacall gave a well-prepared coy response to the inquiry about the jeweled band with a whistle attached. "A fellow by the name of Mr. Bogart gave this to me in honor of *To Have and Have Not*, the first picture in which we appeared together," she said of her husband. "It was prompted by a line I said in the picture—I don't know whether you remember it or not, but the line goes something like this: 'If you want anything all you have to do is whistle. You know how to whistle, don't you? You just put your lips together and blow.'"

One of the most anxiously awaited *Person to Person* interviews was with Marilyn Monroe in the spring of 1955. Murrow visited with her while she was a guest at the Connecticut home of photographer Milton Greene and his wife Amy. After spending several hours applying light make-up and selecting a simple, tight-fitting, dress, the actress began to wonder if she might look too "dowdy." "When a CBS cameraman tried to calm her," writes Monroe biographer Donald Spoto, "saying that she looked fabulous and that millions of Americans would fall in love with her on the spot, Marilyn became very nearly paralyzed with fright." But the producer was able to reassure her by saying, "Just look at the camera, dear. It's just you and the camera—just you two."

Even though Murrow's questions to the movie queen were uninspired— "Do you like New York?" "Do you like Connecticut?"—she managed to turn the program into a memorable one and keep her image intact. "Your picture has been on the cover of almost all popular magazines, hasn't it?" the host wondered. "Not the *Ladies Home Journal*," she cooed.

The impact of an appearance on *Person to Person* was often quite tangible to those who had been interviewed. It could be measured in an increase in record or book sales, movie or theater attendance, TV ratings, or fan mail.

The commodity of celebrity became increasingly institutionalized in postwar America. After World War II the public relations industry experienced remarkable growth. As the Hollywood studio system became extinct, stars began to retain personal press agents and publicists to nurture and tend to their fame. The importance of TV exposure in any game plan was paramount.

In his landmark 1961 book, *The Image*, historian Daniel Boorstin analyzed the evolving concept of celebrity in the television age. It was, he wrote, "a new kind of eminence." Unlike the old-fashioned kind, it was not necessarily based on morality or heroism, but personality. Boorstin defined a celebrity in the modern world as "a person who is known for his well-knownness."

To illustrate his point Boorstin offered the example of a massive 1959 publication called the *Celebrity Register*, a compilation of more than 2,200 biographies. Boorstin noted that the Dalai Lama was listed beside the sexpot TV comedienne Dagmar and that Pope John XXIII came right after Mr. John the hat designer.

As television took hold of American life, an ever-expanding panoply of famous people offered examples of personal style. Inciting fascination, not admiration, was the goal of their publicity campaigns. What mattered most was making an impression.

Intoxicating Charm

The life of the party always had a drink in his hand. In the 1950s, alcohol was routinely presented on TV in a positive social fashion. Cocktails and highballs were the mark of a glamorous and sophisticated crowd. On the 1953 series *Topper*, for instance, George and Marian Kirby, the good-looking young ghosts who haunt their posh former home, now owned by Cosmo and Henrietta Topper, ran with a hard-drinking bunch before they were killed by an avalanche on their fifth wedding anniversary. Even in death, the Kirbys' "zest for life" could not be quenched. Their alcoholic St. Bernard dog, Neil, also perished in the accident. Scenes of the ethereal pooch sporting an ice bag on his head to relieve a hangover were a recurring gag.

The *Playhouse 90* production of J.P. Miller's script *The Days of Wine and Roses* in 1958 was a notable exception to the rule. The story of a young married couple and their drift into alcoholism conveyed a different picture, one of damaged lives rather than carefree consumption.

But TV in the swinging sixties continued to define out any adverse effects of alcohol use. It was a seemingly required activity for successful young professionals. On *Bewitched*, advertising executive Darrin Stephens was unlikely to get through a day without imbibing. If he was running dry on creative ideas, a martini would lubricate the brainstorming. If his over-bearing mother-in-law was visiting when he returned home, his loving wife Samantha would fix everyone a drink to break the tension. When he and his boss Larry Tate entertained clients, their glasses were continually freshened.

Countless situation comedy plots perpetuated the myth that drinking alcohol was an effective means of coping with everyday stress and that cold showers and drinking coffee could return a person to sobriety. Another falsehood the medium relayed was that a stock character, the town drunk, was a lovable and harmless member of the community.

Otis Campbell, who is well-acquainted with all the moonshiners in Mayberry, regards the jailhouse as his home away from home on *The Andy Griffith Show*. More of a town mascot than a menace, he would lock himself up and enjoy Aunt Bee's home cooking while he recuperated after a night of carousing. "Now I know I must be drunk," Otis says as he tries to jump into the cell bed that had been propped up on its side. "I never fell onto the wall before!"

In 1965, *The Dean Martin Show* greatly bolstered the notion of drunkenness as a lark. The handsome host of the variety show had been the partner of comedian Jerry Lewis in the 1940s and 1950s, but in the early 1960s he became known as a member of the Rat Pack—a show biz drinking circle that included Frank Sinatra, Sammy Davis, Jr., actor Peter Lawford, and comedian Joey Bishop. Booze was their bond.

Martin's TV persona was of a relaxed crooner, always a little looped and often downright sloshed. "Every time it rains, it rains bourbon from heaven," he'd sing. Hiccupping in his tuxedo, Dean Martin was the convivial dipsomaniac.

The unfortunate message of his extremely successful television show was that liquor enhances life. Those who drink were made out to be colorful and engaging characters. Disapprovers were cast as self-righteous, out-of-date moralizers. The joy of being plastered was that one could escape the constraints and responsibilities of adult life. "I got picked up the other night on the suspicion of drunk driving," Martin joked. "The cop asked me to walk a white line. I said, 'Not unless you put a net under it.'"

The fear and embarrassment alcoholics caused their families were comic fodder. "I had Thanksgiving dinner in bed," the tipsy host said. "I really didn't plan it that way. It was just that when I woke up, I was on the kitchen table."

The pervasive presence of alcohol on prime time did not wane as the 1970s began. Jokes about heavy drinking remained a staple of television entertainment. A young viewer learning about the grown-up world would logically infer that everybody drinks, it's fun to do, and nothing bad happens to you if you do it.

Kids expressing the desire to partake of alcohol was a common occurrence on situation comedies. "In five and a half years I'll be able to drink," the teenaged daughter Barbara eagerly informs her mother on *One Day at a Time*. When Arnold, the little lead character in *Diff'rent Strokes*, is refused a drink of wine at the dinner table, he asks, "Can I smell the cork?" Even if the adults in the stories reminded their children that a person can be grown up without drinking, the presentation of alcohol as a forbidden fruit added to its allure.

Researchers studying adolescents were concerned about the depictions. "Television, it is clear," an expert in the field wrote, "serves as a *de facto* health educator in general and an alcohol educator in particular."

A comedian named Foster Brooks joined the supporting cast of regulars on *The Dean Martin Show* in 1970. His stand-up routine consisted of him slurring through a number of jokes about his excessive drinking. In 1973, a new feature, the "Man of the Week Celebrity Roast," appeared on the show and Brooks became one of several celebrities seated at the banquet dais tossing comic insults at the guest of honor. The segment was so popular that when the show ended in 1974, NBC ran the roasts as a series of occasional specials. Gags about alcohol abuse were a fixture of the concept.

"I look forward to being part of this glowing tribute," Dean Martin said in 1977 to open the roast for actress Betty White. "And about 3:00 this afternoon I got started on my glow." When Brooks stepped up to the podium he told the assembled, "It's a thrill to sway before you tonight." As he said of Betty White, "We go way back," he fell over backwards and hit the floor.

The other celebrities included a few zingers for Dean Martin along with their remarks about Betty White. "He likes staying at the MGM Grand Hotel," said actress Georgia Engel about the venue of the broadcast. "They have fourteen bars here and they're all within staggering distance." Milton Berle complimented Martin's appearance, "Your eyes are so shiny and bright. Drinking that Windex again?" Defending himself against the comic barbs, Martin explained, "Just because I have red eyes and a white face doesn't mean I'm a drunk—I could be a rabbit!"

Drinking immoderately without serious consequences was a television convention. In real life, tragedy was too often the result. One such horror story occurred in 1980 and reverberated throughout the country.

In Fair Oaks, California, thirteen-year-old Cari Lightner was walking to a church carnival when a car swerved out of control and hit her. She was thrown 120 feet; less than an hour later she died of massive internal injuries. The driver, who fled the scene, was Clarence Busch, a forty-six-year-old man with a long record of arrests for intoxication. Two days before he killed Cari he had been bailed out of jail on another hit-and-run drunk-driving charge.

The victim's mother, Candy Lightner, was told by a police officer that it was unlikely Busch would spend any time behind bars for his crime because drunk driving was "just one of those things." The night before her daughter's funeral, the thirty-three-year-old real-estate agent decided she would start an organization to change the system.

Lightner's first step was to visit California governor Jerry Brown and try to persuade him to set up a task force on drunk driving, a social problem that was killing about 28,000 Americans every year. When the governor would not receive her, Lightner went to his office every day and soon a good deal of publicity was generated. Brown finally acted on her request.

The resulting organization, Mothers Against Drunk Driving, adopted the acronym "MADD," which reflected the mood of its members, many of whom had lost children in similar ways. The crusade targeted lenient laws and weak judicial response to the crime of drunk driving. Each success brought MADD more media attention, such as the 1981 passage of a California law that imposed mandatory imprisonment of up to four years for repeat offenders. The group's membership grew rapidly and gave rise to the formation of Students Against Driving Drunk (SADD). A made-for-TV movie added to MADD's prominence. Mariette Hartley portrayed Candy Lightner in an Emmy-nominated performance.

By the mid-1980s there was a measurable reduction in the annual number of drunk-driving fatalities and a detectable change in the way drinking was presented on television. The awareness provided by MADD served to deflate the humor in intoxication. More storylines highlighted the possible conse-quences of irresponsible behavior. In a 1985 episode of *Mr. Belvedere*, the seventeen-year-old son Kevin signs a parent–youth contract that states if he drinks at a party he will not drive, but instead will phone his parents for a ride home. They, in turn, promise not to harp on him if that occurs. When Kevin gets drunk at the prom, both sides honor the contract. His father tells Kevin, "We're proud of you, pal—in a disappointed sort of way."

But when Kevin gets drunk again a few days later and needs a ride home, his father gets angry. The housekeeper, Mr. Belvedere, has a talk with the hungover teenager about his recent escapades. Kevin says that alcohol gives him courage. "You were at the prom," Mr. Belvedere replies, "not the Russian front." The story concludes with the understanding that drinking is not a manly rite of passage.

An initiative launched by the Harvard Alcohol Project in 1988 had a concrete impact on the portrayal of alcohol consumption on television. Spearheaded by Professor Jay Winsten of Harvard's School of Public Health, the mission of the project was to make the "designated driver" concept a cultural norm. The lobbying effort with writers and producers resulted in many TV characters displaying more responsible attitudes about alcohol. "I don't think we should drive," said April Stevens of *Dallas* to her sister, "I'll call a cab." On the show *Hunter* a waitress asks her customers, "Who gets the soda water? You? Well, I guess somebody has to drive."

Producer Leonard Stern was one of those who made changes. "When I was producing *McMillan and Wife* sixteen years ago," he said in 1988, "I'd have Rock Hudson as McMillan come home and immediately swallow a couple of drinks to relax. Today, I probably wouldn't allow that to happen." *Variety* reported that members of the production community were "more aware than ever before of the power of their TV programs to influence the way people behave."

Making "the designated driver" a household phrase by the early 1990s "was no accident," it was reported in 1993, "but the result of hundreds of references to the dangers of drunken driving deliberately planted in *Roseanne*, *Cheers*, and other top shows through a collaboration between Hollywood and Harvard."

Instead of happy-go-lucky drunks, recovering alcoholics became familiar in prime time. On *The John Larroquette Show*, for example, lead character John Hemingway is introduced in the pilot episode as he addresses an Alcoholics Anonymous meeting: "Hi, my name is John and I'm an alcoholic. Tonight I start a new job. And folks I really, really, really have to make it work this time. Tonight may be the most important night of my life. And all I have to do is get through it without taking a drink."

By the mid-1990s, though, there was evidence in American popular culture of what *The New York Times* called "a fading drumbeat against drunken driving." A British comedy import, *Absolutely Fabulous*, on the cable network Comedy Central developed a cult following. The lead characters were two aging party-girls employed in the fashion trade and who like to drink.

American TV picked up on the relaxation of the anti-alcohol trend. "The climate of this country has been so heavy for the last 10 years," said the producer of the CBS sitcom *High Society* in 1995. "We wanted to let some steam out of the pressure cooker." The lead character of his series, Ellie Walker, is an author of trashy novels and is frequently seen drinking or hungover, even passed out on a friend's dinner table. Ellie has blackouts at parties, and as for rehab, she "thinks 12-stepping is a country dance."

The creator of the comedy series *Cybill* called the title character's best friend Maryann a "joyful drunk." She guzzles martinis out of water bottles. Coincident with television's new willingness to show attractive women boldly hitting the bottle was a rise in alcohol abuse among white females between the ages of eighteen and twenty-nine—the medium's prized demographic. "Maryann drives but she's never been in a crash," pointed out Alyse Booth of the Center on Addiction and Substance Abuse about the unrealistic depiction. She "hasn't even thrown up."

As the number of drunk-driving deaths began to creep up again in 1996, so too had the number of TV characters who drank alcohol irresponsibly. Professor Winsten contended there was "a direct relationship between media coverage and drunken driving fatalities."

"There were two periods of unusually high media attention to drunk driving," Winsten explained. "The first was in 1983 and 1984 and it was largely the work of groups like MADD. The second was in 1989, '90, '91, and '92 with a hefty representation of the designated driver." "During each high-media period," he continued, "alcohol-related traffic fatalities, correcting for vehicle miles driven, fell twice as rapidly as during the intervening low-media periods."

As the 1990s drew to a close, the picture of alcohol use and abuse on television continued to loosen. For every depiction of alcohol as a harmful substance—such as the several-episode *Party of Five* storyline concerning Bailey's disintegrating life at home and college when his drinking gets out of control—there were many more representations of alcohol as an elixir.

The young and winsome coterie on *Friends* enjoy Jell-O shots at a party and everyone has a blast. When Rachel tries to get over Ross's involvement with another woman, she accepts a date with a different suitor and proceeds to get blotto. It's framed in the show as cute, not reprehensible, behavior. In one episode, Rachel's reaction to her mother's embarrassing conduct at a wedding is to ask Monica, who has catered the affair, "There's more alcohol, right?"

On the *Drew Carey Show*, beer was the *raison d'être* of the lead character and his pals. They often reminisce about the alcohol-induced escapades of their glory days. On the 1996 series *INK*, actor Ted Danson played newspaper columnist Mike Logan. He and his ex-wife's new beau bond while they polish off a bottle of scotch. Drunk and silly, they have a great time together.

Commenting one night in his topical monologue on the *Tonight Show*, Jay Leno was incredulous about a news item regarding a fraternity that outlawed alcohol at its social functions. "Drinking is the only reason you have a fraternity," he joked to the appreciative laughter of the audience.

After years and years of unconcern about portrayals of alcohol abuse, the television industry was prodded into an acknowledgment of its danger. A personal tragedy became a mother's crusade that could not be ignored. But when the direct pressure eased, a relapse was evident in many network offerings that once again were suggesting a fun-loving personality could be found in a bottle.

Fashion Sense

Whatever "look" was in at any given moment in postwar America, there was a television connection. No fad or fashion could survive without a stamp of approval from the majority medium.

Singer Pat Boone's trademark was wearing white bucks. When *The Pat Boone Chevy Showroom* went on the air in 1957, his footwear became a much-copied style. "There were a lot of bucks in those bucks," Boone laughed about all the money he made by attaching his name to a shoe line. His clean-cut image also helped sell more than thirty other products, including "April Love" perfume, named after one of his hit records, and an official Pat Boone cardigan sweater.

When the Beatles appeared on *The Ed Sullivan Show* on February 9, 1964, a fashion revolution was launched. Long hair on boys instantly became a craze. Beatle-boots and mod collarless jackets were quickly added to the wardrobes of young men who wanted to impress their classmates.

During the mid-1960s two prime-time rock 'n' roll shows, *Shindig* on ABC and *Hullabaloo* on NBC, were showcases for the top recording artists of the time, from Motown to the Mersey Beat. But the programs also popularized Carnaby Street fashions. The mini-skirted *Hullabaloo* Dancers turned white go-go boots into a must-have item for every hip young lady.

In the late 1960s the fashions of the counterculture were mainstreamed through television. Love beads, peace medallions, bell-bottom pants, and psychedelic prints moved from Haight-Ashbury in San Francisco to Main Street in small towns across America. What started out as a rebellious challenge to the status quo became standard attire. A 1966 TV series about a rock band, *The Monkees*, inspired by the Beatles movie *A Hard Day's Night*, influenced young viewers to buy not only their records, but also items like wire-rimmed sunglasses known as Monkee-shades. J.C. Penney, the department store of the middle class, purchased the licensing rights to use the name on a clothing line that included Monkee pants, Monkee shirts, and Monkee boots.

The impact of television on women's fashions in the 1970s was strongly felt. Designer Bob Mackie, who created the outrageous outfits worn by Cher on *The Sonny and Cher Comedy Hour*, takes credit for invigorating the sales of halter tops. The style had been introduced in the early seventies, but "they weren't selling," according to Mackie. "Cher has a beautiful back and shoulders so when I put her in backless dresses, women started to become more experimental, feeling that 'If she can look like that, so can I.'"

The biggest fashion splash of the 1970s, though, was "The Farrah Phenomenon." When *Charlie's Angels* premiered in 1976, it was assumed that actress Kate Jackson would be the commanding presence among the three lead characters, which also included actress Jaclyn Smith. But within the first weeks of the series it was clear that the three angels were not equally appealing to the viewers. Farrah Fawcett-Majors, who played the role of Jill Munroe, emerged as a superstar.

The ABC publicity department was deluged with requests for photos and interviews with the petite thirty-year-old blonde with a dazzling, toothy smile. Just why she generated such fanatical interest among viewers was a subject of much speculation in the press by psychologists and other experts in human behavior. The most common verdict was that Farrah's hair was responsible. "That mussed-up blonde mane looks as if she just got out of bed and is immediately ready to get back into it," explained a college professor from Ohio.

"The key to the whole thing," a Los Angeles psychiatrist offered, "is that men think of her as a sexpot and women invariably describe her as 'adorable.' When women call another woman 'adorable,' that means she poses no threat to them in terms of seducing their husbands. Maybe that's because they read about this girl's happy marriage to Lee Majors and that she even hyphenated her last name with his."

Farrah's manager thought the reason for her success could be summed up in one word—nipples. "Innocent of bra," as she was described, Farrah inspired the timid to follow her lead. "Jaclyn Smith and Kate Jackson were reluctant at first," it was reported in *TV Guide*, "but Farrah Fawcett pushed for it." Soon young women around the country who might never have considered it without the impetus of *Charlie's Angels* adopted the no-bra policy.

The stampede to license Farrah merchandise resulted in T-shirts, dolls, lunch pails, a signature line of shampoo, and a pin-up poster that sold two million copies in less than four months, breaking a speed-sales record previously held by Fonzie of *Happy Days*. In a 1977 poll conducted by *Scholastic* magazine, more than fourteen thousand junior and senior high school students said that Farrah Fawcett-Majors was their Number One personal hero. President Jimmy Carter came in at number sixteen.

Hairdressers were beleaguered with requests for Farrah's distinctive haircut with wing-like wisps on each side. Those whose clients possessed thick and luxurious hair could copy the layering and produce a close replica. But, when girls and women with fine, straight hair came in to the shop and asked for "a Farrah," beauty operators cringed.

In the early 1980s, haute couture was the fashion trend, fueled in part by the elegance and opulence of First Lady Nancy Reagan. "Suddenly it was okay to take the diamonds out of the vault," wrote the notorious fashion critic, Mr. Blackwell, "resurrect the sables from storage and wrap yourself in resplendent Reagan red." The prime-time soap operas of the era, Blackwell believes, reflected the Reagan style and furthered the American appetite for such glamour.

"When 100 million people worldwide are watching a show," said *Dynasty* costume designer Nolan Miller, "it has to have some influence on fashion." The resurgence of hat-wearing among stylish women, Miller said, had a boost from the character of Alexis. And Krystle was the reason, he contends, large shoulder pads became so in vogue.

As a fashion forum for teenagers in the 1980s, MTV was a powerful force. Videos that showed women in sexually provocative costumes crawling between the legs of men in sadomasochistic poses defined the sleazy-look as an acceptable style for young women.

No pop star had more impact on retail clothing sales than Madonna. Even junior high and elementary school girls became Madonna "wannabes." "I see 12-year-old girls wearing tight skirts and spiked heels," said a saleswoman of Madonna-wear, a signature line of "sports-wear for sexpots." The wardrobe included lace tank tops and T-shirts and a $30 tube skirt that could be "rolled down for public navel maneuvers."

"Madonna says 'I'm gonna dress the way I want and act the way I want, and if you don't like it, tough tooties,'" one of her emulators explained. Referring to themselves as "Boy Toys," her fans adopted the brassy style of wearing underwear as outerwear. Mr. Frederick's of Hollywood lingerie stores across the country were delighted with the trend as teens packed in and put their money on the counter.

Madonnaesque strapless, lacy prom and party dresses accounted for approximately $60 million in sales in 1984 and 1985. The grateful Council of Fashion Designers of America gave MTV an award in 1985 for the network's influence on fashion.

On the cable network's fifteenth anniversary in 1996, the president of MTV, Judy McGrath, reflected on its viewers over the years. "If you're an MTV fan," she said, "you like all the stuff that's on MTV. You like all the junk pop cultural stuff. That's how you know who you are and what to wear and what you're like."

The proliferation of "entertainment journalism" in the 1980s with the increasing popularity of shows like *Entertainment Tonight* brought a new level of newsworthiness to the clothing choices of all kinds of stars. Reporters sent to cover the Oscars, the Emmys, the Golden Globes, the People's Choice, and numerous other award presentations devoted the lion's share of their commentary to fashion hits and misses.

A prime-time trendsetter of the 1990s was the character of Amanda Woodward, played by Heather Locklear, on the series *Melrose Place*. She was the president of an advertising agency and wore power suits to the office. But hers were not traditional or conservative. Amanda's jackets were described by one columnist as "sausage-tight" and her skirts "placemat size."

Retail stores began offering suits with the same body-skimming silhouette. "Amanda may be fictional," a newspaper story reported, "but her wardrobe has become a real influence for clothing makers such as Trilogy, Baramai Studio, Gallay and Bebe. . . . Trilogy, a line launched by the company Rampage, has suits named after Locklear's Amanda."

In the mid-1990s, *People* magazine reported that the hairstyle of a TV character had become "the biggest hair craze since Farrah Fawcett feathered her tresses back in the 70s." An editor of *Vogue* described the craze for her readers in 1996 with a touch of hyperbole: "Right this minute everybody thinks she can look like Rachel, Jennifer Aniston's character on the insanely popular *Friends*. I watched about 15 minutes of *Friends* once, and I have to admit it was entertaining. But it's not so much the show as this girl's poufy shag that has captured the imagination of everyone on the planet."

Early in the trajectory of the trend, a Los Angeles hairstylist actually had clients who flew in from New York to get the haircut. Soon such an extravagance was unnecessary, *Vogue* reported, "since by now every salon in every mall in America offers a version of the Rachel."

The surge in cigar smoking among young adults in the mid-1990s, including women, worried health care professionals. It had always been an oddity in American culture for a woman to smoke a cigar. But several prime-time shows jumped on the bandwagon and validated as fashionable an activity that had once been considered socially unacceptable.

In a column entitled "Must-Smoke TV"—a take-off on NBC's "Must See TV" slogan—*TV Guide* reported in 1996 that "it was just a matter of time before TV's leading ladies started smoking up a storm." It was "a strange coincidence," the piece noted, that "the women of NBC's Thursday-night comedy lineup all got the urge to light up on the same evening, Sept. 19, during the season premieres."

On *Friends*, *Seinfeld*, and *Suddenly Susan*, smart and attractive gals had no compunction about puffing a stogie. "There's something slightly rakish about it," explained the executive producer of *Suddenly Susan*. "We want to establish that Susan is a very decent person who wants to experiment a little bit." The ironic message was that cigars are an accouterment of young women who can think for themselves.

Television has always given Americans ideas on how they want to look and helped them compose their fashion statements. But however essential outer trappings are in revealing and defining human personality, how one talks, acts, and reacts to others is the true measure.

Codes of Conduct

When Miss Landers' fifth-grade class at Grant Avenue Elementary School was having its picture taken for the yearbook, in a 1961 episode of *Leave It to Beaver*, all the girls had on their nicest dresses and the boys wore jackets and ties. Beaver Cleaver, goaded by his conniving friend Gilbert, made a funny face by pulling down his lips and sticking out his tongue just as the shutter clicked. His stunt got him in big trouble.

In a meeting with Beaver's father, Principal Rayburn explains there's no time to have another picture taken, the yearbook has already gone to press. "Well, I guess it's going to be quite embarrassing for all of us," Ward says. Mrs. Rayburn gently hints that he's missing the point; there's more than embarrassment at stake. She's used to boys pulling pranks now and then, she says: "But it's what this implies, Mr. Cleaver. It shows the other students that Theodore has no respect for his school, his classmates, that it's just one big joke."

Back at home a contrite Beaver worries about the humiliation he'll feel when the yearbook comes out. Ward asks Beaver to think also of how Miss Landers, Mrs. Rayburn, the other children, and their parents will feel. "When you do something bad, Beaver, or break a rule," he says, "it can affect and hurt a lot of people."

In TV households throughout the 1960s good manners were essential. Children asked to be excused before leaving the dinner table and adults never engaged in shouting matches or argued in mean-spirited ways. Perhaps for most viewers it was an unrealistic picture of family dynamics, but it offered a model of respectful and loving communication.

In the 1970s, politeness on prime time took a nosedive. The rush to relevance in the wake of *All in the Family*'s success raised the decibel level of family discussions on TV sitcoms. Sarcasm and name-calling became commonplace. "The main comedy technique is the insult," wrote a critic about the genre of shows that included *Maude*, *Good Times*, *Sanford and Son*, and *The Jeffersons*.

Television's influence on how Americans express themselves has always been easy to detect. The slogans of TV commercials and the sayings of TV characters infiltrate everyday speech. Fonzie's greeting of "Aaaaaay" accompanied by a thumbs-up gesture and J.J.'s explosive affirmative response "Dy-no-mite!!" on *Good Times* were repeated to distraction by young fans in the early and mid-1970s. In the same time period, the medium was also validating the lobbing of biting insults as a defensible mode of disagreement. Caustic comments made by lead characters in sitcoms were presented not as rudeness but as the hallmark of a clever and feisty personality. The more acrid the insult, the more it was rewarded with laughter and applause.

Another incursion into America's deteriorating sense of personal decorum came with the rise of *The Gong Show*. The syndicated offering from producer Chuck Barris, which ran from 1976 to 1980, featured amateur performers being evaluated by a panel of celebrity judges. Talent was not a requirement for the contestants. One of the most memorable acts, according to Barris, was The Popsicle Girls—two attractive young women dressed in shorts and halter tops who stood before the cameras and provocatively sucked away on the frozen phallic symbols.

The role of the judges was to comically express their contempt for the players by banging on a huge gong when the performance became intolerable. At the sound of the gong, the act was ejected from the stage while the judges exchanged glib mockery about what they had just witnessed. Exhibitionism and ridicule were at the heart of the formula. Barris denied that he had made his fortune by degrading anyone, saying that between "95 percent and 97 percent" of the people involved were "having a ball." He added that it is impossible to "purposely, knowingly humiliate somebody because a person knows in advance that it's coming and they can avoid it if they have any brains at all."

Game shows in which people were made to look foolish had long been part of American television. *Beat the Clock*, for instance, which began in 1950, had contestants from the studio audience perform various stunts within a given time limit. Typical tricks included stuffing inflated balloons into an oversized pair of long underwear or trying to spring a series of mousetraps with a frankfurter on the end of a fishing pole line. Relay races involving whipped cream and custard pies ensured that a messy time would be had by all. But, like a parlor game of charades, it was silly, not mean.

What was different about *The Gong Show* was the element of hostility it introduced. Barris's follow-up program, *The $1.98 Beauty Show*, was even more spiteful. The contestants were described by one critic as "women, many homely, obviously talentless, and seemingly desperate for attention." The show, which included a talent and swimsuit competition, was, the critic explained, "ostensibly a parody of the Miss America Pageant," but was "in reality a study in female degradation."

By the 1980s, television was validating and rewarding crudeness each and every day. "The wages of trash are high," a social observer wrote about American culture in the early part of the decade. It was a lesson that TV was teaching well to viewers of daytime talk shows. General managers of local stations, who in the past felt a responsibility to program with a public-interest yardstick, were steadily succumbing to a marketplace standard.

There seemed to be a race among TV talk show hosts, a media analyst observed, "to see who could stoop the lowest and make the most noise doing it." Searching for the bottom limit of what viewers would accept, producers mined flagrantly shocking topics. Hookers, strippers, transvestites—even people who claimed to have had sex with animals—joined the parade of guests.

Beyond selecting trashy subject matter, though, producers also encouraged boorish, confrontational behavior among those being interviewed, as well as those in the studio audience. A host would instigate gross rudeness, and the show would be rewarded with publicity when provocations resulted in physical clashes. Geraldo Rivera, a pioneer of this kind of trash television, made the cover of *Newsweek* when his nose was broken in an on-camera fight between black activists and white supremacists. Those who profited from the debasement of the airwaves appeared to be shameless.

Some pinned the sad trend of deteriorating standards on the Federal Communications Commission (FCC) led by Reagan appointee Mark Fowler. "Deregulation has brought a new breed of broadcaster to whom public service matters less," said Andrew Schwartzman, director of the Media Access Project. "They're willing to close their eyes and say 'Go ahead and put it on.' This creates pressure for broadcasters who know better and say privately they hate this kind of programming but have to do it to compete."

In the late-1980s, *The Morton Downey Jr. Show*, dubbed as "confrontainment," revolted those who thought the medium had already reached its nadir. The star of the program was a chain-smoking abrasive host whose purpose was not to shed light on the issues being discussed but to generate angry verbal clashes that verged on physical conflict.

Downey assumed the role of a liberal-hating arch conservative. He insulted and bullied those who disagreed with him, as the studio audience, composed primarily of young white men, cheered him on. "Zip it, puke breath" or "Suck my armpit" were typical retorts to guests with opposing points of view. On one 1988 show, Downey wrapped an American flag around himself, gestured to his buttocks and challenged an Iranian guest to "kiss it."

American popular culture, led by television, was sinking ever deeper in the muck. "We have lost the aesthetic category of the vulgar because we have been overwhelmed by it," wrote James Twitchell, the author of *Carnival Culture: The Trashing of Taste in America*. "We have ceased to recognize it because it has become the norm, in computer jargon—the default mode of taste."

Even Americans who rarely or never watched TV were affected. As the language of television grew coarser, so too did the language of people on the streets. As the 1990s arrived, many citizens identified with the complaint of commentator Andy Rooney. "I'm increasingly aware," he said, "walking around in public, of the cacophony of obscenities bombarding my ears."

As in every period of TV history, there was ample evidence that viewers of the 1980s and 1990s incorporated the language of the medium into their own. In 1986, actor William Shatner, who had played Captain Kirk on *Star Trek*, appeared in a comedy sketch on *Saturday Night Live*. The skit satirizes Star Trek Conventions at which devoted fans asked trivia-filled questions of the series' stars. Shatner, playing himself, becomes frustrated with the proceedings and tells the trekkies: "I'd just like to say, move out of your parents' basements and get a life! I mean, for crying out loud, it was just a TV show." The phrase "get a life" immediately caught on and even became the title of a TV show about a young adult with a severe case of arrested development. Ten years after the *SNL* sketch aired, a national poll conducted by a Michigan university voted the phrase one of the most overused in the English language.

But it wasn't the benign phrases that were troubling. When children imitated the greeting "I'm Bart Simpson, who the hell are you?" parents had a hard time explaining why it was acceptable for a ten-year-old boy in a cartoon to address adults with such rudeness but it wasn't for real children.

In the early 1990s the amount of objectionable language on television, defined as profanity, epithets, and scatological words, skyrocketed. A research study conducted by Professor Barbara Kaye of Southern Illinois University found that between 1990 and 1994 such language increased by 45 percent in prime time and 94 percent in the traditional family hour between 8:00 and 9:00 p.m.

Vulgarities became standard modes of expression from lead characters. The use of the phrase "you suck" by a six-year-old girl on the CBS sitcom *Uncle Buck* created some trepidation for the network and sponsors in 1990. But by mid-decade the word "suck" in all of its forms was so commonplace that it no longer raised an eyebrow in broadcast standards departments.

Viewers also became accustomed to hearing the word "bitch" used without reservation. A typical usage occurred on an episode of *Friends* in which Rachel gets to know the new girlfriend of a young man on whom she has a crush. When it turns out that the girlfriend is a charming and dear person, Rachel reacts by saying "That bitch!" The demeaning word is meant to prompt a laugh.

In 1994, when Fox moved *Melrose Place* to a new night, the network promoted the change with the slogan, "Mondays are a bitch." Posters featuring the slogan scrawled graffiti-style over the face of Heather Locklear's Amanda were plastered on bus shelters and mall kiosks throughout the country. "The *Melrose* campaign not only reflects a Neanderthal view of strong-willed women," wrote a Los Angeles TV critic, "it also is bound to provoke a lot of discussions between parents and children about 'naughty words we don't use.'"

But the effects of television were hard to undo as a source of social learning. If the good and funny guys on TV used expressions like "pissed off," "bite me," and "kiss my ass," requests for decorum in real-life conversations seemed prudish to youngsters who had been conditioned to crudeness in language. "I've been a principal for 20 years and I've seen significant changes. And one of the factors is TV," said Jim Freese of Homestead High School in Fort Wayne, Indiana. "I'm seeing more instances of inappropriate language around school. It's part of the vocabulary, and often they don't think about some of the words because they hear them so often on TV."

In the 1990s, uncouth conduct as well as vulgar language were epidemic on American television. The heavily promoted premiere of Michael Jackson's music video "Black or White" was simultaneously broadcast in November 1991 on the Fox network, MTV, and Black Entertainment Television. In the hope of maximizing the number of children and preteens in the audience, the cameo appearances of Bart Simpson and Macaulay Culkin, the child star of the hit movie *Home Alone*, were well-advertised.

The video opens with Culkin happily listening to loud music in his room. When his father orders the boy to turn it down, the youngster hauls some huge amplifiers and speakers downstairs, tells his father "Eat this!" and then raises the volume of the music so high he literally blows the father through the roof.

The most controversial part of the video, though, was a dance segment in which Michael Jackson repeatedly grabs his crotch. Along with close-ups of his pants zipper being pulled up and down, the performance included what was described as "an exaggerated simulation of masturbation."

Those who spoke and acted obscenely on television were often chastised in the short term by commentators and columnists, but they never became cultural pariahs. Self-centered displays, ill-manners, and the refusal to display embarrassment were rewarded with publicity and attention.

Madonna's appearance on the *Late Show with David Letterman* in the spring of 1994 is a case-in-point. "Why are you so obsessed with my sex life?" the guest asked the host, who for months had been using Madonna's alleged promiscuity as monologue material. "Well," Letterman replied, "I have none of my own." "David," Madonna responded, "You are a sick fuck."

Thirteen times during her twenty minutes on the air, the pop star used the f-word. Each time it was bleeped by the network for the home audience. Madonna also told Letterman there was a pair of her panties in his desk drawer. "Aren't you going to smell them?" she asked. Later in the interview she discussed the benefits of "peeing in the shower." "It fights athletes' foot. I'm serious. Urine is an antiseptic. It has to do with the enzymes in your body."

Madonna's performance, reported *The New York Times*, "produced tabloid headlines and extensive television coverage." "She certainly got attention," said Robert Morton, the producer of Letterman's show. "I had to wonder, are the people in Madonna's camp slapping each other five over this?"

The star's publicity agent, Liz Rosenberg, proffered, "What do people expect from Madonna?" Noting all the press about the incident, the agent commented, "They fall for it every time, don't they?" Asked if the negative reactions troubled her client, Rosenberg said it didn't bother her, that the star was on to the next project, adding, "Madonna isn't much of a reflective girl."

As the 1990s advanced, so much of entertainment television seemed to be a celebration of pure irresponsibility, designed to shock and appeal to the most base instincts in human nature. The comical presentation of unconscionable acts, such as torturing a cat in a *Beavis and Butt-Head* cartoon, had taken on the mantle of avant-garde despite its crass commercial intentions. Those on television who violated commonly held canons of decency or politeness achieved prominence and profit, with no apparent penalty to be paid.

Symptoms of a resulting decline in American standards of comportment were everywhere. Opinions seemed to split along generational lines when, in 1994, a seventeen-year-old high school student asked President Clinton at an MTV-sponsored forum on youth and violence whether he wore "boxers or briefs?" Older Americans regarded the question as an undignified impertinence and found it hard to imagine that a young lady could muster the gall to pose it to the commander-in-chief. But teenagers, kids who had grown up with different TV models, thought it was funny and harmless.

Caught off-guard by the question, the President answered "Usually briefs" to "his gleeful audience of 200 college and high school students"—and, of course, the TV audience. The *Washington Post* reported that after President

Clinton responded to the question, he shook his head and "sounded just a bit peeved" when he proclaimed "I can't believe she said that."

Laetitia Thompson, who had intended to ask the President a serious question about drug legalization, was in the media spotlight after the event, fielding questions from the press, such as, "How long have you been wondering about Clinton's underwear?" Explaining her change of heart regarding her query, the "willowy blonde with cover-girl good looks" said: "That's what people want to know about. He's a real human being. He's very sexually oriented, and people are always interested in that."

By the late 1990s the American press was brimming with analyses and articles like the USA Today cover story, "Excuse Me, But.... Whatever Happened to Manners?" There was a growing consensus in the country that the quality of public life in the United States had dramatically eroded. The great majority of citizens—89 percent according to a U.S. News and World Report poll—believed "their country is becoming a nasty place to live, where bad manners, uncouth drivers, unholy language, and unruly kids are crowding civility out of society." Every serious discussion of why Americans were behaving so badly as the new century approached considered television as one of the major contributors to the problem.

In the fall of 1999, the wholesome ABC game show Who Wants to Be a Millionaire became a national sensation, a seeming antidote to the rising tide of crudeness on American television. The genial host Regis Philbin asked contestants a series of increasingly difficult multiple-choice questions. Three "lifelines" were available to the person in the hot seat— a "50/50" that would eliminate two of the four answers, an "Ask the Audience" that polled the members of the studio audience, and a "Phone a Friend" that allowed the contestant to place a call to one of five preselected pals with expertise in different fields. Philbin's question before each selection was accepted, "Is that your final answer?" caught on as a ubiquitous catchphrase. Who Wants to Be a Millionaire was a show families watched together. Despite its modernistic set, it was an old-fashioned program.

But, Who Wants to Be a Millionaire was an exception. Television still favored the edgy. Reality television was the new prime-time phenomenon on the horizon by the summer of 2000. The first season of Survivor on CBS followed the exploits of sixteen adventurers stranded on the island of Pulau Tiga, twenty miles off the coast of Borneo. Initially the contestants were divided into two competing "tribes." The challenges leading to one person's ultimate $1 million victory were both physically and psychologically demanding. Executive producer Mark Burnett explained that *Survivor* was about "Machiavellian politics at their most primal."

The following summer NBC introduced *Fear Factor*, another non-scripted reality show that became a quick hit. Contestants engaged in dangerous stunts involving speed or height and gross stunts like eating bugs or animal parts or being submerged in disgusting substances. The series was criticized for its premise that any indignity was worth enduring if there were a big enough financial pay-off.

The MTV series *Jackass*, which debuted in fall 2000, was criticized for celebrating stupidity for stupidity's sake. The program carried both an oral and print disclaimer that read, "The following show features stunts performed by professionals and/or total idiots under very strict control and supervision. MTV and the producers insist that neither you and/or anyone else attempt to recreate or perform anything you have seen on this show." MTV claimed to target the program to viewers between the ages of eighteen and twenty-four, but at least a third of the show's audience was seventeen or younger.

Reports of kids copycatting *Jackass* stunts began to surface. Some of the imitations were moronic, such as the young man in Minnesota who disrupted traffic on a rainy day by running around dressed in a hospital gown and brandishing a chainsaw. Others were tragic. A thirteen-year-old boy in Connecticut and his friends decided to mimic a *Jackass* act of daredevilry in which the show's host and creator Johnny Knoxville wore a fire-resistant suit covered with raw meat and reclined over a lighted grill to barbeque himself. The boy ended up in the hospital in critical condition suffering from second- and third-degree burns. As had become the norm in TV-inspired misfortunes, the producers expressed sympathy while adamantly denying even the slightest responsibility for influencing impressionable viewers.

Beginning in the post-World War II era, the broad reach of television was socializing the national personality in sundry ways. Over the decades it brought harmless trends that enlivened daily lives and interactions. But, by the end of the 20th century, it was also defining as acceptable lewd and selfish behaviors that diminish and weaken communities.

Fig. 9 Charles Van Doren, an English instructor at Columbia University, who won $129,000 in fourteen appearances on the quiz show *Twenty-One*, ultimately confessed to his complicity in the rigging of the contests. (*Broadcasting and Cable* collection, Library of American Broadcasting.)

CHAPTER 9

Deep Focus:
Television and the American Character

Kate Smith's stirring rendition of "God Bless America" was a radio tradition during World War II that inspired and comforted. On February 1, 1944, the singer instituted a new custom in American broadcasting—the pledge drive. In a 'round-the-clock appeal, Smith made fifty-seven appearances on the CBS network urging the purchase of War Bonds. It was an extraordinary feat that resulted in the sale of more than $100 million worth of bonds.

When *The Kate Smith Evening Hour* came to television in 1951, she opened each show with her signature version of "God Bless America." The song evoked the recent past but also suggested to viewers that new challenges faced the country, which called for the power of prayer. In the early postwar years, religion was a growing aspect of American family life. Church membership climbed and new congregations proliferated to serve expanding suburban communities.

"The family that prays together, stays together" was an often-repeated motto. In 1954, Congress amended the Pledge of Allegiance to say that America was one nation "under God." The following year, the phrase "In God We Trust" became a required feature on all U.S. currency.

Television acknowledged religion's importance. The networks maintained religion departments and worked with various groups, such as the National Council of Churches, in the production of ambitious Sunday morning programming. Series like *Lamp Unto My Feet* and *The Eternal Light* offered dramatized stories illuminating the common perspectives of the major faiths.

In February 1952, the DuMont television network brought religion to prime time with a simple one-man show called *Life Is Worth Living*.

The star was a fifty-seven-year-old Catholic Bishop, Fulton J. Sheen. "He's a dead duck," was the consensus among industry insiders when Sheen's show was scheduled on Tuesday nights at 8:00—opposite Milton Berle's wildly popular *Texaco Star Theater*. But the benevolent bishop surprised the doubting Thomases. He caught on.

An unanticipated chemistry occurred at the Adelphi Theatre in midtown Manhattan when Bishop Sheen took the stage to meet his audience for the live broadcast. Not many Tuesday nights passed before the big-gun competition began to feel a little squeeze in the ratings. While Milton Berle cavorted in drag, Sheen glided on set in full-blown regalia—a long cassock, a gold cross and chain at his breast, a purple cape flowing from his shoulders to the floor, and a skull cap, called a zucchetto, perched on his graying hair. The visual impact was dramatic.

With a boyish smile of acknowledgment for the applause of the studio audience, Bishop Sheen would begin his talk. "Friends, thank you for allowing me to come into your home again." Then by way of anecdote he would introduce the topic for the evening: "The other day I was in an elevator in a department store. . ." It was always a universal theme, such as humor, art, science, or the nature of love. "Starting with something that was common to the audience," Sheen wrote of his technique, "I would gradually proceed from the known to the unknown or to the moral and Christian philosophy." His messages were ecumenical parables, never direct presentations of Catholic dogma.

Each week Bishop Sheen spoke for twenty-eight minutes without notes or a TelePrompTer from a simple set designed to look like a rectory study. Occasionally he would write a word or draw a diagram on a blackboard, the way a university lecturer might to emphasize a key idea. When he moved away from the slate and addressed another one of the three cameras, a crew member—out of TV viewers' sight—would wipe the board clean. It became a running gag on the show that Sheen had a divine helper assigned to erasing duty—"my angel Skippy."

Some of Sheen's personal friends and admirers, who knew the true depth of his erudition winced to hear him make corny jokes on TV. "I'm going to buy my angel a bottle of Halo Shampoo," he quipped one night. Skippy, he explained to viewers, was a union man. He belonged to Local 20 of the Cherubim.

Bishop Sheen also became hot copy. *Life*, *Look*, and *Time* magazines ran flattering feature stories. The number of stations carrying *Life Is Worth Living* jumped from three to fifteen in less than two months. Fan mail flowed in at a rate of 8,500 letters per week. There were four times as many requests for tickets as could be filled. The sponsor, Admiral Appliances, which paid the modest production costs in exchange for a one-minute commercial at the open of the show and another minute at the close, was feeling the gratification of someone who does a quiet good deed and ends up getting the key to the city.

NBC soon began to covet its neighbor's success and tried to persuade Bishop Sheen to leave the DuMont network. But if there was any temptation to jump to a bigger ship, the new celebrity's loyalty overcame it.

As National Director for the Society for the Propagation of the Faith, an organization that sponsored Catholic missions throughout the world, Bishop Sheen discovered his television exposure was a fund-raising bonanza. Gifts ranged from dimes taped on index cards to will bequests of considerable sums. But Sheen was not a precursor to latter-day TV evangelists who hoodwinked the faithful for personal reward. Solicitation was not the foundation of the show. Spontaneously sent gifts, which ran into millions of dollars, built hospitals and schools. "Every cent," Sheen assured, "found its way to some poor area of this earth."

As with any television personality, Bishop Sheen received all sorts of requests. Children asked for a hat like his or if he might give a poor girl a pony, which he did. One letter came from an aspiring actor named Martin Estevez. Although in later years having an ethnic surname would be an asset to a screen career, in the 1950s it was still a hindrance. So the young man wanted to know if he could borrow the Bishop's name. He became Martin Sheen and ascended to stardom.

By Halloween of the Bishop's first season, if a kid went trick-or-treating wearing his sister's Brownie Scout beanie, his dad's cummerbund, and a satin cape that went with his mother's evening gown, everyone knew he was supposed to be Bishop Sheen.

Nominees for the 1952 Emmy Award for Most Outstanding Television Personality included Jimmy Durante, Edward R. Murrow, Lucille Ball, Arthur Godfrey, and His Excellency, the most Reverend Bishop Fulton J. Sheen. When the clergyman's name was announced as the winner and he accepted the statue, he graciously credited others for his success: "I wish to thank my four writers, Matthew, Mark, Luke, and John."

Sheen's adroitness as a television performer amazed his directors. He understood he was not preaching from a cathedral pulpit and avoided thunderous flourishes in favor of personalized communication. "The several thousand people in the Adelphi Theatre are not my audience,"

Sheen explained. "My words are aimed at little family groups seated about their television sets in their own living rooms."

"Truly uncanny," one of Sheen's directors, Hal Davis, remembered, "was his ability to pace himself so shrewdly that he could build to a climax of emotion at the precise second. He never required time cues, as I remember it, but worked from the clock set above the floor monitor."

The Bishop moved about spiritedly as he spoke, seldom remaining in a fixed position very long but rather striding across the set. There were no blocking rehearsals for *Life Is Worth Living*, though. Sheen shifted freely but knew how to telegraph his moves to the director by looking over to the direction he was about to travel. The only non-extemporaneous segment of the program was the closing. Each week Sheen prepared a peroration of precisely two minutes. He would always end his remarks by lifting both arms up and out at waist level with palms directed heavenward and saying, "God love you."

The amazing appeal of a priest's weekly talk could not be attributed solely to his mastery of the mechanics of television speaking. It was the content and context of his message that touched a responsive chord in so many Americans at mid-century. The generation that had lived through ten years of the Great Depression and sacrificed for the duration of World War II had matured with prescribed exigencies. First came the fight for survival in a cruel economy. And then the national purpose was simply and totally to defeat the enemy. But what was the sustaining goal now that the challenges had been met and defining crises had passed into history?

The hunger for normalcy, for convention, for predictability and order, was a natural craving in men and women whose young lives had been so unsettled for so long. Once the pieces were picked up, though, and the country was back on an even keel, there was an emptiness that accompanied the stability. People who for years had meaning and purpose imposed on them now had to discover for themselves profundity in everyday living.

Sheen intuited the void in postwar Americans. He sensed their frustration and aimlessness. His remedy was a spiritual life with assured values. On the very first broadcast of *Life Is Worth Living*, he stated the premise of the series succinctly: "Life is monotonous if it is meaningless, it is not monotonous if it has a purpose." What Bishop Sheen offered in his television talks was the opportunity for viewers to find purpose in their lives through belief in a personal God.

But however effective television could be at cultivating the spiritual side of the American character, the medium's top priority was cultivating materialism in viewers. Advertising and a great deal of programming were encouraging viewers to find purpose in their lives by acquiring material possessions. The message of Bishop Sheen and other men of religion on television in the early 1950s, such as evangelist Billy Graham, resonated with many members of the G.I. Generation, but the core values of younger Americans were being formed with the backdrop of commercial television.

The 1950 book *The Lonely Crowd*, by David Riesman, an analysis of the American character, examined changes that Riesman and his collaborators Nathan Glazer and Reuel Denney attributed to the growth of mass communication. Americans in the past, the social scientists described, were more "inner directed," meaning they had an internal moral compass. Once their values were formed through church and family traditions, these principles remained solid touchstones throughout life. But children in postwar America, they wrote, were growing up to be "other directed," seeking the social approval of peer groups and displaying "flexible values." By the time the second edition of *The Lonely Crowd* was published in 1961, television as a "tutor of consumption" had become prevalent in American culture and the rise of "other-directed" values was apparent.

As the 1950s drew to a close, *Christian Century* magazine asked, "Are we a nation of liars and cheats?" The television-age morality play that prompted such a sharp question began more than four years earlier when the first major TV quiz show, *The $64,000 Question*, made its debut in 1955. The game quickly won a huge audience and reaped enormous profits for the sponsor, Revlon cosmetics. By 1957, forty-seven half-hour network periods were occupied by quiz shows. As many as five quiz programs per week appeared in the list of top-rated shows.

In 1956, a handsome young English instructor from Columbia University decided to try to make it as a contestant on one of the quiz shows. However prestigious his academic appointment was, Charles Van Doren was not especially well-paid in his profession. If he were lucky enough to win a few thousand dollars from a game show, it would be a windfall.

When Van Doren showed up to take the test for a modest daytime contest called *Tic-Tac-Dough*, his name rang a bell with the producers. His father, Mark Van Doren, was a Pulitzer Prize-winning poet, his mother, Dorothy Van Doren, was a successful novelist, and his uncle, Carl Van Doren, was a biographer of Benjamin Franklin. A week later, Charles was invited to appear on *Twenty-One*, a prime-time quiz with big money prizes. Van Doren would be the challenger to Herbert Stempel, an Army veteran who was a student at New York's City College and who had already dispensed with several opponents.

Twenty-One premiered on NBC in September 1956, sponsored by Geritol, a tonic for "tired blood." The show was modeled after the card game of the same name. Two players answered questions ranging in difficulty from one to eleven points, the winner being the person who stopped with the higher total short of twenty-one or with exactly twenty-one points. The questions were drawn from 108 separate categories, so narrow expertise in one subject was not enough to secure a win.

The first few shows were dismal. Not many contestants could be found who had such encyclopedic knowledge. Players floundered and tie scores of zero-zero frustrated the program's producer, Dan Enright, who then decided to add more entertainment value to the show. He thought that viewers would root for someone like Herb Stempel, a common man, from a poor background, who was intellectually gifted.

Enright visited Stempel at his home in Queens the night before he was to appear on *Twenty-One*. The producer pulled out a packet of cards and began reviewing questions and answers. "After having done this," Stempel would later testify to Congress, "he very, very bluntly sat back and said with a smile, 'How would you like to win $25,000?'"

Stempel willingly entered the "unholy alliance." Enright instructed him to wear a shirt with a frayed collar and an ill-fitting suit the next day and to get a "marine-type white-wall haircut." Stempel was told to stutter when asking for high-point questions. He was to bite his lip, pat his brow, and always refer to the host of the program as "Mr. Barry," never Jack.

Stempel was a quick study and a big winner. Within eight weeks he had amassed $49,500. People recognized the "common man genius" wherever he went. But, unbeknownst to Stempel, Van Doren—upper crust through and through—was being brought in to become the new champion.

When Charles Van Doren was presented with the proposition that he would defeat Stempel in a series of dramatic ties, which would have to be rigged, he was not anxious to participate. He wondered why he couldn't try to beat him fairly. He was told that the rigging of quiz shows was commonplace; they were merely entertainment. Producer Al Freedman suggested to Van Doren that he would actually be helping an important cause. The skeptical contestant later testified that Freedman "stressed the fact that by appearing on a nationally televised program, I would be doing a great service to the intellectual life, to teachers and to education in general, by increasing public respect for the work of the mind through my performances."

"Less swiftly than Stempel, but just as surely," wrote Walter Karp, a chronicler of the scandal, "Charles Lincoln Van Doren had taken the leap into fraud." He accepted questions and answers and coaching on how to perform in the isolation booth to give the appearance of struggling to come up with the correct response.

When the "script" for the first match-up between Stempel and Van Doren called for a draw, Stempel assumed the Ivy Leaguer was being built up for a dramatic fall. He trusted that the triumph of the common man over the privileged son was the operative formula. But a few days later Stempel was informed that *Twenty-One* needed a new champion. He was to lose to the fair-haired boy by missing an easy five-point question— "Which movie won last year's Academy Award?" The answer was *Marty*, the film version of the television drama, Stempel's favorite movie. The whole scenario was galling to him, but Stempel had little choice but to take his $49,500 in winnings and return to obscurity.

Van Doren became a sensation. Week after week, from late November 1956 through March 1957, he amazed the nation with his well-rounded knowledge. He was "a new kind of TV idol," wrote Jack Gould in *The New York Times*. "Of all things, an egghead . . . whom many a grateful parent regards as TV's own health-restoring antidote to Presley." In February 1957, *Time* magazine did a cover story on the "wizard of quiz" that examined "the fascinating, suspense-taut spectacle of his highly trained mind at work."

Inevitably, Van Doren had to give way to a new champion. But he won $129,000 before his defeat to "lady lawyer" Vivienne Nearing. He left *Twenty-One* as a household name and a star. He made guest appearances on *The Steve Allen Show* and signed a $50,000 per year contract with NBC to offer commentary on education and culture on the *Today* show.

Stempel's cries of foul to newspaper reporters were dismissed as sour grapes. But serious rumblings of large-scale quiz show rigging started circulating in the summer of 1958 when a stand-by contestant on the show *Dotto* found a notebook while backstage. It contained the answers to questions asked on the broadcast, which had also been furnished to the champion by the producers. When *Dotto* was abruptly canceled, reporters grew more interested in Stempel's allegations.

While a grand jury investigated, denials were issued by everyone involved with *Twenty-One*. On the *Today* show, Van Doren disavowed Stempel's accusations. He told United Press International "at no time was

I coached or tutored." The hope was that the fuss would die down. Instead, Congress entered the picture when Representative Oren Harris, a Democrat from Arkansas, called the House Legislative Oversight Committee to probe the TV quiz shows.

In the autumn of 1959, Charles Van Doren was invited to appear voluntarily before the subcommittee. But he was not yet ready to face up to what he had done. He and his wife fled to New England, away from the reporters camped outside their door. Dan Enright, though, had already conceded that his show had been rigged for many years. When the subcommittee issued a subpoena ordering Van Doren to testify, he had no choice but to publicly confess his sins.

"I was involved, deeply involved, in a deception," Van Doren said on November 2, 1959. By the time he finished his story ninety minutes later, he had explained in painful detail the fraudulence of his fourteen appearances on *Twenty-One*. "I would give almost anything I have to reverse the course of my life in the last three years."

Scores of people were entangled in the trickery, but it was Van Doren's admission of guilt that ignited the debate over television's role in a decaying American morality. How could a man considered to be above reproach, a teacher, allow himself to be turned into a paid cheat? The nation was stunned. On the *Today* show, Dave Garroway cried at the revelation. President Eisenhower declared the deception "a terrible thing to do to the American public."

Commentary in the national press was harsh and unforgiving. The *Chicago Tribune* called Van Doren "a spectacular sell-out." But the problem was deeper than one man's venality. The *Atlanta Journal* postulated that "the frantic urge to make a fast buck" was "a kind of disease that's eating away at the moral tone of our nation." The sobering lesson of the Van Doren episode was that in postwar America, in a culture that so glorified getting and spending, objective standards of honesty could be easily rationalized away.

Poverty and Greed on Display

When *Strike It Rich* appeared on television in 1951, it quickly generated a debate. Defenders saw it as testimony to American generosity and critics believed it was a callous exploitation of human misery. Either way, viewers were drawn by the sad personal stories of needy contestants who hoped for a jackpot of cash, gifts, and offers of help from complete strangers.

As the show's host Warren Hull would coax players to tell their tales of woe, he would often get teary-eyed himself. *Strike It Rich* participants were frequently in need of money for medical treatment or had simply fallen on such hard times that they were desperate. Contestants were asked quiz questions and won cash for correct answers. But the crux of the show was the "Heart Line," when the telephone lines were open and viewers were invited to pitch in what they could to help ease the contestant's suffering. Money, goods, services, even job offers were called in on a telephone placed in the middle of a heart-shaped set piece.

A sailor whose six-year-old son needed an operation for a club foot received $800 from a listener in California and the offer of free medical attention from a Florida hospital. On one broadcast a young violin prodigy explained that he needed to strike it rich for somewhere between three and four hundred dollars to replace his instrument, which had been stolen. When he finished his story, he played beautifully for the audience on a borrowed violin. The virtuoso, Franz Kreisler, who was watching the show at his New York apartment while nursing a broken leg, spontaneously called and said, "I want the little fellow to have my three-quarter-size Stradivarius."

Most Heart Line calls were pre-set, though. "We'd arrange with donors to phone in gifts for a particular contestant," said the show's creator and producer, Walter Framer. "If a widow with six children came on to explain the pressing need for a new roof for her house, we would contact ahead of time a roofer to set up a donation of his services. He got a 'plug' for his company, and if the woman won some money, well, it was there for other necessities. If someone told about needing a sewing machine in order to take in work as a dressmaker, a firm like Singer might donate a machine— it had to be called in in advance of the contestant's appearance."

On one *Strike It Rich* show, a young mother who had been deserted by her husband, and had recently undergone an operation, said that unless she came into some money quickly, she was going to give up her baby for adoption. The suspense mounted as she struggled through the quiz portion of the game, but finally she answered all the questions correctly for $500. Then an offer of help came from a man who volunteered to provide her with $40 a month until she was able to find another husband. "Is this entertainment?" an appalled Jack Gould asked in his *New York Times* column. "The crises that occur in the lives of individuals must not become grist for the morbid mill of TV."

Because no one left *Strike It Rich* empty-handed, its lure was great. Would-be contestants were encouraged to write to the program and tell why they needed help. Between 3,000 and 5,000 letters arrived each week. The show's producer and several secretaries would dig in the mound of mail and look for the most provocative candidates. Twenty or so of the best sob story authors were invited to appear in person for an interview with Walter Framer and his staff. Of those, a half-dozen were picked to appear on either the afternoon or prime-time version of the show. Another one or two candidates would be selected from the studio audience.

Many destitute people, including some encouraged by the show, journeyed to New York just hoping to be picked from the studio audience, but then were not chosen to appear. A good number of the unlucky candidates ended up stranded in the big city and eventually applied to be on the relief rolls. Welfare agencies and charitable organizations such as the Salvation Army complained bitterly about the false hope *Strike It Rich* was holding out to the most vulnerable citizens.

The New York City Commissioner of Welfare denounced *Strike It Rich* as "a disgusting spectacle and a national disgrace." The supervisor of The Travelers Aid Society, an organization which was grappling with many of those rejected by *Strike It Rich*, said, "We don't know if the successes on the show balance off against the human misery caused by it. But from what we see, I'd say they didn't. . . . Putting human misery on display can hardly be called right." In light of the criticism, the show began to warn the home audience not to travel to New York unless specifically invited to do so. *Strike It Rich* also stopped choosing contestants from the studio audience.

The controversy over the morality of making a public spectacle of victims of poverty, illness, and everyday misfortune, however, did not dampen the appeal of seeing fellow Americans in dire straits. Another program that put contestants in the position of begging for charity, *Queen for a Day*, began its nine-year TV run in 1955. Within months it became the number-one daytime show, reaching a daily audience of around thirteen million.

The format of *Queen for a Day* was simple: Five women selected from the studio audience each told their hard-luck story to the show's host, Jack Bailey. The same studio audience then chose the one it thought most deserving. The "applause meter" would appear on the screen to measure the reaction as Bailey stood behind each woman and reminded viewers of her problem: "Candidate Number 3, whose mother is coming to spend her few remaining years with her, and she desperately needs a bed."

As soon as a winner was chosen, the other women were promptly forgotten. "The show had an embarrassing weakness," its producer Howard Blake confessed. "Only one of the five daily candidates could be elected Queen and have her wish granted. The other four, no matter how desperate their needs, supplied their share of entertainment, but had to settle for a small consolation prize—a radio, a toaster, a dozen pairs of stockings. Sometimes they would burst into tears, but we never let the camera see that. Once the Queen was elected, the losers were deliberately ignored."

The Queen was draped with a sable-collared red velvet robe and a jeweled crown was placed on her head as Jack Bailey bellowed, "I now pronounce you...Queen for a Day!" Then, while seated on her throne, the lucky lady was shown her torrent of prizes, all provided by the manufacturers for promotional consideration. Very often the Queen would be in tears as lovely models paraded by with silverware, china, make-up, fashions, blankets, pillows, appliances, and such. Bigger items like washers and dryers, refrigerators, and furniture appeared on the set with more pretty girls who gestured to the merchandise with gently flowing arms. Eventually *Queen for a Day* was expanded from thirty to forty-five minutes to fit more commercial plugs in the broadcast.

"No candidate for Queen was ever planted, prompted or rehearsed," explained Howard Blake to those who might have wondered if the show was rigged in any way. "Our integrity, however, had limits. Our holiness had holes. When it came to picking the women to appear on the show, the general assumption was we chose the most needy and deserving. But the most needy and deserving usually had to be dumped. A lot of the women desperately needed a doctor or lawyer, for instance. We could never provide either because there was no way of telling what it might eventually cost. And no doctor or lawyer would work for free in return for a plug. We investigated. A candidate had to want something we could plug. . . . Some of the women were ugly, some were incoherent, they had to be dumped too, deserving or not. . . . We had only one aim—to pick the woman who would provide the best entertainment."

Novelist Denise Giardina remembers watching *Queen for a Day* as a child growing up in Appalachia. "The women, dressed plainly and often weeping," she recalled more than two decades later, "poured out their sorrows before the whole world, and the studio audience judged by their applause which woman was to be pitied most." Surrounded by poverty, Giardina rarely saw her world on television, until she saw this game show. "*Queen for a Day* was in shockingly bad taste, but children care nothing about taste," she wrote.

"I was fascinated by the program because the real women who pleaded their cases were the only people on TV who reminded me of my neighbors. They were plain, good-hearted and distraught. They put me in mind of the woman next door whose husband was killed in the mine, and my Sunday school teacher, who bought her children's shoes from the church rummage sale. The difference was that the people I knew would rather have died than beg on national television."

Producer Blake conceded, "Sure *Queen* was vulgar and sleazy and filled with bathos and bad taste. Everybody was on the make—we on the show, NBC and later ABC, the sponsors and the suppliers of gifts. And how about all the down-on-their-luck women who used us to further our money-grubbing ends? Weren't they all on the make? Weren't they after something for nothing?" With befitting crassness, the producer defended his work by telling his critics: "*Queen for a Day* was a typical American success story. And if you don't like it, either try to change the rules of the game or go back where you come from."

In postwar America, surrendering one's dignity on national TV for prizes and cash was not the exclusive domain of the downtrodden, however. A new genre of shopping-oriented game shows emerged in the late 1950s and had respectable denizens of the middle class lose their inhibitions and make spectacles of themselves as they shrieked wildly, jumped up and down uncontrollably, danced, cried, and hugged and kissed anyone on the set. Ecstatic excitement, near orgasmic joy, became a standard reaction to winning not only cars, but even modest prizes.

Game shows like *The Price Is Right*, which debuted in 1957, did not require academic or esoteric learning, but rather knowledge of consumer culture. Four contestants competed with each other as they tried to guess the retail price of merchandise. The contestant who came closest to the price without going over it won the item. No real intellectual demands were made, but the premise was that good consumers deserved to be rewarded. *The Price Is Right*, in the words of social critic Morris B. Holbrook, was "the essence of the modern Ethos of Consumption; the unrestrained, rafter-shaking adoration of Products on Parade; the unfettered, shameless worship of Commodities on Stage; the uncontained, mind-numbing celebration of Merchandise on Display."

In 1965, the game show *Supermarket Sweep* valorized the accumulation of material goods beyond the need, or even capacity, to use them. In actual supermarkets around the country, three husband-and-wife teams competed to have the highest total at the checkout counter. In the first leg of the competition, which was announced in play-by-play fashion, the husbands raced through the store and crammed as much merchandise of the greatest possible value into their shopping carts. Careening around corners and dodging each other, most headed directly for the high-priced items in the meat counter. Hams were grabbed in a frenzy. The wives got to play and add to the total by guessing the retail value of various items.

"It's time for *Supermarket Sweep*," the announcer told viewers, "the TV game show that travels to your home town and lets you run wild through your supermarket." Just why seemingly upright citizens would behave in such untoward ways mystified some viewers and horrified many critics. Even the show business trade journal *Variety*, which had a high threshold for the excesses of popular culture, called the show "a study of conspicuous greed in an affluent society." The review pointed out that a program spotlighting men racing around to load up their grocery carts as their wives egged them on was not likely to be a big success in the export market. "Even the French, who know a thing or two about grubbing the buck, might squirm at the *déclassé* doings."

But shopping-oriented game shows justified a way of life. American materialism was approximating a religion in which "things" gave meaning to human existence. Jubilant hysteria over consumer goods became a cultural norm. Those who regarded it as a dangerous and sad symptom of an ailing national character were simply dismissed as killjoys and self-righteous moralists by true believers.

Aging American Style

Lily Ruskin of *December Bride*, played by actress Spring Byington, was an unusual lead TV character in 1954. She was old. She was in her sixties. But the running gag of the show was that she didn't act like other old people on the screen. She wasn't sick or cranky, she wasn't set in her ways or narrow-minded. She lived with her daughter and son-in-law and they were pleased to have her in their home. Lily was meant to be a rare but inspirational flower. "This show makes every dame over forty-five think she's still desirable," said the producer of *December Bride*, giving a good indication of what was considered over-the-hill in the 1950s.

A more typical TV senior citizen of the era was Amos McCoy of *The Real McCoys*, played by Walter Brennan. "He was the grandpa," a reviewer wrote.

"But he was really the child. He was stubborn and ornery and had to be taken care of by his grandchildren." Grandpappy Amos walked with a limp and seemed to be in a constant state of dyspepsia.

Reverence for age and the wisdom it brings was not a major ingredient in American television entertainment as the 1950s gave way to the 1960s. The youth culture of the new decade glorified the contemporary, the trendy, and the fresh. But as television ignored or disparaged those who had survived many decades of history, the American population was experiencing a profound change. Life expectancies were increasing and the postwar rise in the standard of living was sharpest for elderly Americans. By the 1970s, real-life senior citizens were healthier, far more independent, and more active than most of their television counterparts.

In 1970, a sixty-five-year-old woman named Maggie Kuhn was forced to leave her job as a journal editor at the United Presbyterian Church in New York City because she had reached the mandatory retirement age. Instead of slowing down and relaxing, however, Ms. Kuhn and several friends founded an organization seeking a ban on mandatory retirement and championing the rights of older citizens. At a time when the militant civil rights activists, the Black Panthers, were much in the news, Kuhn and her cohorts were quickly dubbed the Gray Panthers by a New York talk show host. As their cause gained widespread attention, the term "ageism" took its place alongside racism, sexism, and militarism as one of the oppressive forces of the era.

In the mid-1970s, Media Watch, a volunteer group created by the Gray Panthers, monitored and commented on television's treatment of senior characters. Lydia Braggar, the chair of the group, who was in her seventies as they undertook their work, told audiences around the country that old people on TV were depicted as "ugly, toothless, sexless, incontinent, senile, confused, and helpless. . . . Old age has become so negatively stereotyped that it has become something to dread and feel threatened by."

A recurring sketch on Johnny Carson's *Tonight Show* featured the host costumed in an 1890s-style dress, with a gray wig and wire-rim glasses. He was the insufferable Aunt Blabby, "TV's definitive silly old lady," according to *The New York Times*. Aunt Blabby could have been a first cousin of Maudie Frickert, another silly old lady character performed often on television by comedian Jonathan Winters.

The Blabby character reinforced the idea that the elderly invariably suffered debilitating losses of bodily functions and of their faculties. "Good to see you," says Carson's sidekick Ed McMahon welcoming Aunt Blabby to the set. "Good to see you," she replies. "At my age it's just good to see." "Has there been much crime in your neighborhood?" McMahon continues. "It's been terrible," Aunt Blabby replies. "They steal everything. My furniture, my silverware, my furnace. Worst of all, they even stole my toilet." "Your toilet!? Well that's terrible," McMahon responds. "Well it's all right," Blabby assures him. "I seldom use it anyway."

In 1977, Maggie Kuhn was a guest on the *Tonight Show* and took the opportunity to explain why Aunt Blabby and so many other TV images fostered harmful stereotypes. Kuhn told Carson the nation was full of elderly women who weren't dingbats. She hoped her gift to him of a Gray Panthers T-shirt would remind Carson of the vital, older viewers in his audience and cause him to rethink the character. "So far, it hasn't helped," the press reported a short time after Kuhn's appearance. "Aunt Blabby is as hopelessly giddy as ever."

Another television superstar who was disappointing to the Gray Panthers was Carol Burnett. Her popular comedy-variety show was built around a stable of memorable characters. In one recurring sketch, she and cast regular Harvey Korman portray two elderly people rocking on the porch and contemplating what might have been if they had made other decisions early in life. "I wish Carol would be a little less vicious," said a Gray Panther spokesperson. "She's funny, but at a terrible expense to the dignity of older people."

Other groups, including the American Association of Retired Persons, also got involved in the late 1970s in the attempt to influence television's portrayals of seniors. The National Council on Aging formed a Media Resources Center, which set up an office in Hollywood to lobby television's creative community to "do a little better by the old." The exception to TV's stereotyping of the elderly, particularly elderly women, as feeble-minded was in daytime serial dramas. Soap opera matriarchs, such as Phoebe Tyler on *All My Children*, had agile minds and long, clear memories.

"One of our biggest objections," explained Nadine Kearns of the Media Resources Center, "is to the idea that people suddenly start doing dumb or terrible things because they are old." In reference to a popular show of the time, *Mary Hartman, Mary Hartman*, in which the title character's elderly father began exposing himself in public, Kearns said, "We never objected to the Fernwood flasher, per se. What we didn't like was the implication that he turned flasher because he was old."

As the decade drew to a close, the complaints of senior-citizen activists were supported by a 1979 research study that found elderly on TV were routinely portrayed as being treated with disrespect and they were less likely to play serious roles. But the 1980s brought an increased awareness of America's aging population, beginning with the election of near seventy-year-old Ronald Reagan as President of the United States. The TV networks and advertisers began to pay more heed to those who fell on the far side of the traditional eighteen- to forty-nine-year-old target audience.

In 1984, CBS introduced *Murder, She Wrote*, starring sixty-year-old Angela Lansbury as Jessica Fletcher, an author of mystery novels who achieved her celebrity status late in life after a more mundane career as a substitute teacher and PTA volunteer. The series seemed to be a long shot for success based on standard observations. The leading lady wore sensible shoes and there was minimal sex and violence on the screen. But the show was a runaway hit.

"Jessica is a sincere, down-to-earth woman who is vitally interested in people," said Lansbury about the role-model potential of her character. "She isn't an eccentric prissy old lady like Miss Marple or somebody's maiden aunt from East Nowhere. This character says to the audience that older women are bright, energetic and capable of doing a great job."

That same season, a male senior citizen was also the star of a prime-time show. *Crazy Like a Fox* starred Jack Warden as Harry Fox, a private eye who outwitted master criminals many years his junior. The biggest senior splash of the mid-eighties, though, was *The Golden Girls*, which premiered in 1985. Three women in their mid-to-late fifties shared a home together in Miami, a city full of retirees. Blanche, the owner of the house, was a lusty Southern belle widow. Rose, a naïve country gal from Minnesota with a tendency to tell long and pointless stories about her childhood, was also a widow. Dorothy, a divorcée and substitute school teacher, was the most outspoken of the housemates. Dorothy's salty-mouthed mother, Sophia, joined the household when her retirement home was destroyed by a fire.

The Golden Girls presented aging as a challenge, not a curse. When their home is burglarized, Rose worries that the thieves were after drugs. "We have Maalox and estrogen," Dorothy tells her. "How many junkies have gas and hot flashes?"

The trend of stars in the over-fifty-five category on top-rated shows in the mid-1980s was called "television's new wrinkle." Ever since prime time began, *Newsweek* reported, "showing disrespect for our elders seemed a sacrosanct video imperative." But advertisers grew more aware of the buying power of the elderly. Senior Americans in the 1980s had more discretionary income than ever before. The reason was a combination of Medicare benefits, pension payments, and, naturally, fewer dependents than younger consumers. Alienating seniors with Aunt Blabby-type characters was no longer a wise move.

American culture did not lose its obsession with youth, though. Prime-time shows continued to be populated with young people in numbers disproportionate to real-life statistics. In the early 1990s, despite improvements in TV depictions of senior citizens, research studies showed that only about 2 percent of the fictional characters on TV were sixty-five years or older, yet that age group accounted for 12.5 percent of the U.S. population. "Symbolically," said one of the professors conducting the content analysis, "it says that old people don't have much importance."

In 1994, a commercial for Dorito Tortilla Thins displayed an attitude toward the elderly that harkened back to the 1970s. A gray-haired woman shuffling along the street munching the tortilla chips is oblivious to a runaway steamroller barreling down on her. Comedian Chevy Chase attempts a rescue by climbing aboard a swinging wrecking ball. He's successful in his heroic effort—but the joke is that he saves the bag of chips the old gal was eating and allows her to be plowed into wet cement.

Senior groups and various agencies representing the interests of older Americans strongly objected to the spot. The company apologized by sending cases of free chips to food banks and producing another commercial in which Chase gets fired from his position as spokesman.

By the mid-1990s, TV viewers past age fifty were the fastest growing segment of the American population. But the trend of featuring older performers, which began a decade earlier, was in reverse. The success of the Fox network in the late 1980s and 1990s in programming to young viewers was one factor in the equation. Advertisers were willing to pay more for younger audiences. "Ad agencies don't want to pitch their wares to older, wiser folks," a TV columnist reported. "They may have more money, but advertisers think they're too careful how they spend it."

Another factor was the realization that although younger viewers were unlikely to watch shows designed for older audiences, such as *Murder, She Wrote*, older viewers would tune into youthful shows such as *Friends* and *Seinfeld*. "The new reality in prime time," a critic wrote in the fall of 1995, "is that you can no longer build a show around a character who's over 50." Several shows with older lead characters, such as *Matlock*, *In the Heat of the Night*, and *Empty Nest*, were canceled that season.

Putting the best spin on prime-time television's waning interest in depicting the lives of senior citizens in the late 1990s, CBS vice-president David Poltrack explained: "In the last 20 years, age has become an increasingly irrelevant life-style indicator. Older people are healthier, more dynamic. A 35-year-old, college-educated professional has much more in common with a 50-year-old from the same background than he does with a 35-year-old blue-collar worker with a high school education."

In 2000, the associate research director for the American Association of Retired Persons, Robert Prisuta, addressed the forum "The Missing Image: Older People in the Media." He reported that although 13 percent of the U.S. population were sixty-five years or older, only about 2 percent of the characters in prime-time television were in that age group. And even though women represented 60 percent of the senior population, only one-third of the older characters in prime time were women. "So they virtually are invisible in prime-time network television," he said.

"If you look at the resolution of outcomes in dramatic fictional programming," Prisuta noted, "usually an unsuccessful or ambivalent resolution is associated with older people. In a nutshell, older people don't come across as effective in problem solving, in dealing with issues as do younger characters."

The good news, as the 20th century gave way to the 21st, was that Americans were living younger longer. The bad news was that entertainment television was doing little to acknowledge that life experience—aging—is a positive and universal adventure.

All God's Children

A lead character in a wheelchair was an unusual twist for a TV series in 1967 when *Ironside* debuted. Actor Raymond Burr played Robert Ironside, a twenty-five-year member of the San Francisco Police Department. He was chief of detectives when an assassination attempt on his life failed, but the bullet grazed his spine and left him paralyzed from the waist down. Ironside became a special consultant to the force. With a specially equipped police van he was able to continue his lifelong war on crime.

Wheelchairs on the small screen were usually confined to fund-raisers, such as *The Jerry Lewis Labor Day Telethon,* and were often occupied by children. Although Lewis's connection with the Muscular Dystrophy Association went back to the early 1950s, his annual Labor Day TV event began in 1966. Over the years viewers came to expect that big stars like Sammy Davis, Jr., would cajole them into generosity. When they tuned in, they could also be sure their heartstrings would be tugged with sad stories of children and families whose lives had been devastated by one of the many forms of the disease.

But hope for a cure was always the overriding theme. An announcement of triumph—such as when the vaccine for polio was discovered in 1955—was the goal. Each year at the end of the broadcast, as the final pledge totals were displayed, Jerry Lewis would sing a slightly off-key version of "You'll Never Walk Alone." Tears flowed, checks poured in, and a tremendous number of people were helped. Medical research was endowed, wheelchairs were purchased, and summer camps financed.

By 1990, when the Americans with Disabilities Act was passed, *The Jerry Lewis Labor Day Telethon* was a well-established institution in American culture. It was carried on more than two hundred television stations around the country and, according to *Business Week* magazine, "attracted Super Bowl-size audiences of up to 100 million viewers." The legislation, which went into effect in the summer of 1992, was a groundbreaking anti-discrimination law that emphasized mainstreaming the disabled. It required that public accommodations and transportation be accessible to the disabled and it outlawed employment discrimination.

During the 1980s, the number of TV characters with disabilities increased in part due to the efforts of the Media Access Office, a liaison group between Hollywood and disabled performers. The roles were often guest shots or supporting parts, such as the character of Geri Warner on the sitcom *Facts of Life*. Geri, who appeared occasionally for three seasons, was the cousin of lead character Blair Warner and, despite the handicap of cerebral palsy, was determined to become a comedienne. The actress, Geri Jewell, was in real life coping with the same affliction.

The Media Access Office particularly advocated roles in which a character's disability was incidental to the story. The former chairman of the organization, Alan Toy, once appeared in a commercial in which he portrayed an ordinary business executive carrying a briefcase and walking on crutches, which is how he really transported himself. "If only we could get that image of normality projected more," he said, "the more audiences would get used to seeing us as human beings, and the less aghast they'll be when they meet us in the street."

In 1989, the ABC drama *Life Goes On* broke new ground when it introduced an eighteen-year-old mentally challenged teenager, Corky Thatcher, as a central character. The role was played by actor Christopher Burke, a young man with Down's Syndrome. In 1991, the series *Reasonable Doubts* featured deaf actress Marlee Matlin as a district attorney whose hearing impairment was secondary to the plotlines. Matlin would later have a prominent role as a political consultant in the NBC drama *The West Wing*, and again her hearing impairment was inconsequential.

By the early 1990s, television programs and commercials were featuring disabled people more frequently and in more varied roles. "There has emerged a new spirit of self-identification and activism among the disabled community," wrote Jack Nelson, a media analyst studying the images of disability in popular culture. "Changes are taking place in how society treats the disabled, and how they are portrayed in the media. These improvements are partly fueled by the Americans with Disabilities Act of 1990 and by a growing awareness that those with disabilities are first of all people and only secondarily defined by any impairment they might have."

As the activism of the disabled grew throughout the 1980s, the fund-raising techniques of *The Jerry Lewis Labor Day Telethon*—what some called "pity-mongering"—seemed increasingly out of sync with a self-empowerment movement. Before 1990, those who were critical of Lewis's approach kept their thoughts to themselves. But a cover story Lewis wrote for *Parade* magazine in September 1990, entitled "If I Had Muscular Dystrophy," convinced several activists to challenge the man who had raised more than one billion dollars to treat neuromuscular illnesses.

Writing from the vantage point of a child with muscular dystrophy, Jerry Lewis referred to his wheelchair as "that steel imprisonment." Reflecting on his imagined condition that made him feel "trapped and suffocated," he wrote, "When I sit back and think a little more rationally, I realize my life is half, so I must learn to do things halfway. . . . I may be a full human being in my heart and soul, yet I am still half a person. . . . I just have to learn to try to be good at being half a person."

The article angered and saddened a wide range of advocates for the disabled. "My wheelchair isn't an imprisonment—it's a tremendous vehicle of liberation," responded Carol Gill, president of the Chicago Institute of Disability Research. "What's a steel imprisonment is those negative images that Jerry Lewis and the Muscular Dystrophy Association (MDA) promote. The stereotypes keep us locked in a cell of discrimination and prejudice."

Two former Chicago-area Muscular Dystrophy poster children, Michael Ervin and his sister Cris Matthews, were roused into forming a group called "Jerry's Orphans"—a sardonic comment on Lewis's habit of calling muscular dystrophy patients of all ages "my kids" as an expression of endearment. "I think the term 'Jerry's Kids' is insulting and antiquated, and counterproductive to anything but the MDA's fund-raising purposes," Ervin claimed. "It reinforces the childlike stereotype: it infantilizes and emasculates people with disability."

The damaging message of telethons, activists believed, was that a disabled person needs a cure in order to have a life worth living. They hoped for a new understanding to penetrate public consciousness. They wanted Americans to realize that for most "victims of disease," civil rights were ultimately more important. "At its simplest," reported *The Nation*, "the disability rights philosophy says that disability is not really the cause of an undignified harsh life. The real cause is lack of access to buildings, jobs, transportation; segregation and denial of services. The cure charities believe that in order to raise money, they must continue to convince society that the only thing that will help disabled people is a cure."

For those who were not paying much attention to the growing disability rights movement, the protests accompanying the 1992 *Telethon* were shocking and confusing. Demonstrations against the broadcast were held at stations in more than two dozen cities, including New York. It seemed unbelievable that disabled citizens, many of whom had benefited from the MDA, were speaking out against Jerry Lewis.

Laura Hershey, a former poster child from Denver, helped organize the Tune Out Jerry Coalition, claiming the telethon fed the cultural myths that disabled people led sad lives. She criticized the telethon for focusing on the small number of children who die, rather than the far greater number of adults who live with one of the forty neuromuscular conditions covered by the MDA. "Jerry Lewis's approach is a relic of the past," Hershey said. "There's still a sentimental feeling about him because he's been working at it for so long, but the kind of approach he's using doesn't have any place in how our community feels about itself now."

On one side of the dispute, critics argued that telethons led viewers to believe disabled people should get what they need as a matter of charity, not as a matter of right. Telethons, they said, discouraged Americans from accepting disability and finding ways to accommodate it permanently in the social fabric. On the other side, defenders of Jerry Lewis proclaimed him to be a humanitarian who was entrapped in the web of political correctness. They believed only a handful of discontents who confused compassion with pity was generating a disproportionate amount of news copy.

But the support of the highest-ranking disabled person in President George H.W. Bush's administration gave the anti-telethon protesters an added degree of credibility. Evan Kemp, Jr., an attorney and chairman of the Equal Employment Opportunity Commission, had long been critical of the "pity approach to fund-raising." As someone with a neuromuscular disease, Kemp believed that "Stereotyping, which the pity approach reinforces, leads to all kinds of discrimination. . . . Why should an employer hire someone who, admired public figures on the telethon tell them, is really helpless?"

Although *The Jerry Lewis Labor Day Telethon* was the most watched fundraiser, each year three other major telethons were aired—for Easter Seals, the Arthritis Foundation, and United Cerebral Palsy. The four annual broadcasts, according to Professor Paul Longmore, a historian specializing in the history of the disabled, "are the single most powerful cultural mechanism defining the public identities of people with disabilities in our society today, mainly because they reach so many people. . . . Collectively, they have a combined audience of 250 million people."

Protests against telethons were an attempt to change the ideology surrounding disability in the United States. "Primarily, these are events which define culturally appropriate handicapped behavior, (being a good cripple)," wrote author Marilynn Phillips in the journal *Social Science and Medicine*, "and which serve to demonstrate predictable interactions between nondisabled and disabled persons."

Some opponents wanted telethons reformed, not eliminated. The group Jerry's Orphans hoped to "neutralize" the annual event by pressuring Jerry Lewis out of the picture. The work of MDA fund-raising for research and equipment could be carried on, they felt, without characterizing people with disabilities as childlike, dependent victims.

The head of the National Easter Seal Society said that his group's annual telethon actually started making more money after it listened to the complaints of disabled people. The broadcast put greater emphasis on independence. The majority of profiles presented were of disabled adults who were in control of their lives.

But others believed there was no redeeming value in the format. "Telethons, no matter how much they might try to 'reform,'" wrote Bill Bolte, whose disability was from polio, "should be done away with. They degrade those who are different or need support, make human beings into symbols of what no one wants to be."

When the Easter Seal Society of Southeastern Michigan discontinued its annual telethon in 1996, Yvonne Duffy, author of the "Disabled in America" column for the *Detroit Free Press*, who herself had been a regional poster child years earlier, welcomed the change. "At last," she wrote, "one nonprofit organization serving people with disabilities has finally had the courage to sever the sympathy cord."

Duffy continued: "This debasing spectacle is not inconsequential. Long-held stereotypes of people with disabilities as dependent cripples in need of charity are again reinforced. The repercussions are also economic. Who will hire us to run their businesses or plead their cases in court, for example, after viewing us paraded across television screens as sad, helpless children? That a few telethons a year can undermine the considerable strides we've made to become equal, contributing members of society is disheartening."

Reporter John Hockenberry, in his 1995 book *Moving Violations: War Zones, Wheelchairs, and Declarations of Independence*, recalled a fellow patient at his rehabilitation center calling out to anyone who would become frustrated or angry, "Hey, look over there; it's one of Jerry's kids." The insult, Hockenberry wrote, "fused two powerful and contradictory themes in American life: sympathy and self-reliance." In rehab, he explained, people were taught not to ask for help or let anyone push their chairs. "We were proud crips who were going to play basketball and win races and triumph over our disabilities," Hockenberry said. But outside the rehab center, "self-reliance was a high-risk proposition. To people raised on telethons, it looked suspiciously like a chip on the shoulder. Somewhere between bitterness and anger and Jerry's kids, we would all have to live."

In the 1990s, American perceptions of disability were evolving and maturing. When Heather Whitestone was crowned Miss America of 1995, viewers saw and heard a deaf woman communicate unselfconsciously. During her tenure and after, numerous television appearances made Whitestone a familiar figure.

The accident in which Christopher Reeve, star of *Superman* movies, became a quadriplegic underscored the significance of the term "temporarily able bodied"—the term the disability rights movement uses to describe those without handicaps. Reeve's TV appearances with Barbara Walters, Larry King, on the 1996 Academy Awards broadcast, and that year's Democratic National Convention resulted in far less pity than admiration for his strength of character.

As the stigma of disabilities diminished, young students of American history were surprised to learn that most citizens never knew of President Franklin Roosevelt's paralysis and dependence on a wheelchair. At the end of the 1990s, it seemed incredible not only that newspaper and newsreel photographers were willing to participate in the "splendid deception" of never showing the President in his wheelchair, but, even more so, that it was considered necessary.

It's How You Play the Game

The role of sports grew tremendously in postwar America, primarily due to television. In each passing decade, as sports programming increased in amount and cultural significance, children became more likely to name professional athletes when asked who they considered to be their heroes. By the 1990s, presidents, astronauts, and Nobel laureates were a meager source of inspiration to America's kids compared to the superstars of sports.

Wide-scale concern over a conspicuous decline in sportsmanship began to emerge in the 1970s. As the salaries of athletes skyrocketed, so too did unsportsmanlike conduct on the field of play. "In a more innocent age," wrote a social commentator in 1978, "violence in professional sports—except for boxing—was limited to an occasional spike-high slide into third base or a not-so subtly thrown beanball. It was rough, but it was individual and sporadic. Today, violence, or the possibility of violence is systematic throughout most sports events. Violence, after all, makes good television. . . . Television does more than simply report or reflect this violence: it idolizes it."

In the 1980s, as salary statistics became as important as performance statistics on TV sportscasts, game "highlights" often included fistfights, brawls, and cheap shots as if they were an expected and entertaining part of the event. Players who exhibited cockiness rather than sportsmanship were rewarded with media attention. For instance, National Football League star Deion Sanders added to his fame by high-stepping the final yards of his touchdown runs to embarrass the players chasing him. His teammate, Andre Rison, performed a "Highlight Zone strut" after every touchdown, regardless of the score. Arrogance and contempt for the principles of fair play became part of the marketing of pro teams. The Detroit Pistons were promoted as the Bad Boys; the Cincinnati Reds as the Nasty Boys.

Trash talk to taunt opponents became more acceptable as a legitimate part of game strategy. "There may be only a few of us alive who remember that in the days of two-hand set shots and five-figure salaries, a certain decorum prevailed on the floor and in the stands," mused *Newsday* sports columnist Fred Bruning. "A player did not, for instance, sink a basket and then suggest his next conquest would be the other fellow's girlfriend."

The irony, Bruning observed, was that when it came to TV commercial endorsements, "Some of the nastiest players get some of the sweetest deals because we have become an in-your-face society. . . . Swagger sells. Chest-thumping is a lifestyle choice. You see it everywhere—one the road, in the schools, across the back fence. Too many Americans go through life looking for an excuse to throw a punch and sprawl into the stands."

In the early 1990s, a national debate was stirring over the impact of the sports world on the broader American culture. If star athletes had an obligation to set a good example for youngsters, many of them were shirking their duty. The controversy came to a boil with a 1993 television commercial for Nike shoes. Charles Barkley, a top-flight NBA player known for his intimidating style, stared into the camera and said, "I am not a role model. . . . I am paid to wreak havoc on the basketball court. Parents should be role models. Just because I dunk a basketball doesn't mean I should raise your kids."

Barkley's NBA colleague Karl Malone took issue with that point of view in a column in *Sports Illustrated*:

> Charles you can deny being a role model all you want, but I don't think it's your decision to make. We don't choose to be role models, we are chosen. Our only choice is to be a good role model or a bad one. I don't think we can accept all the glory and the money that comes with being a famous athlete and not accept the responsibility of being a role model, of knowing that kids and even some adults are watching us and looking for us to set an example. I mean, why do we get endorsements in the first place? Because there are people who will follow our lead and buy a certain sneaker or cereal because we use it.

Malone's sentiments were widely applauded but did nothing to stem the tide of outrageous conduct by professional and collegiate athletes and their coaches. A columnist for the *National Review*, Taki Theodoracopulos, who played on the professional tennis circuit from 1956 through 1967, including Wimbledon and the Davis Cup tournaments, recalled in 1993, "Back then tennis was fun and the great players acted like champions on and off the court." He lamented the changes in his game during the intervening years: "Money, of course, is partly to blame. The stars seem to forget that the end does not always justify the means. As I write this I have just seen [John] McEnroe playing Andre Agassi and, although losing badly, abusing the umpire with four-letter words I would not use against a Serbian rapist. And every word is being heard because of the mikes situated next to the chair. McEnroe has a lot to answer for."

In the 1990s, there was growing evidence that young children and teenagers were emulating the behavior of the athletes they saw on TV. Unsportsmanlike conduct had become defined as the norm. Some public school leagues eliminated the postgame mandatory handshake because too often the ritual touched off fistfights. A father of a ten-year-old hockey player whose team banned the postgame handshake reported, "Trash talking in the handshake line had reached an art form in my son's league, and some boys were spitting into their own hands before the congratulatory shake." The traditional show of goodwill and respect for one's opponent, a handshake, had always been considered an integral part of American sports.

"I can't remember a single ugly incident during a postgame handshake when I played organized sports 20 years ago," the father continued. "No one I know can remember one either. What I do remember is a firm and unswerving commitment to sportsmanship from every adult around me. To show up an opponent, or taunt him, was not tolerated. Hotdogging was reviled. Lipping off to the ref or the coach got you a quick seat on the bench. And handshakes and cheers after the game were important."

If sportscasts, as suggested by *New York Times* TV critic John J. O'Connor, "reflect the true soul of the nation," there was much to contemplate about the American character in the 1990s. "Once there was something called sportsmanship," O'Connor wrote, "having to do not with winning but the way one played the game. Today, even as more athletes command salaries that are a little short of obscene, grabbing attention is the name of the game and violence is a handy weapon. . . . The spectacle of Michael Jordan slugging players on a basketball court, for example, probably sends a more immediate and damaging message to the youth of this country than all the violence on network entertainment programs."

Even the most egregious breaches of sportsmanship rarely resulted in serious punishment. As the 1996 baseball season drew to a close, a shocking incident repulsed virtually everyone who saw it replayed on television. During a game between the Baltimore Orioles and the Cleveland Indians, umpire John Hirschbeck mistakenly called the Orioles' second baseman Roberto Alomar out on a third strike when the ball was outside. Heated words were exchanged and after Alomar reached the dugout, he raced back to the plate and spat directly into Hirschbeck's face.

The next day, the American League president announced that Alomar would be suspended for five games, but not until the following April. He would still be eligible to compete in post-season play. Although no one defended Alomar's incivility, his punishment was less than a slap on the wrist. "No way should he be playing," wrote sports columnist Mitch Albom. "Not after what he did. A baseball player spits in the face of an umpire, and here he is, Tuesday afternoon, taking swings in the play-offs as if nothing happened? What's it take to get suspended in this game? A gunshot? Right is right, wrong is wrong. And in your heart you know the difference."

In postwar America, television became a symposium on national values, prompting soul-searching about truth and lies, launching vigorous debates about how images affect perceptions, and sparking concern over the examples set by those who play games that are metaphors for the struggles of everyday life.

As children in the 1950s and 1960s, virtually all baby boomers—about 96 percent—were raised in a tradition of faith. They attended Sunday school and religious classes in record numbers. But in their adolescence and early adulthood in the late-sixties and 1970s, a majority of that generation abandoned their churches and temples. Together, baby boomers and television grew more secular. In 1980, *TV Guide* reported that religion was the most ignored aspect of American life on prime-time television.

Highway to Heaven, starring Michael Landon as an angel who helps and inspires ordinary people on earth, while performing an occasional miracle, aired from 1984 to 1989. It was a well-received oddity, particularly by older viewers and those with long-established religious ties.

An episode of *Roseanne* in the late 1980s reflected the sentiments of many younger religious drop-outs. The Conners' young son, D.J., asks his mother and father why their family doesn't go to church and pray. He asks what religion they are. Roseanne and Dan reply that even though they don't practice a formal religion, they try to be good people, and to them that is like a religion.

In the 1990s, prompted by mid-life assessments, members of the first TV generation began to make more room in their lives for spiritual matters. Rather than returning to a single organized religion, though, they explored their beliefs in individualistic ways. While denominational loyalties remained weak, interest in spirituality climbed. Along with other media, television began to reintroduce faith as motivation for living a moral life. "The God of pop culture is not necessarily a Judeo-Christian God," wrote a magazine columnist examining the trend. "He (or she) can be any form of pure love and power."

Two shows with spiritual themes, *Touched by an Angel* and *7th Heaven*, began long prime-time runs that would extend into the decade. Both avoided denominational specificity. "We talk about a Supreme Being, who loves us all," explained Della Reese, the star of *Touched by an Angel*. "Religion is a man-made thing. We deal in spirituality. That's a God thing."

The biggest prime-time hit of the 1990s, though, had nothing to do with soul searching. The four lead characters of *Seinfeld* were self-absorbed, self-indulgent, single New York apartment dwellers in their thirties. Jerry, Elaine, George, and Kramer were described in the *National Review* as "four desperately selfish and ludicrously childish friends who behave in a way that can be described, in clinical terms, as sociopathic. They fall in and out of bed with a gaggle of partners, none of whom measure up, and spend a portion of each show in a local coffee shop, kvetching. Who would like these people? Who would want to have them as friends? They wear life like an itchy sweater—grumbling, grouchy, and always trying to wiggle out of a responsibility."

Plenty of viewers, though, were willing to spend at least thirty minutes each week in their company. *Seinfeld*, a series that claimed to be "a show about nothing," was heralded as the defining sitcom of the era. Larry David, co-creator with Jerry Seinfeld, eschewed the conventional wisdom of sitcoms by describing his guiding principle as "no hugging, no learning," the definition of an empty life turned into "Must-See TV."

An episode of *Seinfeld* was like a well-told offensive joke—funny but not humane; easy to appreciate on one level, yet naggingly troublesome on another. Some critics speculated that the popularity of the series rested with its rebuke of the perceived pieties of political correctness. The lives of the principal cast members were regularly inconvenienced by people of different cultures and different life experiences.

In *The New York Times*, John J. O'Connor, described one particularly controversial episode as coming "queasily close to sick-joke territory." When George can't find a parking space at the mall, he uses an area designated for the handicapped. This forces a woman in a wheelchair to park on a lower level. When her wheelchair batteries give out halfway up the ramp to the next level, she is injured in an accident. "She couldn't use her hands?" George mutters. Jerry, defensive about their boorish decision to park there, says, "It's not as if we stuck a broomstick in her spokes and she went flying." Later in the episode, Kramer falls in love with the victim.

"She got everything I ever wanted in another human being—except for the walking." "You don't go out that much anyway," Jerry reminds him.

Even sudden death is a laughing matter. George, who has been trying to weasel out of a proposed marriage, is relieved when his fiancée dies after licking toxic glue on their wedding invitation envelopes. When Elaine, Jerry, and Kramer show up at the hospital and learn the shocking news, they are unmoved. They shrug in "that's life" resignation and urge George to join them for coffee.

When the series ended its nine-year run, the hype surrounding the final episode reached frenzy status in the popular culture. Would the characters become real adults and recognize their selfish ways? No. They stayed true to form. Their plane to Paris is forced to land for repairs and they find themselves stranded in the small town of Latham, Massachusetts. As they stand in the street, they witness a carjacking but do nothing to help the victim, and instead crack wise about the overweight man behind the wheel. Kramer videotapes the crime. They're charged with breaking the "Good Samaritan Law" and put on trial.

The lawyer for the "Seinfeld Four" offers the defense, "You don't have to help anybody. That's what this country is all about." But they're found guilty and when the judge sentences them to a year in jail, he says, "Your utter disregard for everything that is good and decent has rocked the very foundation upon which our society is built." The defendants feel no contrition; the narcissistic cycle continues.

The role of television in fashioning personal beliefs about the meaning of life and what constitutes moral behavior is not an easily quantifiable entity. It is part of the mystery of how and why souls are touched. But in the decades since the mid-20th century, TV has undeniably contributed to the formation of individual value systems that have in turn shaped a collective American character.

Fig. 10   The testimony of John Dean, former counsel to Richard Nixon, implicating the President in the Watergate scandal, mesmerized TV viewers in 1973. (*Broadcasting and Cable* collection, Library of American Broadcasting.)

CHAPTER 10

The Webbed Republic: Democracy in the Television Age

From the moment Pearl Harbor was bombed until the Japanese surrender, virtually every American citizen joined in a united commitment to defeat the enemy and defend a cherished way of life. Even conscientious objectors searched for ways to serve their country and still abide by their personal beliefs. "Not once in the years 1941 to 1945," recalled a Quaker who was exempt from military service, yet joined the Navy nonetheless, "did I hear a single American inveigh against the war."

Everyone who wasn't in uniform did what they could. Hollywood stars sold war bonds and schoolchildren bought them. Families grew "victory gardens" and collected scrap metal. Housewives saved cooking fat that could be processed into the glycerine needed for gunpowder. Perhaps no one had more power to help the cause, though, than journalists. Print and radio reporters covering the war were generally not neutral in their dispatches. It was rare that they would question the government or second-guess military matters. If cooperation meant the war might end one day sooner, they gave it.

The U.S. Army's Chief of Staff, General George C. Marshall, routinely briefed top members of the Washington press corps, but the sessions were for background only. The arrangement allowed reporters insight into the conduct of the war and the general never worried that the trust would be violated.

Ten days before the Allied invasion of Sicily in 1943, General Dwight Eisenhower explained to thirty reporters the planned assault in specific detail, even identifying which divisions were scheduled to hit the beaches. No security breaches occurred. As the invasion progressed an interesting story emerged. General George Patton had slapped an American soldier said to be suffering from shell shock. At Eisenhower's personal request, field reporters in Sicily agreed to sit on the item.

The Office of War Information coordinated the release of all news announcements and decided what should or should not be said over the air. Radio stations were asked to voluntarily censor any information pertaining to troop movements, casualty lists, and rumors. Even live person-on-the-street interviews were avoided just in case someone said something subversive or harmful to the war effort.

Despite these self-imposed limitations, World War II brought out the best in radio journalism. Americans heard Edward R. Murrow broadcasting from London during the German blitz. They could hear air raid sirens in the background and the sounds of bombs exploding nearby. They listened to Eric Sevareid describe the experience of being forced to jump from a disabled plane while on his way to cover the battle of Burma. They were riveted by on-the-spot D-Day reports. During the war years, the American public grew devoted to radio news, depending on it for fast, accurate, and thorough information.

When the war ended and television started to gain attention, its potential for entertainment was clear. But the medium seemed an especially poor competitor to newspapers and radio when it came to news. It offered neither the in-depth analysis of print nor the instant coverage of events that radio had mastered. Early TV newscasts were primitive productions. A story about a house fire was once illustrated by setting a crude model of a home ablaze in front of a studio camera. Those who dismissed television as a force in American journalism, though, would soon have a different view.

In 1950, CBS newsmen Edward R. Murrow and Fred Friendly began a documentary and news series on radio called *Hear It Now*. The following year, the duo brought the program to CBS television with the title *See It Now*. "This is an old team trying to learn a new trade," Murrow told the audience on the first broadcast.

During World War II, the long-standing disagreements between the United States and the Soviet Union were put aside. But the fundamental differences between the two powers could not be ignored after the Allied victory. The United States was intent on spreading a vision of freedom and economic opportunity around the world. The Soviet Union, devastated by the war and concerned about its own security, demanded that its neighbors be politically sympathetic with a socialistic ideology. Capitalism and communism were on a contentious course.

As *See It Now* began its prime-time run on CBS, the Cold War was affecting all aspects of American life. The sense of mission that sustained Americans during World War II was being recast. The new enemy was communism and its containment was the keystone of American foreign policy.

When North Korean forces invaded South Korea with Soviet-built tanks in June 1950, President Truman responded vigorously. American naval and air power were ordered into battle. The United States also went to the United Nations Security Council and secured UN assistance in repelling the aggression.

The war in Korea was not easily covered by fifteen-minute network newscasts. When newsreel-style footage was available, it offered only a limited picture of the conflict. But in December 1952, *See It Now* presented an hour-long report called "Christmas in Korea" that brought the war home in an unprecedented way. Murrow, along with a camera crew of fifteen men and five additional reporters, gave viewers a close-up look at war. From the front lines of combat to the hospital ships, from the military barracks to downtown Seoul, American soldiers—as well as those from France, Britain, and Ethiopia—were interviewed. The war was presented in graphically human terms.

On the homefront, the Cold War was also having an impact on daily life as the suspicion of communist infiltration in American institutions began to rise. Loyalty oaths and blacklists, which produced serious violations of civil liberties, were accepted by most Americans, who believed the procedures were necessary to root out any traces of communism within the United States.

Recognizing an issue that was likely to mobilize voter support, Senator Joseph R. McCarthy, a Republican from Wisconsin, seized on the public's alarm about the communist threat. He selected assorted targets and lobbed unfounded accusations of communist ties. For instance, McCarthy referred to Secretary of State Dean Acheson as "Red Dean of the State Department."

In 1952, the Republicans won control of the Senate and McCarthy's power grew. As chairman of the Government Operations Committee his anti-communist witch-hunt intensified. Even President Eisenhower was becoming uneasy with his tactics but was reluctant to challenge him because public opinion polls indicated a majority of citizens supported Senator McCarthy's crusade.

The damage that resulted from this twisted sense of patriotism was the subject of the *See It Now* broadcast of October 20, 1953. "The Case of

Lt. Milo Radulovich" was the story of a twenty-six-year-old University of Michigan student who lost his Air Force Reserve commission and was separated from the service as a security risk—not because of actual charges against him, but because he maintained a relationship with his father and sister, both of whom were suspected of "questionable activity" by unnamed sources.

Murrow and Friendly challenged the Armed Forces with their report to "protect national security and the rights of the individual at the same time." Five weeks later, the secretary of the Air Force appeared on *See It Now* and announced that it had been decided "it is consistent with the interests of national security to retain Lt. Radulovich."

In December 1953, a second "Christmas in Korea" program aired. Broadcast historian Michael Keith writes that the documentary was "especially courageous in the McCarthy era" since it tried to be objective and "show the truth about some of the horrors of war, and avoid phony patriotism and the exploitation of the country's Communist phobia."

Earlier in 1953, one of McCarthy's loyal assistants was drafted into the Army. When he was not given preferential treatment of any sort, the senator retaliated by investigating army security and even top-level army leaders themselves. The Army charged that McCarthy had gone well beyond the bounds of his authority and was flagrantly abusing power. The U.S. Senate agreed to investigate the complaint.

The Army–McCarthy hearings were scheduled for April 1954. A few weeks before the hearings commenced, on March 9, *See It Now* presented its most famous broadcast, "A Report on Senator Joseph R. McCarthy." The program consisted primarily of film of McCarthy in action and revealed his bullying tactics. The strength of the case against McCarthy didn't come from the narration by Murrow; rather the newsman allowed the footage of the senator to speak for itself. McCarthy's peculiar facial expressions and bizarre laughter—qualities that could not be conveyed as vividly in print or radio reports—suggested to many viewers that he was an unstable personality.

The broadcast ended with a postscript by Murrow articulating the conclusion that he hoped his audience had reached—that McCarthy's unsubstantiated accusations were ruthless and dangerous. But also, American citizens needed a better understanding of their own democracy—they needed to recognize the difference between dissent and disloyalty. "The actions of the junior Senator from Wisconsin have caused alarm and dismay amongst our allies abroad and given considerable comfort to our enemies," Murrow explained. "And whose fault is that? Not really his. He didn't create this situation of fear, he merely exploited it, and rather successfully. Cassius was right: 'The fault, dear Brutus, is not in our stars but in ourselves....' Good night, and good luck."

The following week *See It Now* offered "Annie Lee Moss Before the McCarthy Committee." Moss, a middle-aged black woman, was interrogated and accused by Senator McCarthy of representing a danger to national security. The widow, a former cafeteria worker in the Pentagon, had been employed as a low-level communications relay machine operator for the Pentagon code room and later transferred to a clerical position in the supply section.

Mrs. Moss denied that she had ever been a member of the Communist party. When Senator Stuart Symington asked if she had ever heard of Karl Marx, she replied, "Who's that?" Eventually Annie Lee Moss regained her job when the Pentagon proved that McCarthy's charges were baseless.

A month after the first *See It Now* report on McCarthy, CBS provided thirty minutes of reply time to the senator. He chose to attack Murrow's allegiance: "Now, ordinarily, I would not take time out from the important work at hand to answer Murrow. However, in this case I feel justified in doing so because Murrow is a symbol, the leader and cleverest of the jackal pack which is always found at the throat of anyone who dares to expose individual communist traitors."

Murrow wrote in response:

> Senator McCarthy's reckless and unfounded attempt to impugn my loyalty is just one more example of his typical tactic of attempting to tie up to Communism anyone who disagrees with him. . . . I take no back seat to Senator McCarthy or anybody else in my dedication to this country and to its aims and ideals, nor are my views about the danger of Communism or Communist infiltration into the affairs of this country less uncompromising than those presumably held by the Junior Senator from Wisconsin. . . . When the record is finally written, as it will be one day, it will answer the question—who has helped the Communist cause, who has served his country better—Senator McCarthy or I? I would like to be remembered by the answer to that question.

After McCarthy's scurrilous attack on the premier newsman and most trusted voice of World War II, President Eisenhower could no longer remain silent on McCarthy's activities. As the Army–McCarthy hearings were about to begin, the President took sides by publicly stating that he counted Murrow among his friends.

ABC decided to carry the hearings live. It was the network with the least to lose by scrapping its daytime programming. ABC's ratings increased by 50 percent. For thirty-six days a fascinated audience watched McCarthy and his chief aide Roy Cohn reveal themselves as if the television lens were an x-ray of character. The contrast between their crude manner and the soft-spoken, gentlemanly testimony of Joseph Welch, an Army attorney rebutting a McCarthy charge that one of his young associates was a communist, was a turning point for many viewers. "Have you no sense of decency, sir?" Welch asked the badgering McCarthy. "At long last, have you left no sense of decency?" Historian Erik Barnouw has written of Senator McCarthy, "A whole nation watched him in murderous close-up—and recoiled."

The *See It Now* broadcasts and the televised hearings destroyed McCarthy's credibility. The Senate finally summoned the courage to formally condemn his conduct. Television showed more effectively than any other medium that McCarthyism was the antithesis to Americanism.

The downfall of a demagogue marked the ascent of TV journalism. In less than a decade after World War II, television's power to shape national events and influence opinions had been convincingly demonstrated. But patriotism in the Cold War era was not as easily defined as it had been in World War II. Radio had been a nation-binding propagandist for freedom, but in the television age—and the atomic age—the conflicts were more complex and the enemy not always so clear.

The Living-Room Wars

In a memo to his staff as they prepared to expand their nightly newscast from fifteen to thirty minutes in 1963, NBC News executive producer Reuven Frank reminded them: "The highest power of television journalism is not in the transmission of information but in the transmission of experience."

The truth of his statement had already been profoundly proven by television's coverage of the civil rights movement. Martin Luther King, Jr., understood the visceral power of the medium. Television became "the chosen instrument of the revolution." King developed into a skillful teledramatist, scheduling his protests to accommodate the deadlines of network newscasts. Favorable coverage by *The New York Times* was wonderful, but King knew that stirring newsfilm on ABC, CBS, and NBC was a far more coveted prize. It was television that forced Northern viewers to take notice of the struggle for desegregation and television that helped engender a solidarity among Southern blacks.

In the spring of 1963, Birmingham, Alabama, was targeted for a major protest by the Alabama Christian Movement for Human Rights. That organization joined forces with Martin Luther King and the Southern Christian Leadership Conference in what was called Project "C," for Confrontation.

The protest was launched just before Easter to disrupt one of the busiest shopping seasons in the year for downtown merchants. The demands of the black citizens were simply for the right to use the same lunch counters, drinking fountains, and rest rooms as white customers in businesses that profited by black patronage. They also asked that some black sales clerks be employed and that a biracial committee be set up to examine ways to desegregate the public school system. As the largest segregated city in the United States, Birmingham was pivotal. If change came to Birmingham, no other Southern city could hold out for long.

In early April, volunteers began sitting down at lunch counters and picketing in front of stores. As arrests were made, new demonstrators continued to stream into downtown Birmingham. It was a peaceful demonstration designed for television coverage. The police chief, the infamous Bull Connor, attempted to cut off media access to Martin Luther King. The motel in which King was staying was surrounded by Birmingham police. The only way to get past the blockade was to present press credentials issued by the Birmingham Police Department. Reporters requesting a press pass were likely to be asked: "What the hell you ovah here for, wantin' to give all these niggers mo' publicity?"

On Good Friday, April 12, when King was arrested and thrown in jail, national and world media attention focused on Birmingham. Over the next few weeks the drama was played out on the evening news and special reports. Every day there were more arrests. As the campaign wore on and morale among some volunteers was sagging, Martin Luther King reminded them that their cause was being seen on the *Huntley–Brinkley Report*. "We are not alone in this," he assured them. "Don't let anyone make you feel we are alone."

The willingness of Birmingham's black citizens to be arrested baffled and frustrated the segregationist authorities. On May 2, the jails were overflowing when the demonstrations took a new and phenomenally newsworthy turn. For the first time, children joined the protest. Thousands of black children marched. More than nine hundred were arrested.

This ploy to elicit compassion and media attention angered Bull Connor. The following day the Birmingham Police Department gave up on the arrests and began to physically repel the marchers. Nightsticks, high-pressure fire hoses, and police dogs were their weapons. The violence committed against the demonstrators in Birmingham, so many of whom were children, was captured by news photographers and soon became symbolic of the American struggle for civil rights.

The bared fangs of lunging German shepherds and the overpowering streams of water directed at terrified women and children was a television sight that "sickened" even the President of the United States. "I can well understand," John Kennedy said, "why the Negroes of Birmingham are tired of being asked to be patient."

It wasn't information—facts and figures on segregation—that convinced the American public that civil rights was a moral issue that could not be ignored one hundred years after the Emancipation Proclamation. It was television's transmission of experience. The images on film and video offered a dimension of understanding not contained in words.

When Reuven Frank wrote his prescient memo in 1963, a painful chapter in American history that would provide even more commanding evidence of Frank's insight was just beginning to unfold. The United States was steadily increasing its support of South Vietnam in a bitter civil war against the communist North, led by Ho Chi Minh.

South Vietnamese leader Ngo Dinh Diem was rapidly losing support within his own country. He had no tolerance for those who criticized his government and he imprisoned thousands of dissidents. Americans viewed with horror TV newsfilm of Buddhist priests in South Vietnam burning themselves alive in protest. American officials gave up hope that Diem would reform. In 1963, after receiving assurances the United States would not object to an internal coup, South Vietnamese military leaders assassinated Diem and seized control of the government.

Shortly after Diem's assassination, President Kennedy was murdered in Dallas and Lyndon Johnson inherited the war. Johnson, like Kennedy, believed the lesson of World War II was that aggressors had to be stopped. Whether or not President Kennedy would have eventually withdrawn and let the Vietnamese solve their own problems no longer mattered. "I'm not going to lose Vietnam," LBJ vowed, "I'm not going to be the president who saw Southeast Asia go the way China went."

Even though during the presidential campaign of 1964 Johnson told voters, "We are not going to send American boys nine or ten thousand miles away from home to do what Asian boys ought to be doing for themselves," the American military escalation began early in 1965 with the bombing of North Vietnam. A few months later the President sent ground troops into action. At the beginning of 1965, there were 25,000 soldiers in Vietnam. By the end of the year there were 184,000 and the numbers would swell to 543,000 in 1968.

Johnson hoped to control the public's perception of the war. But television was presenting pictures that caused Americans to question the mission in Vietnam. In August 1965, CBS newsman Morley Safer and cameraman Ha Thuc Can were traveling with a marine unit when it came to the South Vietnamese village of Cam Ne, just outside of Da Nang. Earlier in the day, the marines had been fired on from the village; three were wounded. After the Viet Cong slipped away, the angry American soldiers were primed for payback.

"This is what the war in Vietnam is all about," Safer told his viewers. Footage then showed U.S. Marines using cigarette lighters to set fire to thatched huts, ignoring the anguished peasants begging to return to their homes to retrieve food, pets, and other possessions. Old men, women, and children were rousted with bayonets.

With the Viet Cong long gone, explained Safer, the Americans engaged in an action that "wounded three women, killed one baby, wounded one Marine and netted four old men as prisoners." Safer added: "There is little doubt that American fire power can win a military victory here. But to a Vietnamese peasant whose house means a life of backbreaking labor, it will take more than presidential promises to convince him that we are on his side."

Safer's report challenged the definition of American soldiers as heroes, so ingrained in the popular imagination. The American boys were the villains in Cam Ne. Viewers were accustomed to news coverage that incorporated patriotic sentiments. In the early stages of the U.S. involvement in Vietnam, TV reporters followed what Safer later called "the old rules of reporting the war." "The identification between the trooper and the reporter was very close," he explained. "You were on his side, the enemy was wrong. . . . Those rules were probably quite valid in the Second World War and perhaps even Korea. But there was something very smelly about Vietnam that everyone was aware of and nobody wanted to talk about."

After Safer's story from Cam Ne appeared on the *CBS Evening News with Walter Cronkite*, the network was flooded with calls from people complaining that what they had just seen could not possibly have happened.

No one, though, understood the impact of altering the definition of American military action more clearly than Lyndon Johnson. The President was angry about the report and accused CBS of undermining the war effort. But even Johnson, a master in the art of intimidation, would have little success in controlling the power of television to transmit the experience of Vietnam.

By mid-decade color television was becoming more common in American homes. One of the first CBS News specials to be broadcast in color was *Christmas in Vietnam* in 1965. Producer Russ Bensley recalled: "The switch from black and white to color was significant in two ways. The country, for one thing, looked prettier. It was green and not nearly as depressing or horrible looking as it seemed in black and white. Yet, on the other hand, when the blood started flowing it looked much more terrible than it had in black and white."

Nightly television reports of death and destruction in Vietnam—and the American body count—inevitably caused many Americans to question the purpose of the fighting. Antiwar activism first flourished on college campuses, where "Make Love Not War" became a ubiquitous slogan.

When *The Smothers Brothers Comedy Hour* joined the CBS Sunday line-up in February 1967 as a midseason replacement, no one expected it would give the popular western *Bonanza* much competition. But the variety show, hosted by a clean-cut folksinging team, quickly caught on with young viewers. It was TV's first counterculture showcase.

As the program's popularity grew, the network eased its standards on sexual innuendo, but the social satire was growing more political. Pointedly antiwar messages began punctuating the skits. CBS Director of Programming, Michael Dann, insisted that antiwar themes could not be part of the show. When folksinger Joan Baez appeared as a guest on *The Smothers Brothers Comedy Hour* and introduced a song by dedicating it to her husband, then in jail for resisting the military draft, the network trimmed her remarks. In the edited version, viewers heard her say, "I want to dedicate this song to my husband—who is in jail." The reason he was incarcerated remained unspoken. Defining draft resistance as a noble act was the most threatening of anti-establishment values. Those who supported American policy in Vietnam believed the Smothers Brothers were making antiwar protest—and disrespect for authority—fashionable.

The appearance of folksinger Pete Seeger brought the issue to a head. After being banished from television for seventeen years because of being blacklisted, Seeger was invited by Tom and Dick Smothers to be a guest on their show in the fall of 1967. He chose to sing "Waist Deep in the Big Muddy," a song that told of a World War II incident in which a commanding officer ordered his platoon to cross the Big Muddy River on a training march. Not knowing the river was deep and dangerous, he nearly drowned the entire company before he was swept away himself.

Seeger made sure the audience understood the metaphor of President Johnson's handling of the war in Vietnam. He pointed out that by reading the newspapers, viewers realized they were once again "Waist Deep in the Big Muddy," while "the Big Fool Says to Push On." Michael Dann ordered the segment removed before the show aired. Pete Seeger made the dispute public by phoning a *New York Times* reporter to relay the story. "It's important for people to realize," Seeger told the press, "that what they see on television is screened, not just for good taste, but for ideas."

Tom and Dick Smothers increased the heat on the network by inviting Seeger back for a return engagement. The storm of bad publicity after the first incident, coupled with the show's continuing success in the ratings, complicated the situation. CBS relented. On February 25, 1968, *The Smothers Brothers Comedy Hour* featured Pete Seeger singing "Waist Deep in the Big Muddy."

This time the significance of the metaphor was even more conspicuous. Just a few weeks earlier the Tet Offensive stunned Americans who had believed the Johnson administration's optimistic assessments of the war's progress. The Tet Offensive was a bloody, massive assault by Viet Cong and North Vietnamese forces throughout South Vietnam. It revealed the enemy was much stronger than Americans had been told.

During the three weeks that the battles raged and casualties mounted, television was influential in shaping the American reaction to Tet. Although strategists argued it was, in the final analysis, a military victory for the United States, the pictures told a different story. "More than 60 million people watched the network news shows every evening," historian William Chafe writes. "Editors in New York, choosing five or six minutes of footage out of the multiple stories they had to select from, inevitably exercised profound influence in defining the reality of the war to Americans. . . . What were Americans to say about the democracy of their ally when they saw, in glaring color, the chief of South Vietnam's national police execute a Vietcong suspect in the middle of a Saigon street?"

After visiting Vietnam for a news special on the Tet Offensive, CBS newsman Walter Cronkite—considered by most Americans a nonpartisan, dispassionate teller of the truth—was convinced of the futility of the war. Many were surprised on February 27, 1968 when he closed *Report From Vietnam by Walter Cronkite* with the suggestion that negotiations with the Viet Cong and the North Vietnamese might be the only rational way for the United States to end its involvement in Southeast Asia. Instead of a certain bloody stalemate, Americans should disengage, he said, "not as victors, but as honorable people who lived up to their pledge to defend democracy and did the best they could."

After President Johnson watched Cronkite's report, he worried about being able to sustain public support for his policies. "If I've lost Cronkite," he told his press secretary, Bill Moyers, "I've lost middle America." This, coupled with the stark reality of the ability of the enemy to move at will, triggered an in-depth reconsideration of U.S. policy in Vietnam. Weeks later, the President's advisors painted a bleak picture, and at the end of March, Johnson made a television address on the state of the war in which he announced a halt to the U.S. bombing. He then shocked the country by declaring he would not seek nor accept the nomination to run for another term as President. His withdrawal from politics, he hoped, might help heal "the division in the American house."

By the time the Democratic Convention opened in Chicago in August 1968, the divisions were even deeper. Thousands of young antiwar protesters who were denied parade permits for their demonstrations by Mayor Richard Daley clashed with police and National Guardsmen in what would later be judged a "police riot." Clubs, rifle butts, tear gas, and Mace were used to keep the protesters from marching on the convention hall. Their chant, "The whole world is watching," convinced many horrified viewers that the event would not have occurred at all had it not been for the presence of television cameras.

Even though the amount of time the networks devoted to coverage of the violence was minimal—NBC, for instance, spent only twenty-eight minutes on the demonstrations outside the hall out of a total of thirty-five hours of convention coverage—television was criticized for paying too much attention to the demonstrators. By showing this traumatic tear in the American fabric, network news was accused of giving aid and comfort to the enemy. The dilemma for television news gatherers was that a basic scientific principle—observation changes the character of the subject being observed—applied to their work as well.

In the decade of the 1960s, television transmitted experiences that changed American history. Television critic for *The New Yorker*, Michael Arlen, had called Vietnam "the living-room war"; the psychological frontlines were on the screen. With images of high emotion it influenced the course of both the civil rights movement and the war in Vietnam. In postwar America, television became the primary forum of democracy, the place where citizens formed the impressions that guided their consciences and their votes.

Framing the President

It was the "new" Richard Nixon who made a cameo appearance on *Rowan and Martin's Laugh-In* in January 1968. "Sock it to Me?" he asked. The catchphrase that was sweeping the country had a special irony when said by the politician hoping to make a comeback. Television had socked it to Nixon pretty hard earlier in the decade.

In the presidential campaign of 1960, the camera fell in love with John Kennedy, and Nixon paled in comparison. The first of the Great Debates between the candidates emphasized the image gulf. "That night," recalled *New York Times* reporter Russell Baker, "television replaced newspapers as the most important communications medium in American politics."

Nixon's bitterness toward the mass media reached a climax after his loss in the 1962 gubernatorial campaign in California. In a press conference to announce his retirement from public life, he told the assembled reporters, "You won't have Nixon to kick around anymore."

By 1968 he had a change of heart and was ready to try again for the Republican nomination and a run for the presidency. But this time, Nixon's campaign advisors would control his use of television. He attempted to create a new public image by employing the techniques of public relations and advertising. The successful strategy was to avoid TV reporters in uncontrolled circumstances and instead to conduct informal, impromptu interviews.

Once in the White House, Nixon continued to deflect live television coverage as much as possible. During the span of his presidency, Nixon held fewer press conferences than his TV-age predecessors. Beginning in 1969, Nixon's Vice-president, Spiro Agnew, launched a vigorous attack on the news media, especially television. Agnew claimed that the news on network television came filtered through the biases of liberal New Yorkers who didn't understand or care about the real pulse of the country.

In his campaign for reelection in 1972, Nixon's successful strategy was to isolate himself from traditional open forms of political communication and again market himself in controlled environments. Reporter David Broder likened Nixon to a "touring emperor" rather than a candidate for the American presidency.

On June 17, 1972, an odd story broke. Viewers of the *NBC Nightly News* heard Garrick Utley report it this way: "Five men wearing white gloves and carrying cameras were caught early today in the headquarters of the Democratic National Committee in Washington. They were caught by a nightwatchman. They did not resist arrest when the police showed up. They apparently were unarmed and nobody knows yet why they were there. The film in their cameras hadn't even been exposed. Anyway, they're being held."

The story of the break-in at the Watergate building wasn't initially one in which the television networks invested much enterprising reporting. The lack of pictures diminished its value for the evening news. But two young reporters for the *Washington Post*, Bob Woodward and Carl Bernstein, were bloodhounds on the trail. They produced a steady stream of stories suggesting a tie-in between the White House and the burglary. Democratic presidential candidate George McGovern hoped the matter would become a campaign issue about the integrity of the incumbent. But, with television virtually ignoring the story, Watergate didn't register with most voters as an issue of consequence. The administration's dismissal of it as "a third rate burglary" played in Peoria. Richard Nixon was reelected by a landslide.

During the first months of Nixon's second term, however, mounting evidence hinted the White House itself played a role in the attempt to spy on the Democrats. In March 1973, the Senate began an inquiry into the numerous charges of impropriety.

Not knowing how many weeks or months the inquiry might drag on, the television networks were reluctant to make a costly commitment to preempt their daytime programming indefinitely. After the first week, in which all three networks carried the sessions live, they worked out a rotation plan. Each day one network would broadcast the Watergate hearings, and the other two would maintain their regular schedules. The Public Broadcasting Service, however, carried the hearings live each day and then rebroadcast them later in the evening for viewers whose work or school schedules didn't allow them to watch in the afternoon.

As the hearings progressed, public interest didn't wane, it increased. Senator Sam Ervin of North Carolina, chairman of the Senate Judiciary

Committee during the Watergate hearings, became a TV folk hero. The graduate of Harvard Law School liked to describe himself as "a simple country lawyer." With his Southern drawl he'd sometimes quote from the Bible. The contrast between the white-haired, courtly Ervin and the smooth-talking slick-backed Nixon accomplices was a perfect TV-drama conflict.

For five consecutive days at the end of June, all three commercial networks decided to carry the testimony of former Nixon counsel John Dean. His were the most damaging charges. But his words alone, stating his belief that President Nixon had not only been aware of the cover-up but probably directed it, were not what mesmerized the audience. "Viewers saw the entire frame of their screens filled with his face," wrote media analyst Gregor Goethals about Dean's testimony. "Sometimes the camera moved in with a tight shot in which every motion of his eyes could be followed. Cameras monitored every expression that might assist or damage his credibility as a witness. In the political drama being enacted, John Dean's persona symbolized doubt and distrust of the president."

The question that gripped the country was, "What did the President know and when did he know it?" In July, a former Nixon aide, Alexander Butterfield, revealed that an elaborate audio taping system in the White House had probably recorded many of the meetings that would shed light on the question. The committee requested the tapes but President Nixon refused to release them. In August, the Ervin committee adjourned for vacation. The months of testimony had produced no hard evidence, but they resulted in a tremendous change in public opinion. The confidence of the American people in their president plummeted.

The pressure on Nixon was evident in his television appearances. In one press conference he nervously addressed his mounting troubles by claiming, "I am not a crook." When CBS White House correspondent Robert Pierpoint asked Nixon at a press conference what it was about television news that so aroused his anger, Nixon responded: "Don't get the impression that you arouse my anger. You see, one can only be angry with those he respects."

In April 1974, Nixon delivered a televised speech asking the country to put Watergate aside and move on to more important things. The President was seated near stacks of bound volumes of edited transcripts of the tapes that had been subpoenaed. He explained that his demonstration of cooperation proved he had nothing to hide.

Nixon vainly hoped the great volume of material would discourage close scrutiny. But television news, as if to make up for its foot-dragging early on, zeroed in with tenacity. All three networks presented special broadcasts featuring the reading of transcript excerpts. Even though not all the requested tapes had been included in the transcripts, and they were heavily edited with many indications of "expletive deleted" and "unintelligible" passages, they revealed a petty and profane president with little regard for the rights of those he considered his enemies.

The House Judiciary Committee opened formal impeachment hearings on July 24, 1974. Television carried three days of debate on the pros and cons. Instead of partisan rhetoric, though, what viewers saw and experienced was the deep personal anguish of each committee member.

On Saturday, July 27, a formal vote was taken on the first article of impeachment. "In a scene reminiscent of Studio One's 'Twelve Angry Men,'" a critic wrote, "the TV cameras focused on each member's face for the roll call voice vote. Throughout the country viewers shared the drama and tallied the score as the camera panned from member to member, each speaking only the word: 'yes' or 'no.'" The motion passed twenty-seven to eleven.

Before the full House approved a resolution of impeachment, which would lead to a trial in the Senate, Nixon announced voluntarily in a prime-time speech on August 8 that he would resign his office. The following morning, with no apparent contrition for his wrongdoings, Nixon allowed television to broadcast his emotional farewell to the White House staff. Although he was a defeated man, the 37th President of the United States flashed his trademark "double V" for victory symbol as he climbed into the helicopter waiting to take him to the airfield for his return home to California. The irony of the image seared itself on America's collective memory.

"I'm a Ford, not a Lincoln," the new president told his countrymen. Gerald Ford's corny, self-deprecating humor was a much-appreciated attempt to brighten the grim days following Nixon's resignation. It was also a way to frame himself as a hardworking, but unflashy chief executive.

In his first year in office, Gerald Ford's image began to gel as a man of good intentions, but modest gifts. He was not an eloquent speaker or impressive fielder of questions from the press. But it was his occasional trips over his own feet—the kind of missteps that everyone makes—that became magnified in the public mind when captured in television pictures.

In 1975 the debut of a late-night sketch comedy show called *Saturday Night Live* cemented the image of Gerald Ford as a bumbler. Comedian Chevy Chase assumed the character of the President. Without special make-up or any attempt to mimic Ford's voice, Chase played up his perceived clumsiness with huge pratfalls and extreme physical comedy.

In one skit Gerald Ford's press secretary, Ron Nessen, played by comedian Buck Henry, devised a plan to counter the President's image for clumsiness. The idea of "Operation Stumblebum" was that every time the President stumbled, so would all the aides around him, so that the mishap wouldn't seem out of place. By the end of the routine, the President, played by Chase, his press secretary, and two secret service agents were fumbling around the stage, falling on the floor, banging themselves on the head, and ripping their clothes.

The real Ron Nessen, who considered the media portrayals of his boss as a fumbling lightweight a serious liability, happened to see that program. He began to watch *Saturday Night Live* every week. The gags were cutting. A regular feature was "Weekend Update," a mock newscast that once reported Gerald Ford's new campaign slogan was, "If he's so dumb, how come he's President?"

Nessen decided to deal with the *SNL* problem by proving that the Ford administration had a good sense of humor. The press secretary planted the idea that he would like to appear on the show as a guest host. "You lose by getting all huffy and demanding they stop it," Nessen believed. "You win by showing you can laugh at yourself and take part in the thing."

President Ford agreed to videotape three brief clips to be integrated into the show which Nessen would host. His lines were: "Live from New York, it's Saturday Night," "Ladies and gentlemen, the press secretary of the United States," and "I'm Gerald Ford and you're not."

The producers of *SNL* wanted the high profile of having the President and his press secretary appear on their show, but they were also determined not to be used for political purposes. Ron Nessen told the *Washington Post*: "When we first talked about this I told them I can't do anything truly embarrassing or in bad taste to the White House. And they agreed there'd be nothing like that on the show." But producer Lorne Michaels informed Nessen that *SNL* wouldn't change its ways in deference to his position.

Although Michaels denies the program intentionally set out to undermine Nessen's strategy to define President Ford as a good sport, many of the show's writers told a different story to Dong Hill and Jeff Weingrad, authors of *Saturday Night: A Backstage History of Saturday Night Live*: "They say, without equivocation, that *Saturday Night* was out to get Nessen." The attitude was characterized by one of the writers as, "The President's watching. Let's make him cringe and squirm."

Knowing that Nessen would be looking out for politically offensive material in his own sketches, the writers "feinted left and went right," in the words of one of the team. Raunchy material, even by *SNL* standards, was prepared for the surrounding skits.

The opening bit of the April 1976 show was the kind of funny business that everyone expected. Nessen joked that among the things he learned as press secretary was how to remove the President's tie from a helicopter blade—while he was still wearing it. Chevy Chase as Gerald Ford stumbled around the Oval Office and eventually stapled his ear and signed his hand.

But as the show unfolded, a vulgar tone replaced the familiar ribbing. The sketches that Nessen hadn't paid attention to in rehearsal included one in which cast members came up with disgusting names for a fictitious product called Flucker's jam. Among the suggestions were Dog Vomit, Mangled Baby Ducks, Death Camp, and Painful Rectal Itch. On the "Weekend Update" segment, Gilda Radner as the confused commentator Emily Litella questioned the value of television's concentration on "the presidential erection." Another sketch had to do with flavored, carbonated feminine douches. Still another featured a couple making love while Supreme Court justices stand around the bed to prevent any kinky activity from taking place.

President Ford and his family were not pleased with the broadcast. The President made no public comment, but Betty Ford said she regretted that her husband's taped appearances might give the impression he endorsed the distasteful sketches. Several newspaper columnists complained that the show damaged the dignity of the presidency. The most painful remark for the press secretary, though, must have been from the *Washington Post*. Columnist Bill Gould wrote that one of his readers commented that if Gerald Ford allowed Ron Nessen to appear on *Saturday Night Live*, then, "I don't see how I can vote for a man who could be so dumb."

It is impossible to quantify how much the image as a befuddled klutz damaged Gerald Ford's election campaign. But the legacy of his short presidency will never be untangled from the irreverent television series that pushed the envelope of American satire in the mid-1970s.

President Jimmy Carter's first few hours in Washington were a successful exercise in presidential television. His surprise inaugural walk down Pennsylvania Avenue with Rosalynn Carter at his side symbolically announced the true end of Nixon's imperial presidency. During his first year in office Carter was an effective television communicator. His daughter Amy went to public school and the President carried his own suitcase. He portrayed himself as a common man with an uncommon gift of leadership.

Before too long, though, Carter's "good old boy," Washington-outsider image was skewing toward hick rather than rescuer of the republic. In 1978, adman Gerald Rafshoon was hired to fine tune Carter's image. Hoping to create the sense that the President was an international man of broad and deep interests, Rafshoon saw to it that Carter was seen mingling with Andres Segovia rather than Willie Nelson.

No amount of presidential PR could deliver Carter from the Iran hostage crisis that played out on American TV screens from November 1979 through January 1981. When Carter agreed to let the deposed Shah of Iran enter the United States for medical treatment, Iranian student radicals, supporters of Ayatollah Khomeini, seized fifty-three Americans and held them hostage in the American embassy in Tehran.

The undivided attention of network news organizations made Carter a himself hostage of the crisis, unable to divert the attention of the nation away from the humiliation. Khomeini understood that if opportunities for dramatic TV pictures were provided, such as forceful anti-American demonstrations, the networks could not lose interest in the story. The ABC network ran nightly broadcasts called *America Held Hostage*, which eventually became *Nightline*. Walter Cronkite adopted a new sign-off for the *CBS Evening News*: "And that's the way it is, Thursday, December 13, 1979—the 40th day of captivity for the American hostages in Iran." Night by night, Cronkite reminded viewers that Americans were being held and that the United States was apparently powerless to resolve the crisis. The number of days in captivity finally reached 444.

Ronald Reagan had been president for only sixty-nine days when he was shot by John Hinkley as he left the Washington Hilton. Even though the chief executive had already finished his public appearance and was just taking a short walk from the back door of the hotel to his waiting limousine, cameramen were there to record the horrible scene. Ever since President Kennedy had been shot in Dallas with no professional news photographers there to document the crime, a ritual known as "the body watch" became standard operating procedure. Everywhere the President goes, cameras follow.

On March 30, 1981, the first TV bulletins of an attempt on President Reagan's life interrupted daytime programs at about 2:30 p.m. in the east. Within minutes viewers saw an astonishing scene of gunplay. Early reports erroneously said the President had not been hit and that his press secretary Jim Brady had lost his life. But soon Americans knew that both men were gravely wounded. The videotape of the shooting was replayed frequently throughout the day's coverage, sometimes in slow motion, sometimes in frame-by-frame progression.

Some critics questioned the need for the networks, including the Cable News Network (CNN), the new player in 1981, to use the footage so excessively. When John Hinkley was brought to trial, the pictures of the horrible scene were again shown repeatedly, even in promos for newscasts. "It has become just another blob of news footage," wrote *Washington Post* TV writer Tom Shales. "Something terrible and awful has been reduced through over-exposure to a numbingly familiar ritual that passes before our eyes without much effect. . . . In other words, the footage of President Reagan being shot is used by news producers the same way car-chase and car-crash footage is used on *The Dukes of Hazzard* and *CHIPS* . . . An act of monstrous insanity was turned into just another video doodle."

After a month of often painful recuperation, Reagan addressed a joint session of Congress in prime time. Although his purpose was to speak on the economy, the joyous scene, a wave of goodwill and sympathy, was likened to a coronation. The President read a letter he had received from a seven-year-old boy. "I hope you get well quick," the child wrote, "or you might have to make a speech in your pajamas." The President paused for laughter and then delivered the punchline with perfect comic timing: "P.S. If you have to make a speech in your pajamas, I warned you." Reagan's popularity rating rose nineteen points that evening.

In the years that followed, Reagan's success with television, his reputation as "The Great Communicator," stemmed from the ability of his staff to control his TV image. News management as practiced by the Reagan White House involved limiting reporter access to the President himself, stressing issues that favored the President, speaking in one voice for the administration, and repeating the same message again and again. Reagan aide Michael Deaver provided the television networks with a "line-of-the-day" for the evening news. "We figured that if we could dictate as much of the sound bites on the evening news as possible—and dictate it so that our story got out, we could continue to be at fifty-plus in the opinion polls—and that's what really mattered."

Television brought postwar presidents remarkable opportunities to communicate with the American public. But it has also been a devastating factor in the tenures of some modern chief executives. Although presidents strive to frame themselves and their policies favorably through media coverage, leadership in the television age also requires an ability to prevent challenging forces from controlling the image on the TV screen.

The Gathering Place

Schoolchildren around the country were watching TV with their classmates on the morning of January 28, 1986. It was a special event that permitted regular lessons to be put aside for awhile. Along with six astronauts, a school teacher, Christa McAuliffe, was on board *Challenger*, the space shuttle being launched from Cape Canaveral.

Some of the parents and teachers of the children in those classrooms that morning might have reminisced about the excitement of watching John Glenn's lift-off a generation earlier. On February 20, 1962, the normal routines of American life were suspended for the day. Not only in schools, but in stores and restaurants, hospitals and offices, people were preoccupied with the TV screen. In Grand Central Station, ten thousand commuters stood in the central mezzanine to watch on a huge TV monitor that hung above the ticket windows. All three networks covered the story. The country was spellbound.

By 1986, space travel no longer dominated national attention. After the glory of seeing an American flag planted on the moon in 1969, laymen were easily jaded. Only CNN was covering the *Challenger* launch live and few viewers took time out of their workday to watch. But the kids cheered as they saw the rocket boosters clear the launch pad. Then, just a moment later, they witnessed the spaceship explode and disintegrate into trails of smoke—seven lives extinguished before their eyes.

That evening, as all the television networks devoted themselves to the tragedy, the grown-ups who remembered John Glenn were now reminded of the weekend in November 1963 when television united the country after the shock of President Kennedy's assassination. In times of triumph and trauma, the nationalizing effect of television on the American people has been profound. After four days of coverage, culminating with John Kennedy's state funeral of heartbreaking grandeur, the television industry accepted the gratitude of the country for its stellar public service. Few would deny that television helped the American democracy maintain its course in a time of overwhelming crisis. In 1963, television's unprecedented role helped the country come to terms with tragedy by allowing viewers to mourn as a family united in grief.

Before the decade ended, though, viewers would gather around their television sets again and again trying to absorb the reality of sudden, violent death. From election results to State of the Union speeches, live events of great importance to the country have bound television audiences to their screens. But in October 1987, the fate of a single, tiny citizen caused the nation to hold its collective breath. In Midland, Texas, eighteen-month-old Jessica McClure fell twenty-two feet into an abandoned water well shaft. For three days rescuers diligently drilled through rock to try to remove her as she cried for her mama and sang nursery rhymes to herself.

Along with CNN, all three networks covered the last stage of the rescue live. The First Lady of the United States, Nancy Reagan, who had just been told she had breast cancer, refused to leave her room for a biopsy until she saw Jessica pulled from the well. Shortly after the baby was recovered, President Reagan placed a telephone call to her parents and told them, "Everybody in America became godfathers and godmothers of Jessica while this was going on."

In the early weeks of 1991, the Persian Gulf War commanded the national attention. A coalition led by the United States was attempting to force Iraq to withdraw from Kuwait, a country it had invaded five months earlier. In its first few days, Operation Desert Storm was covered by the American television networks on an intensive, almost minute-to-minute basis.

Unlike Vietnam, though, on television the Gulf War seemed antiseptic. Convinced that disturbing television pictures from Vietnam had turned the American public against the mission, the Defense Department was determined to have this war covered on its own terms. Military restrictions on the press were imposed. Instead of footage of wounded soldiers, television news was filled with selectively released videos of "smart" bombs devastating their targets.

The war, as seen on TV, had the feel of a video game. Sam Donaldson of ABC News, for instance, trumpeted the pinpoint accuracy of the U.S. air-defense system in a report about an enemy scud missile attack. Referring to the incoming warhead, he boasted: "And rising to intercept it—a U.S. Patriot missile. Bull's eye! No more Scud."

Throughout the weeks of the conflict, the Persian Gulf War was covered as a highly personal contest between America and the villain Saddam Hussein. Network and local news broadcasts employed special logos, dramatic openings, powerful music, and memorable visuals, such as a fighter-bomber taking off at sunrise. Patriotism soared, as measured by flying the flag, wearing yellow ribbons, donating blood, and attending rallies. "It was, in the end," said media scholar Daniel Hallin of TV's coverage, "a story of the firmness of American leaders, the potency of American technology, and the bravery, determination and skill of American soldiers. It was the story of a job well done."

Not all of the events that compelled Americans to gather around the television screen in the early 1990s, though, offered reassurance that the country was strong and unified. In October 1991, much of the nation was transfixed by a two-day hearing before the Senate Judiciary Committee considering the nomination of Judge Clarence Thomas to the U.S. Supreme Court. Daytime programming was interrupted for a spectacle that made the preempted soap operas seem wholesome in comparison.

Anita Hill, who worked for Thomas from 1981 to 1983, was interrogated on her charges that he sexually harassed her with unwanted advances and crude discussions of pornography and his own sexual prowess. In graphic detail the soft-spoken thirty-five-year-old law professor described her boss's behavior and recounted his words. She explained what it meant to be victimized in this way and how her fears and embarrassments prevented her from coming forward at the time. Hill's credibility as a witness, especially among women who had similar experiences, was bolstered by the fact she had apparently nothing to gain by her appearance before the committee.

But, at the same green-draped table in the Senate Caucus Room, Thomas's denials and anguish over being accused were no less believable. In record numbers, Americans watched a TV drama far more gripping than any episode of *Perry Mason*. The only apparent truth was that one of the witnesses was lying. In the days and weeks that followed, bitter arguments filled TV panel discussions. The hearing was frequently referred to as a case of "She said, He said," reinforcing the notion of a wide gender gap in American society.

In March 1991, a citizen with a new video camcorder captured a scene on the streets of Los Angeles that jarred the conscience of the country.

The videotape revealed the blurry image of a man being kicked, clubbed, and shocked with a stun gun by a group of uniformed members of the Los Angeles Police Department as he writhed on the ground. The video, shown repeatedly on television, convinced most viewers that even though Rodney King might not have been an entirely praiseworthy person, he was a victim of excessive police force.

So, a little more than a year later, after the video had become ingrained in American culture, it was a surprising turn of events that twelve jurors in Ventura County, California, decided there was not enough evidence on the tape to convict the police officers of wrongdoing. The acquittal of four white policemen brought denunciations from political and community leaders, black and white. But words condemning the verdict and condemning the violence against Rodney King could not prevent the rage felt in South Central Los Angeles from erupting into more violence.

On April 29, 1992, a horrible new scene, shot by a hovering TV-news helicopter, entered American history. In a racial reverse of the Rodney King video, a white gravel-truck driver was dragged from his vehicle and beaten unconscious by angry blacks. Marauding gangs ignited fires, looted stores and offices, and pulled other motorists from their cars. The following morning, as the violence continued, a grim Bryant Gumbel opened the *Today* show with the words, "We'd like to say 'good morning' on this Thursday, but frankly, there is nothing good to be said about this last morning of April 1992." After the helicopter footage of the truck driver's beating was shown, Gumbel's co-anchor Katie Couric said that she nearly became sick watching the "terrible, terrible pictures."

When the violence in Los Angeles finally subsided on May 2, fifty-one people had been killed, 2,300 were injured, and more than 10,000 were arrested. The news footage, shown around the globe, was defining the United States as a racist and violent country. For Americans the pictures confirmed a painful truth about their republic. "What I feel is less anger than sadness," reflected Gumbel. "It's a matter of realizing the depth of the divisions between us, as if we're so far apart it isn't even close."

The breach between black and white Americans was again underscored by an ongoing television saga that began in June 1994. The brutal murder of Nicole Brown, the ex-wife of the former football superstar O.J. Simpson, and her acquaintance Ronald Goldman was a sad story that took an extraordinarily shocking turn. O.J. Simpson was a Heisman Trophy winner who went on to have a glorious career in professional football and then became a sports commentator for NBC television. But even Americans with no interest in sports knew him as an affable commercial spokesperson and occasional movie actor. His public image was golden. Americans were thunderstruck when they learned he was the chief suspect in the crime, and TV coverage exploded.

On June 17, 1994, five days after the murders, Simpson was scheduled to surrender to police at eleven o'clock in the morning. The deadline came and went; even his lawyer didn't know where he was. Simpson was a fugitive from justice. At about 6:00 p.m. a traffic reporter in a helicopter spotted a white Ford Bronco, a vehicle that matched the description of Simpson's. Soon a squadron of police cars began following the Bronco, and so many helicopters from local TV stations joined the chase that at one point they blocked the path of police helicopters.

Television networks began to preempt their regularly scheduled shows to carry the bizarre low-speed chase. At CNN there was no question but to interrupt *Larry King Live* for the breaking story. NBC had a dilemma, though. The network was carrying—at great expense—the season's championship game of the National Basketball Association. So, rather than cutting away entirely, a split screen was used to show both events in a surreal blending of entertainment and news.

For hours the country was in suspense. Would he surrender? Would he shoot himself? Before Simpson gave up, in full view of television cameras, an estimated ninety-five million people tuned in—the largest audience ever to witness a hard news story unfold.

The subsequent televised trial of O.J. Simpson dominated American society. Far more media attention was devoted to the sensational case of the football star suspect, which actually affected only a handful of lives, than the investigation into the first attack on the World Trade Center, which had a direct impact on national security and the lives of every American citizen.

On February 26, 1993, a rented Ford Econoline van carrying a 1,500 pound urea-nitrate bomb was parked in the basement of the Word Trade Center. When it was detonated by a timer, the enormous blast killed six people, injured 1,042, and caused an estimated $300 million in property damage. The perpetrators turned out to be a group of Islamist militants with links to Osama Bin Laden's al-Qaeda network. In October 1995, Sheik Omar Abdel-Rahman, a blind cleric who preached at mosques in Brooklyn and New Jersey, was given a life sentence for masterminding the plot.

But the complicated trials of men with foreign names didn't rivet the attention of viewers or boost TV ratings as successfully as testimony for and against O.J. Simpson. Many restaurant owners complained their lunch business was down because people went home to watch the trial. Shopping malls reported sales were off in the spring of 1995; some analysts attributed it to the fact that the O.J. Simpson trial was replacing shopping as recreation for a sizable number of consumers. According to the Cambridge Human Resources Group in Chicago, American employers lost $27.5 billion in productivity during the first year of the case because workers discussed it on company time.

On October 3, 1995, at 10:00 a.m. Pacific Time, the United States came to a seeming standstill. People gathered around television sets with their families or co-workers, fellow students or club members, even with complete strangers in airport terminals or the appliance departments of discount stores. Tension was palpable as the verdict on O.J. Simpson was about to be revealed. In many public gathering places the words "Not Guilty" brought both anger and relief.

Whether or not television did the right thing by indulging America's obsession with a sensational trial would long be debated—even after the jury in a civil suit found Simpson liable for the two deaths in 1997. Some argued the TV coverage was of great benefit to the country because it brought the issue of domestic violence to the forefront. Others rationalized the excess by claiming it offered a lesson in how the criminal justice system worked. But there was no doubt the O.J. Simpson case exacerbated America's racial divisions. Vastly unmatched views about Simpson's guilt among blacks and whites suggested seemingly irreconcilable differences.

But in April 1995, before the conclusion of the Simpson criminal trial, Americans of every persuasion were united in their disgust as they watched ghastly television pictures from Oklahoma City. The bombing of the Murrah Federal Building, which had an on-site daycare center, was, up until that time, the worst terrorist attack on U.S. soil. The 168 victims comprised an ethnic and demographic cross-section of America.

The initial assumption by many Americans that Islamist extremists were responsible turned out to be wrong. The perpetrator, Timothy McVeigh, was a decorated U.S. Army veteran who had served in the Gulf War and later became an anti-government extremist. After his conviction and death sentence, McVeigh requested that his execution be televised in a public broadcast. The Federal Bureau of Prisons, however, denied his wish, and McVeigh died by lethal injection on June 11, 2001.

Feeding Frenzy

A de-emphasis on hard news and foreign news, and an invigorated empha-sis on profit margins, began in the mid-1980s as the TV networks were subsumed by huge conglomerates. Broadcast news that was once deliv-ered as a public service was now expected to help the bottom line. Costly news gathering, especially the upkeep of foreign bureaus, was trimmed in favor of content that was more cheaply produced and that appealed to larger audiences. At the same time, the rise of the twenty-four-hour cable news networks created an expectation among viewers that coverage of stories that interested them should be ongoing.

By the mid-1990s, the term "feeding frenzy" was commonly used to describe the shark-like appetite TV news had for sensational stories with little genuine extended news value, such as the 1996 murder of six-year-old beauty queen Jon Benet Ramsey. In July 1999, a feeding frenzy of gar-gantuan proportions began with the first report that a single-engine plane was missing carrying John F. Kennedy, Jr., his wife Carolyn Kennedy, and her sister Lauren Bessette. Four days of intensive coverage followed as the search in the Atlantic Ocean off Martha's Vineyard led to the recovery of the three bodies.

John Corporon, former news director at WPIX in New York and presi-dent of the Overseas Press Club, wrote of the coverage, "Anchors, editors, reporters, producers and cameramen took an impressive array of techni-cal tools and put them to work. Satellites, microwaves, digital cameras and graphics, videotape, cellular phones, archives, insider contacts and institutional memories of veteran journalists were blended into such mas-sive coverage as to satisfy the appetites of citizens hungering for minute to minute updates."

But ethical lines were crossed. Kennedy's sister Caroline sought privacy, yet cameras with telephoto lenses were trained on her home. "Such pic-ture taking," noted Corporon, "can be appropriate for spotting Mafia fel-ons, mass murderers or celebrities and public figures who court video coverage, but surely not private citizens in a grief mode who signal: please leave me alone!"

The main problem, with a feeding frenzy, however, is that other news is diminished on the agenda of importance. Social security, health care, international events—stories of significance, but not tabloid drama—are given short shrift. "Who knows how many important developments—in addition to the rise of dangerous Islamic extremism—we missed while we were hot on the trail of Bill Clinton's libido," wrote journalist Cynthia Tucker. Even though Tucker was "disgusted" with the behavior of the forty-second president, she continued, "It is difficult to make a rational argument that Clinton's personal sexual misconduct caused damage to the republic."

Another sex scandal involving a powerful man and a young woman dominated TV news in the spring and summer of 2001. The disappearance of Chandra Levy, a student from San Francisco State University who had come to Washington, D.C., for a government internship, became a feeding frenzy when it was discovered that she was having an affair with Congressman Gary Condit. Although he was never an official suspect, his history of illicit behavior added momentum to the tawdry tale.

The cable news networks went into overdrive and the broadcast networks followed suit. Only Dan Rather, anchor of the CBS Evening News, showed restraint in fueling the national news obsession. ABC's Connie Chung, Barbara Walters, and Diane Sawyer, as well as Don Hewitt, producer of 60 Minutes on CBS, were among those vying for the "big get"—an interview with Representative Condit.

Connie Chung was given the interview, but she had to follow Condit's ground rules, which were that the questioning would be limited to thirty minutes with no questions asked beyond the time limit and the live-to-tape interview would be aired with no editing. "This is journalism? You have to wonder," wrote a newspaper editorialist. "Then again, the ratings will probably go through the roof. Does anything else matter?"

On August 23, 2001, more than twenty-three million people tuned in, the largest audience for a prime-time interview since Barbara Walters' discussion with Monica Lewinsky. Chung elicited no new information. Condit admitted he was "not a perfect man" and maintained that he had no knowledge of what happened to Ms. Levy, whose body would be found in a park near her Washington, D.C., apartment in May 2002. Still it was called "one of the biggest media events of the year" by observers of popular culture. Less than three weeks later, though, on September 11, 2001, the absurdity of the latest feeding frenzy was brought into sharp perspective.

In the American journey since the end of World War II, television played a critical part in how the republic defined itself. At times, a common national vision emerged. At times, fissures came into clear focus. Whether Americans gathered as mourners or as celebrants, supporters or adversaries, the medium allowed them to be participants—regardless of their social status—in the rituals and sacraments of democracy.

At the twilight of the 20th century, television's ability to bring breaking news into American homes was breathtaking. Citizens instinctively switched on TV when they learned from another source that something big had happened. But the sophisticated technology of newsgathering and distribution that allowed viewers such instant access to the world was also capable of distracting viewers from the work of democracy, acquiring the knowledge needed to make informed decisions.

Fig. 11 NBC anchor Tom Brokaw brings devastating news to American viewers on September 11, 2001. (*Broadcasting and Cable* collection, Library of American Broadcasting.)

Epilogue

In many ways, *The Ed Sullivan Show* was a television age metaphor for the American experiment in democracy. The acts had nothing in common. Plate-spinners and opera singers were like different races and religions. But they shared the same stage and, as citizens of show business, they were committed to the same overarching principles.

Viewers of the Sunday night variety program also played a part in making the system work for everyone. When families gathered in the living room, each member had to exhibit a touch of tolerance. There was something for everybody on the bill, but getting there meant sitting through a performance that wasn't necessarily one's cup of tea. Kids looking forward to a good ventriloquist would have to hush when a crooner sang a mushy love ballad that seemed endless.

Watching *Ed Sullivan* gave viewers the opportunity to experience facets of American culture they might not otherwise seek out. When an Irish Catholic grandmother who loved the comedy team of Stiller and Meara tuned in, she might learn something about *Porgy and Bess* as well. Diversity was at the heart of the program's enormous success.

The Ed Sullivan Show represented broadcasting in its purest form. It aimed for a mass audience. Everyone counted. Perhaps this weekly communion is why *Ed Sullivan* looms so large and nostalgically in the memories of those who recall watching television in the 1950s and sixties.

By the year 2000, few television programs still tried to attract a national conglomerate. Hundreds of channels on cable and satellite TV, tens of thousands of easily available movie titles, and countless websites on the Internet relieved Americans of the requirement to pay attention to anything that didn't immediately affect or interest them. This ability of viewers to customize programming to their own tastes diminished the opportunity for shared experiences among American citizens. The fear that resulting social polarization could hurt the day-to-day functioning of the democratic process was increasing as the presidential election got underway.

Campaign 2000 reflected deepening divisions. Television news long used the color red to signify Republican-leaning states and blue to signify Democratic-leaning states. But "red state" and "blue state" became a form of cultural shorthand regarding issues of morality—faith-based opposition to abortion, gay rights, and sexual permissiveness versus secularism and separation of church and state.

The nation was prepared for a close contest between Vice-president Al Gore and Republican governor of Texas, George W. Bush—especially because third party candidate Ralph Nader was expected to siphon votes from the Democratic Party. But no one, not even veteran broadcasters, could have anticipated the astonishing outcome. On election night, the TV networks, beginning with NBC at 7:49 p.m. EST, declared Gore the winner in Florida based on exit polling from the Voter News Service (VNS) and early returns from the state. When CNN discovered a tabulation error in the VNS projection about two hours later, VNS and the other TV networks retracted their call. At 2:16 a.m., November 8, the Fox network declared Bush the winner in Florida and within minutes the other networks made the same call.

Florida tipped the Electoral College vote to the Republican candidate, but various counties in the Sunshine State reported voting irregularities, including ballots rejected by voting machines, paper tags called "hanging chads" that were not completely detached from punch-card ballots, and confusion over the layout of "butterfly ballots." A series of legal challenges kept the election up in the air for several weeks until the Supreme Court of the United States, in a five–four decision, called a halt to the recount process and Florida's twenty-five electoral votes went to Bush.

Suspicions and partisanship hardened in the early months of the George W. Bush administration. Gore had won the popular vote and perhaps had carried Florida. The anger of black Democratic voters in the state who felt that they had been disfranchised did not dissipate as the new president settled in. His campaign promise to be "a uniter, not a divider" would be a tall order while bitterness lingered on both sides.

Although Americans had bid good-bye to the 20th century with Y2K celebrations at the end of 1999, the true end of the 20th century, the

American Century, and the Broadcast Century, occurred at 8:40 a.m. EST on September 11, 2001—the moment that the diverted American Airlines Flight 11, originally en route from Boston to Los Angeles, hit the North Tower of the World Trade Center in lower Manhattan. It was a searing line of demarcation. Within minutes, morning network news shows interrupted their regular programming to show the scene of what was presumed to be a terrible accident.

While cameras focused on the burning North Tower, an even more horrifying vision materialized. Another plane, American Airlines Flight 175, also bound from Boston to Los Angeles, came into view and headed directly into the South Tower. This was not an accident; America was under a terrorist attack.

The collapse of the South Tower at 10:00 a.m. was followed within thirty minutes by the collapse of the North Tower. CNN anchor Aaron Brown was watching with the same disbelief as his audience. "Good Lord," he said, "there are no words." Later Brown reflected: "Nothing I could say was going to be as powerful as what viewers saw. Nothing I could add was going to make people feel better, or frankly, worse. It was all in front of them. I just thought it was a good time to be quiet. It was a country that we all knew in those moments was going to be changed."

As news organizations frantically attempted to get a handle on the story in New York City, air traffic controllers reported that two other commercial airplanes could not be tracked. The frightening scope of the attack emerged as viewers learned that American Airlines Flight 77, taking off from Dulles Airport near Washington, D.C., headed to Los Angeles, slammed into the Pentagon and United Flight 93, leaving Newark, New Jersey, also for Los Angeles, crashed into a field in Shanksville, Pennsylvania, about eighty miles southeast of Pittsburgh. It would soon be learned that a group of passengers on Flight 93 knew of the attacks on the World Trade Center through cell phone conversations with family members. They decided to fight the highjackers and force the plane down rather than let it successfully hit whatever the intended target.

"There were one hundred moving parts to the story," Aaron Brown recalled. "If we were a little slow on something, that was okay. It was okay to be slow, it was not okay to be wrong." Impatient viewers had another option. September 11, 2001, brought the first national security crisis in which Americans could follow the flow of events on the Internet. Websites such as MSNBC.com, CNN.com, and washingtonpost.com were jammed with record traffic. Before the end of the day, CNN.com registered more than 162 million page views. On September 12, the number rose to more than 300 million.

The TV coverage of the rescue mission at the World Trade Center site, now called Ground Zero, was accompanied by heart-wrenching images of people holding pictures of loved ones and scenes of hundreds of missing-person photos posted throughout the area. Families and friends could only hope against hope that someone might recognize the face of an unidentified survivor.

As the evidence pointed to Osama bin Laden, the leader of an international terrorist organization called al-Qaeda, based in Afghanistan, the commercial broadcast and cable networks were scrambling to produce material explaining who he was and what he was after. Only PBS was able to offer an in-depth documentary within two days of the attack by rerunning a program in the *Frontline* series called "Hunting bin Laden" that had been aired originally in the spring of 2000. That broadcast was an update of another *Frontline* program called "The Terrorist and the Superpower" that aired in April 1999 and examined the 1998 bombings of U.S. Embassies in Nairobi, Kenya, and Dar Es Salaam, Tanzania. Media history scholar Thomas A. Mascaro notes, "The program profiled the suspected mastermind of the Africa bombings, Osama bin Laden, three years before most Americans would realize his direct connection to their lives. . . . Among those who were relying on Public Television to help sort out the crisis was Vice President Dick Cheney, who requested a copy of 'Hunting bin Laden.'"

Many journalists at other networks were feeling regrets, however. "September 11, 2001 was my moment of truth," Tom Fenton wrote. "CBS News, like most of the broadcast industry, had been sliding blithely downhill for years; on 9/11, we finally collided with a wall that we should have seen coming. . . . As surely as 9/11 pointed up the myriad failures of official Washington, it also revealed the abject failure of the news media."

The executive editor of ABC's *Nightline*, Tom Bettag, contended that "The summer of 2001 was the low point in American journalism. . . . The networks decided the public was more interested in shark attacks than terrorist attacks. In the three months leading up to September 11, the phrase 'al Qaeda' was never mentioned on any of the three evening news broadcasts—*not once.*"

On September 15, the commercial-free continuous coverage of the disaster ended. The TV networks made a huge financial sacrifice, estimated to be a combined $100 million per day in lost advertising revenues. News professionals who had put themselves in harm's way to gather information were justifiably lauded for their courage. On September 20, Professor Michael M. Epstein analyzed the performance of the TV networks in *The Christian Science Monitor*. "The first day of coverage was TV news at its best: on-the-fly, unchoreographed reporting that echoed Edward R. Murrow's radio dispatches from London during WWII," he wrote. "Caught off-guard with a breathtaking story of unprecedented gravity, reporters and anchors rose to the occasion."

By the end of Day 2, though, Epstein observed that all the networks were manipulating footage with post-production effects, such as "setting slow-motion, digitally altered images of the attacks to music." He described an egregious example: "Fox News Channel uses an image of the North Tower crumbling as a background frame to its coverage. The picture is tinted blue and enhanced to appear grainy. Set to music, it conjures the type of rudimentary surveillance video one might see on a reality show or a tabloid exposé."

In the following days, the conventions of "feeding frenzy" coverage—such as jump-cut editing, canted angles, and providing made-for-TV movie type titles to define the coverage—grew more pronounced. Epstein concluded: "It is a challenge for journalism, in the age of special effects, to make distinctions between news and entertainment. TV journalism has failed to meet this challenge. This is not the time for the networks to make TV news entertaining. It is not the Chandra mystery, the O.J. Simpson trial, or even the Clinton Impeachment. Quite possibly, the future of the nation is at stake. Get rid of the music, the digitally bleached, slow-motion images, and endless replays. Get rid of the jingoistic slogans. Anything less is a disservice to those who died last week, and to all of us."

In the immediate aftermath of 9/11, there was copious speculation in the entertainment industry trade press about the changes the tragedy would generate in audience taste and standards of appropriateness. In all aspects of American life, people were contemplating a "new normal." *Television Week* reported, "It's hard to believe Americans once cared who would win *Big Brother 2* or whether [actress] Anne Heche is crazy. And it's hard to believe that as recently as two weeks ago, that's exactly the kind of pabulum, along with the latest celebrity/politician, sex/murder/kidnapping scandal that dominated television news. . . .We cannot afford to return to the way things were."

Many changes were made in TV programming already in the pipeline to reduce violence and sensational depictions of terrorism. On September 17, *Broadcasting and Cable* magazine reported that the networks were "busy weeding through programs to find content that, after the World Trade Center disaster, seemed inappropriate or insensitive." Tom Feran, TV Critic for the *Cleveland Plain Dealer*, noted that in the wake of other violent tragedies there were predictions of changes in the audience and in the industry. "This time, however, we might lose our taste for Hollywood's imaginings about terrorism and violence, and for the cheap voyeurism of manufactured 'reality,'" he wrote. "How can we not, after seeing so much real heroism and gallantry amid so much real fear, uncertainty and sorrow?"

In the days after the attack, documentarian Ken Burns ruminated on the long-term implications for American entertainment. "You know, I'm a fan of *Entertainment Tonight*," he said. "But I can't watch the show [now]. Who cares? Who are these people? They look like puppets. . . .We've been reset. The old solutions—and I mean that in the most minute literary or artistic choices—are all thrown out. As Lincoln said, we have to think anew and act anew, and that will be where we find ourselves."

The entertainment industry pulled together with amazing speed for a star-studded live broadcast on September 21, 2001. *America: A Tribute to Heroes* was a two-hour telethon to raise money for the United Way's September 11 Fund. The event was simulcast on thirty broadcast and cable networks. In the era of audience fragmentation, a remarkable 65 percent of American households joined the communal ritual of mourning for the victims and accolade for the first responders of the police and fire departments.

The long roster of celebrities spanned the spectrum of American popular culture, harkening back in a doleful way to the inclusive premise of *The Ed Sullivan Show*. After a brief introduction from actor Tom Hanks, Bruce Springsteen and his band opened the program with "My City of Ruin." "Rise up," he sang. "This a prayer for our fallen brothers and sisters."

Media scholar Lynn Spigel described the production style of *America: A Tribute to Heroes*: "While certainly designed to be a global media event, this was a deliberately understated spectacle, achieved through a deliberate display of 'star capital' minus the visual glitz and ego. Staged with 'zero degree' style (just candles burning on an otherwise unadorned set) the program appealed to the desire to see Hollywood stars, singers and sports heroes reduced to 'real' people, unadorned and unrehearsed (or at least underrehearsed), and literally unnamed and unannounced (there was no variety host presiding over the entertainment, no identification of the stars, and no studio audience). This absence of style signified the authenticity of the staged event, thereby giving stars the authority to speak for the dead."

During the broadcast, actor Will Smith introduced Muhammad Ali: "Heroes come in all shapes, sizes, colors, and religions. This man might be the most famous person in the world. He's one of the greatest heroes of our time, and he is a Muslim. It was hate—not religion—that motivated the horrible acts of September 11. And in the wake of the events, nothing could be more un-American that to respond with mindless hatred and blind vengeance. We are strongest when we stand together." The telethon ended with Willie Nelson leading all the other participants in "America the Beautiful."

Pledges amounted to more that $150 million. Viewers who could not travel to Ground Zero and join a "bucket brigade" or bring other skills to the recovery effort had the opportunity to make a monetary contribution and become part of a community based on citizenship, not marketing demographics.

In the autumn of 2001, the United States entered a new era in its history and Americans seemed poised to answer a call for sacrifice and unity. How leaders would harness the strength of the American people and how a great nation would cope with threats and challenges from outside and within will be chronicled in the decades to come. The role of mass communication in 21st-century America might very well be defined by technologies not yet imagined. Future generations, though, will consider television in the 20th century as they ponder the factors that have shaped the country.

Television's documents are critical in illuminating America's story. After World War II, the medium began its rapid rise as the great certifying agent of American culture. Since mid-century, television's most benign power has been to set styles and tastes. "Monday-morning hits" were what record companies called the songs that sold out after a performance on The Ed Sullivan Show.

But television's most transforming power has been to provide social scripts for postwar America. The medium did much more than just hold up a mirror. It provided validation for ideas and behaviors that have had impact on the life of every citizen. It has been the primary means of socialization for baby boomers and their progeny. From the home screen they've derived lessons about what society expects from them and notions of what they expect from society. From the end of World War II through the end of the twentieth century, the national psyche has been permeated, in obvious and discreet ways, by television's defining visions.

Select Bibliography

Prologue

Barfield, Ray. *Listening to Radio, 1920–1950*. Westport, CT: Praeger Publishers, 1996.

Czitrom, Daniel J. *Media and the American Mind: From Morse to McLuhan*. Chapel Hill: University of North Carolina Press, 1982.

Godfrey, Donald G. "First a Line... A Triangle... Then a $ Sign: The Story of Philo T. Farnsworth, the Real Inventor of Television." *Television Quarterly*, vol. XXXI. no. 2, Winter 2004.

Halberstam, David. "America: The Last 50 Years." Lecture at George Mason University, C-SPAN, February 1, 1995.

Henry, William A., III. "The Meaning of TV." *Life*, March 1989.

Kisseloff, Jeff. *The Box: An Oral History of Television*. New York: Viking. 1995.

Moore, Barbara, Marvin R. Bensman, and Jim Van Dyke. *Prime-Time Television: A Concise History*. Westport, CT: Praeger Publishers, 2006.

Powers, John. "Waking Up from the American Dream." *Detroit Free Press Magazine*, April 16, 1995.

Watson, Mary Ann. "Homefront." Media Wars. *Media Studies Journal* theme issue, Spring 1992.

Chapter 1   TV Enters the Picture

Bowie, Donald. *Station Identification: Confessions of a Video Kid*. New York: M. Evans and Company, Inc., 1980.

Bremmer, Robert H. and Gary W. Reichard, eds. *Reshaping America: Society and Institutions, 1945–1960*. Columbus, OH: Ohio State University Press, 1982.

Considine, Shaun. *Mad As Hell: The Life and Work of Paddy Chayefsky*. New York: Random House, 1994.

Corwin, Norman. *On a Note of Triumph*. New York: Simon and Schuster, 1945.

Gorney, Maureen. Communication 555, TV and American History. Oral History Project. Ann Arbor, MI: University of Michigan, October 1987.

Gould, Jack. "TV Makes Inroads on Big Radio Chains." *New York Times*, June 27, 1951.

Grossman, Gary H. *Saturday Morning TV*. New York: Delacorte Press, 1981.

Hawes, William. *American Television Drama: The Experimental Years*. University of Alabama Press, 1986.

Miller, Douglas T. and Marion Nowak. *The Fifties: The Way We Really Were*. Garden City, NY: Doubleday and Company, Inc., 1977.

Montgomery, Kathryn C. *Target: Prime Time*. New York: Oxford University Press, 1989.

O'Connor, John E., ed. *American History/American Television: Interpreting the Video Past*. New York: Frederick Ungar Publishing Co., 1983.

O'Dell, Cary. "A Station of Their Own." *Television Quarterly*, vol. XXX, no. 3, Winter 2000.

Ritchie, Michael. *Please Stand By: A Prehistory of Television*. Woodstock, NY: The Overlook Press, 1987.

Satin, Joseph, ed. *1950s: America's "Placid" Decade*. Boston: Houghton Mifflin Company, 1960.

Tichi, Cecilia. *Electronic Hearth: Creating an American Television Culture*. New York: Oxford University Press, 1991.

Watson, Mary Ann, "Seems Radio Is Here to Stay." *Media Studies Journal*, Summer 1993.

Willis, Edgar E. *Writing Television and Radio Programs*. New York: Holt, Rinehart and Winston, Inc., 1967.

Woolery, George W. *Children's Television: The First Thirty-Five Years, 1946–1981* (Part II: Live, Film, and Tape Series). Metuchen, NJ: Scarecrow Press, Inc., 1985.

Chapter 2   Television and the Melting Pot: Race and Ethnicity

Boulton, Alexander O. "The Buy of the Century." *American Heritage*, July/August 1993.

Braxton, Greg. "Segregated Sitcoms, Why Do TV's Comedies Trail Dramas in Racial Mixing?" *Los Angeles Times* column in *Ann Arbor News*, February 4, 1997.

Campbell, Christopher and Lori Edmo-Suppah. "Television's Troubling Indian Images." *Television Quarterly*, vol. XXXIII, no. 4, Spring 2003.

Chayefsky, Paddy. Cited in "TV From the Inside." *Newsweek*, November 24, 1958.

Clinton, Hillary Rodham. "Save the Oasis of Public TV for Children." *The Detroit News*, August 15, 1995.

Color Adjustment: Blacks in Primetime. Produced for PBS by MTR Productions, aired on the PBS network Fall 1992.

Dates, Jannette L. and William Barlow, eds. *Split Image: African Americans in the Mass Media*. Washington, D.C.: Howard University Press, 1990.

Donn, Jeff. "A Question of Reality." *Detroit Free Press*, April 27, 1992.

Duffy, Mike. "WB, UPN Continue Effort to Win Black TV Viewers." *Detroit Free Press*, August 25, 1996.

Fireman, Judy, ed. *TV Book*. New York: Workman Publishing, 1977.

Gourse, Leslie. *Unforgettable: The Life and Mystique of Nat King Cole*. New York: St. Martin's Press, 1991.

Hamamoto, Darryl Y. *Monitored Peril: Asian Americans and the Politics of TV Representation*. Minneapolis, MN: University of Minnesota Press, 1994.

Jackson, Harold. *From "Amos 'n' Andy" to "I Spy": Chronology of Blacks in Prime Time Network Television Programming, 1950–1964*. Ph.D. dissertation, University of Michigan, 1982.

Jhally, Sut and Justin Lewis. *"Enlightened" Racism: The Cosby Show, Audiences, and the Myth of the American Dream*. San Francisco: Westview Press, 1992.

Lauzen, Martha M. "Diversity in Prime Time: Not a Priority for the Networks." *Television Quarterly*, vol. XXXIII, no. 4, Spring 2003.

Lemann, Nicholas. "How the Seventies Changed America." *American Heritage*, July/August 1991.

Michener, James A. "After the War: The Victories at Home." *Newsweek*, January 11, 1993.

Moore, Frazier. "NAACP Considers TV Network Boycott." Associated Press. November 4, 1999.

Pondillo, Bob. "Saving Nat King Cole." *Television Quarterly*, vol. XXXV, nos. 3–4, Spring/Summer 2005.

"Race – America's Rawest Nerve." *Media Studies Journal* theme issue, Summer 1994.

Shaheen, Jack G. "Arabs – TV's Villains of Choice." *Channels*, Mar./Apr. 1984.

– –. "Hollywood Widens Slur Targets to Arab and Muslim Americans Since Sept.11." Pacific News Service, February 28, 2002.

– –. *The TV Arab*. Bowling Green, OH: BGSU Popular Press, 1984.

Taylor, Ella. *Prime-Time Families: Television Culture in Postwar America*. Berkeley: University of California Press, 1989.

"TV Westerns Draw Fire of Indians." *New York Times*, June 26, 1960.

Unforgettable Nat King Cole, The. Jo Lustig Ltd. Production television documentary in association with BBC TV and Picture Music International, 1988.

Watson, Mary Ann. *The Expanding Vista: American Television in the Kennedy Years*. New York: Oxford University Press, 1990.

Werts, Diane. "Segregation Lives on in Sitcomland." *Ann Arbor News*, January 27, 1996.

Whitfield, Stephen J. *The Culture of the Cold War*. Baltimore: Johns Hopkins University Press, 1991.

Zurawik, David. "Split Growing Between Black, White TV Viewing." *Ann Arbor News*, May 5, 1996.

Chapter 3   Home on the Screen: Gender and Family

Alridge, Ron. "Believe It or Not, Dan Quayle Has a Point." *Electronic Media*, June 1, 1992.

Cassidy, Robert. *Margaret Meade: A Voice for the Century*. New York: Universe Books, 1982.

Clift, Eleanor. "The Murphy Brown Policy." *Newsweek*, June 1, 1992.

Clinton, Hillary Rodham. *It Takes a Village: And Other Lessons Children Teach Us*. New York: Simon and Schuster, 1996.

Coontz, Stephanie. *The Way We Never Were: American Families and the Nostalgia Trap*. New York: Basic Books, 1992.

Dickerson, Marla. "What Happened to the Nuclear Family?" *The Detroit News*, October 2, 1994.

Douglas, William. *Television Families: Is Something Wrong in Suburbia?* Mahwah, NJ: Lawrence Erlbaum Associates, Publishers, 2003.

Friedan, Betty. *The Feminine Mystique*. New York: Norton, 1963.

Halberstam, David. "Discovering Sex." *American Heritage*, May/June 1993.

Harris, Jay S., ed. *TV Guide: The First 25 Years*. New York: New American Library, 1980.

Horn, John. "Will Hollywood Act on Clinton's Urging?" Associated Press, December 11, 1993.

Inside Family Ties: Behind the Scenes of a Hit. PBS documentary, 1988.

James, Caryn. "A Baby Boom on TV As Biological Clocks Cruelly Tick Away." *New York Times*, October 16, 1991.

Lenz, Elinor and Barbara Myerhoff. *The Feminization of America: How Women's Values are Changing Our Public and Private Lives*. New York: St. Martin's Press, 1985.

Lewin, Tamar. "Family Structure Undergoing Profound Change." *Ann Arbor News*, May 30, 1995.

Maddox, Kate and Thomas Tyrer. "'Murphy' Attack Spurs TV Debate." *Electronic Media*, May 25, 1992.

"Networking Women." *Newsweek*, March 13, 1989.

Rosenthal, Phil. "The Impact of Baby Brown." *Ann Arbor News*, January 30, 1994.

Skill, Thomas and James D. Robinson. "Four Decades of Families on Television: A Demographic Profile, 1950–1989." *Journal of Broadcasting and Electronic Media*, Fall 1994.

Skolnick, Arlene S. and Jerome H. Skolnick, eds. *Families in Transition*. New York: HarperCollins Publishers, 1992.

Watson, Mary Ann. "Women's Lives on the Small Screen." *Television Quarterly*, vol. XXVII, no. 2, 1994.

Wines, Michael. "Appeal of 'Murphy Brown' Now Clear at White House." *New York Times*, May 21, 1992.

Chapter 4   The Killing Tube: Violence and Crime

Brownian, Ronald. "Gov. Bush's Recipe for GOP Success: Power to the People." *Los Angeles Times*, 1 May 1999.

Bruning, Fred. "TV Violence Makes Society Violent, Studies Find." *Ann Arbor News*, July 9, 1993.

Christopher, Maurine. "Guns, Congress and the Networks." *The Nation*, August 19, 1968.

Clinton, Hillary Rodham. *It Takes a Village: And Other Lessons Children Teach us*. New York: Siman & Schuster, 1996.

Compton, Neil. "Television and Reality." *Commentary*, September 1968.

"Cut Violence, Clinton Asks Hollywood." *Detroit Free Press*, December 7, 1993.

Dart, Bob. "Executives Plan Less Television Violence." *Detroit Free Press*, December 12, 1992.

Does TV Kill? PBS documentary, aired January 1995.

Duston, Diane. "Survey Finds Majority Object to TV Violence." *Ann Arbor News*, March 24, 1993.

Emerson, Gloria. "The Rewards of Tough." *Vogue*, May 1883.

Erikson, Hal. "*The Sopranos* TV Series." *All Movie Guide*, included in movies2.nytimes.com

"Fighting Violence." *Time*, December 27, 1968.

"General Hospital: Critical Case." *Time*, September 28, 1981.

Goldstein, Warren. "Incest for the Millions: Saying No to David Lynch." *Commonweal*, December 21, 1990.

Grimes, William. "Films and TV Scramble to Edit Bomb Plots." *New York Times*, April 29, 1995.

"Is TV Sex Getting Bolder?" *TV Guide*, August 8, 1987.

"It Pays to Sponsor Television Corn." *Business Week*, October 7, 1950.

Kitman, Marvin. "The Soap Sickness." *The New Leader*, November 30, 1981.

Kolbert, Elizabeth. "In Mounting a Campaign Against Violence, Is the Cable Industry Practicing what It Preaches?" *New York Times*, March 13, 1995.

– –. "Television Gets Closer Look As a Factor in Real Violence." *New York Times*, December 14, 1994.

– –. "TV Execs Get Message: Cool Violence – Or Else." *Detroit Free Press*, July 4, 1993.

Lardner, John. "So You Think You See the Fights on TV!" *Saturday Evening Post*, May 2, 1953.

Lord, Daniel A. "Feature X." *America*, May 9, 1953.

Lutterbeck, Deborah. "Prime Time Politics." *Common Cause Magazine*, Spring 1995.

"MTV's Message." *Newsweek*, December 30, 1985.

"Networks Under the Gun." *Newsweek*, July 12, 1993.

Purdum, Todd S. "Clinton Takes On Violence On TV." *New York Times*, July 11, 1995.

Rader, Benjamin G. *In Its Own Image: How Television Has Transformed Sports*. New York: The Free Press, 1984.

Reeves, Richard. "Guts, Sex, and Common Sense." *Detroit Free Press*, 31 October 1993.

Scanlan, Christopher. "Scholar Engineers Social Change Through TV." *Detroit Free Press*, October 14, 1993.

Signorielli, Nancy. *Violence in the Media: A Reference Handbook*. Santa Barbara, CA: ABC Clio, 2005.

Sniffen, Michael J. "Gun Offenses by Juveniles Rising." *Ann Arbor News*, November 13, 1995.

"Televiolence." *The Detroit News*, June 13, 1993.

"Television Networks Adopt Violence Standards." *Ann Arbor News*, December 12, 1992.

"Television's Hottest Show." *Newsweek*, September 28, 1981.

Thornburn David. Entry on *The Sopranos*. *Encyclopedia of Television*, New York: Fitzroy Dearborn, 2004.

Tobin, Richard L. "On the Hour Every Hour – II." *Saturday Review*, July 13, 1968.

"Vigilante Video." *People Weekly*, January 30, 1984.

Vincent, Richard C., Dennis K. Davis and Lilly Ann Boruszkowski. "Sexism on MTV: The Portrayal of Women in Rock Videos." *Journalism Quarterly*, Winter 1987.

"Violence in Our Culture." *Newsweek*, April 1, 1991.

Werts, Diane. "Prime-time Violence Is Getting Worse? Look Again." *Ann Arbor News*, August 27, 1994.

Wolcott, James. "I've Got Clothes that Jingle, Jangle, Jingle." *New York*, February 28, 1983.

– – . "Talking About TV: Playing It Fast and Loose in Soap-Opera Land." *Vogue*, November 1981.

Yoggy, Gary A. *Riding the Video Range: The Rise and Fall of the Western on Television*. Jefferson, NC: McFarland and Company, Inc., 1995.

Chapter 5   TV Goes All the Way: Romance and Sexuality

Bianculli, David. "Beverly Hills Flop." *New York Post*, October 3, 1990.

Carter, Bill. "Television: In the Rough-and-Tumble World of Daytime Talk Shows, Advertisers Seek To Be Heard but not Seen." *New York Times*, March 20, 1995.

Collins, Rebecca L., et al. "Watching Sex on Television Predicts Adolescent Initiation of Sexual Behavior." *Pediatrics*, vol. 114, no. 3, September 2004.

Diamond, Edwin. "Thy Neighbor's Television, New Light on the Tube's Sex Life." *American Film*, September 1980.

Elber, Lynn. "8 p.m. No Longer Taboo for Racy Fare." *Ann Arbor News*, July 29, 1995.

Elliott, Stuart. "A Divided Approach, Advertisers Choose Separate Tactics for Dealing with Gay Issues." *Detroit Free Press*, February 24, 1994.

Emerson, Gloria. "Love, Sidney Sells Out." *Vogue*, April 1982.

Farber, Stephen. "TV Deals With Sex More Candidly." *New York Times*, April 4, 1987.

Freeman, Michael. "For TV Characters, It's OK to be Gay." *Electronic Media*, September 18, 2000.

Gardiner, Judith Kegan. "Television Intimacy: Paradoxes of Trust and Romance." In *Meanings of the Medium: Perspectives on the Art of Television*. New York: Praeger, 1990.

Gross, Larry. "Don't Ask, Don't Tell: Lesbian and Gay People in the Media." In *Images That Injure: Pictorial Stereotypes in the Media*, edited by Paul Martin Lester. Westport, CT: Praeger, 1996.

Halberstam, David. "Discovering Sex." *American Heritage*, May/June 1993.

Halonen, Doug. "D.C. Heavyweights Take on Talk Shows." *Electronic Media*, November 6, 1995.

Hannah, James. "Sexual Harassment or Not? Sitcoms Often Raise Question." *Ann Arbor News*, December 27, 1994.

Herbert, Bob. "Talk Shows Find a Gold Mine in Sexuality of Troubled Teens." *Ann Arbor News*, March 4, 1996.

Holden, Stephen. "After the War, the Time of the Teen-Ager." *New York Times*, May 7, 1995.

Holloway, Diane. "Sex Replaces Violence as TV's Fare of Choice." *Ann Arbor News*, March 6, 2001.

Kinsey, Alfred C., Wardell B. Pomeroy, and Clyde E. Martin. *Sexual Behavior in the Human Male*. Philadelphia, PA: W.B. Saunders Co., 1948.

Kinsey, Alfred C., and Staff of the Institute for Sex Research at Indiana University. *Sexual Behavior in the Human Female*. Philadelphia, PA: W.B. Saunders Co., 1953.

Lamm, Bob. "Television's Forgotten Gems: The Nurses." *Journal of Popular Film and Television*, vol. 23, no. 2, Summer 1995.

Lieberman, Joseph. "Producers Have Obligation to Viewers, Society." *Electronic Media*, November 6, 1995.

Lorando, Mark. "Sitcoms Treat Harassment Lightly." *Ann Arbor News TV Book*, February 5, 1995.

McCollum, Charlie. "Goodbye *Will and Grace*: Not Just a Gay Show, High Quality Comedy Opened Many Hearts." *San Jose Mercury News*, May 15, 2006.

Marling, Karal Ann. *As Seen on TV: The Visual Culture of Everyday Life in the 1950s*. Cambridge, MA: Harvard University Press, 1994.

Mauertstad, Tim and Beth Pinsker. "TV Cozies Up to Sex." *Detroit Free Press*, September 28, 1995.

Michael, Robert T., John H. Gagnon, Edward O. Laumann, and Gina Kolata. *Sex in America: A Definitive Survey*. Boston: Little, Brown and Company, 1994.

Montgomery, Kathryn C. *Target: Prime Time*. New York: Oxford University Press, 1990.

Moore, Mary Tyler. *After All*. New York: G.P. Putnam's Sons, 1995.

Ness, Carol. "Some See Ellen's Coming Out as Historic." *Ann Arbor News*, March 16, 1997.

O'Connor, John J. "On Teen-Age Virginity, or Its Loss, on Television." *New York Times*, September 21, 1991.

– –. "TV's Closet Door Has Never Been Open So Wide on Gays." *Ann Arbor News*, November 27, 1994.

"Presidential Impeachment Proceedings, *The History Place*, www.historyplace.com/unitedstates/impeachments/clinton.htm

Puig, Claudia. "Children Say They Imitate Anti-social Behavior on TV." *Ann Arbor News*, February 27, 1995.

"Report Cites TV Influence on Young." *Ann Arbor News*, October 17, 1995.

Rich, Frank. "The New Republic." *New York Times*, April 17, 1996.

Schur, Edwin N. *The Americanization of Sex*. Philadelphia: Temple University Press, 1988.

Selnow, Gary W. and Richard R. Gilbert. *Society's Impact on Television: How the Viewing Public Shapes Television Programming*. Westport, CT: Praeger, 1993.

Shales, Tom. "Sexual Dealing." *Electronic Media*, February 17, 2003.

Silverman, L. Theresa, Joyce N. Sprakin, and Eli A. Rubinstein. "Physical Contact and Sexual Behavior on Prime-Time TV." *Journal of Communication*, Winter 1979.

Sklar, Robert. *Prime-Time America: Life On and Behind the Television Screen*. New York: Oxford University Press, 1980.

Stolberg, Sheryl. "'Life's Work' Ignites New Ratings Debate." *Ann Arbor News*, March 2, 1997.

Summer, Claude J. ed. *The Queer Encyclopedia of Film and Television*. San Francisco, CA: Cleis Press, 2000.

Zurawik, David. "TV 'Family Hour' Isn't Going To Be a Family Affair This Fall." *Detroit News*, August 12, 1995.

Chapter 6   The Boxed-In Workplace: Jobs and Professions

Alley, Robert S. and Irby B. Brown. *Murphy Brown: Anatomy of a Sitcom*. New York: Dell Publishing, 1990.

Bayliss, Martha. "TV: Big Bad Businessmen." *Wall Street Journal*, March 23, 1987.

Branegan, Jay. "You Could Call It Wonk Wing: NBC's Hit White House Series Has Become a National Civics Lesson." *Time*, May 15, 2000.

Brooks, Tim and Earle Marsh. *The Complete Directory to Prime Time Network TV Shows, 1946 to Present*. New York: Ballantine Books, 1988.

Bruning, Fred. "Generation X." *Minneapolis Star Tribune*, December 1, 1991.

Chafe, William. *The Unfinished Journey: America Since WWII*. New York: Oxford University Press, 1986.

Crescenti, Peter and Bob Columbe. *The Official Honeymooners Treasury*. New York: Perigee Books, 1990.

Diamond, Edwin. "Is Television Unfair to Labor?" *American Film*, April 1980.

Freed, Roseanne. "The Gripes of Wrath: Roseanne's Bitter Comedy of Class." *Television Quarterly*, Winter 1996.

Gardner, Paul. "Order in the Court: The TV Lawyer Wants to Speak." *The New York Times*, February 16, 1964.

Graham, Ellen. "When Boomers Go Bust." *Detroit News*, November 5, 1995.

Halberstam, David. "America the Last 50 years," Lecture at George Mason universirty, C-SPAN, February 1, 1995.

Houck, Max M. "CSI: Reality." *Scientific American*, July 2006.

James, Caryn. "Pop Culture: Extremes But Little Reality." *New York Times*, March 3, 1996.

Jones, Elka. "As Seen on TV: Reality vs. Fantasy in Occupational Portrayals on the Small Screen." *Occupational Outlook Quarterly*, Fall 2003.

Kolata, Gina. "The Double Life of Dr. Swain: Work and More Work." *New York Times*, September 27, 1994.

Lawson, Herbert, Jr. "Dr. Ben Casey Gets Guidance From Medical Association." *Wall Street Journal*, December 27,1962.

Maloney, Henry B. and E. Jack Neuman. "Mr Novak: Man or Superman?" *Television Quarterly*, Summer 1964.

Marc, David. *Demographic Vistas*. Philadelphia: University of Pennsylvania Press, 1984.

Mastio, David. "Lessons from the oil embargo still count in the 1990s." *The Detroit News*, October 25 1998.

Miller, Douglas T. and Marion Nowak. *The Fifties: The Way We Really Were*. Garden City, NY: Doubleday and Company, Inc., 1977.

Mitz, Rick. *The Great TV Sitcom Book*. New York: Richard Marek Publishers, 1980.

Murphy, Mary. "*The West Wing* Meets the Real Thing, *TV Guide*, July 22, 2000.

Myers, Dee Dee. "Through the Looking Glass Rosy." www.campusprogress.org/soundvision/893/how-west-won-our-hearts

Rose, Reginald. "Law, Drama and Criticism." *Television Quarterly*, Fall 1964.

Rosevear, Paul D. "Is *CSI* for Real?" www.nursetown.com/view_article

Schumach, Murray. "Bedside Manner: 'Doctor Yes.'" *The New York Times*, November 3, 1963.

Serling, Rod. *Patterns, Four Television Plays*. New York: Simon and Schuster, 1957.

Sklar, Robert. *Prime–Time America: Life On and Behind the Television Screen*. New York: Oxford University Press, 1980.

Stein, Ben. *The View from Sunset Boulevard*. New York: Basic Books, 1979.

"Teamsters Charge Archie's the Bunk." *New York Post*, April 4, 1972.

Whyte, William H. *The Organization Man*. New York: Simon and Schuster, 1956.

Williams, Edward Bennett. "The High Cost of Television's Courtroom." *Television Quarterly*, Fall 1964.

Zurawik, David. "Art Imitates Life? Sitcoms Tune Into Our Fears of Dead-end Jobs." *Detroit News*, March 9, 1996.

Chapter 7   Tuning Out Restraint:
Indulgence and Advertising

Barnouw, Erik. *The Sponsor: Notes on a Modern Potentate*. New York: Oxford University Press, 1978.

Black, Jay and Jennings Bryant, eds. *Introduction to Media Communication*. Dubuque, IA: Brown and Benchmark, 1995.

Cherubin, Jan. "Toys Are Programs Too." *Channels*, May/June 1984.

Critoph, Gerald E. "The American Quest for Affluence." In *American Character and Culture in a Changing World: Some Twentieth-Century Perspectives*, edited by John A. Hague. Westport, CT: Greenwood Press, 1979.

Dignam, Monica. "Banning TV Advertising for Kids: Pro's and No's Muster Forces for Hearings." *Television,* vol. 6, no. 2, 1978.

Elias, Marilyn. "How to Win Friends and Influence Kids on Television." In *American Mass Media: Industries and Issues*, edited by Robert Atwan, Barry Orton, and William Vesterman. New York: Random House, 1978.

Elliott, Stuart. "Product Placement Is Under New Attack." *New York Times*, September 2 ,1992.

Gibbons, Gayle and Rebecca Moore. "Can Mr. Machine Save Kids from Count Chocula?" *Television*, vol. 5, no. 1, 1977.

Gray, Ellen. "Some Commercials Start as Soon as the Show Does." *Detroit Free Press*, March 2, 1995.

Harris, Nicole. "Shame on Ads that Use Culture to Sell Liquor." *Detroit Free Press*, August 16, 1993.

"History of TV Advertising" and "50 Best Commercials." *Advertising Age* Internet Feature, (www.adage.com/Features/TV/Index.html), May 25, 1996.

Kaempffert, Walter. "Who Will Pay for Broadcasting?" *Popular Radio*, December 1922.

Klein, Alec Matthew. "'Psychic Friends Network' Not Your Friend." *Ann Arbor News*, July 16, 1995.

Lasch, Christopher. *The True and Only Heaven: Progress and Its Critics*. New York: W.W. Norton, 1992.

Levin, Gary. "The Newest Character on TV Shows: Product Plugs." *USA Today,* September 20, 2006.

McKibben, Bill. *The Age of Missing Information*. New York: Random House, 1992.

Magner, Mike. "Safety Experts Want Brakes Put on Television Car Ads." *Ann Arbor News*, November 19, 1995.

Marin, Rich. "Infomercials Say 'Call Now' and America Grabs the Phone." *New York Times*, October 5, 1992.

"Marketing Revolution in Gasoline: Giant Battle for a Shrinking Market." *Television Magazine*, February 1961.

Melody, William H. *Children's Television: The Economics of Exploitation*. New Haven, CT: Yale University Press, 1973.

Melody, William H. and Wendy Ehrlich. "Children's TV Commercials: The Vanishing Policy Options." *Journal of Communication*, Autumn 1974.

Meyer, John A., M.D. "Cigarette Century." *American Heritage*, December 1992.

Moore, Frazier. "From Health to Hair Grafts, Infomercials Peddle Dreams." *Detroit Free Press*, December 29, 1994.

Muller, Joanne and Janet Brunnstein. "Bikinis and Beer Brew New Image." *Detroit Free Press*, July 29, 1991.

Packard, Vance. "Resurvey of 'Hidden Persuaders.'" *New York Times Magazine*, May 11, 1958.

"Salesman's Decade." *Television Magazine*, February 1961.

Savan, Leslie. *The Sponsored Life: Ads, TV, and American Culture*. Philadelphia, PA: Temple University Press, 1994.

Schwoch, James. "Selling the Sight/Site of Sound: Broadcast Advertising and the Transition from Radio to Television." *Cinema Journal*, vol. 30, no. 1, Fall 1990.

Shorris, Earl. *A Nation of Salesmen: The Tyranny of the Market and the Subversion of Culture*. New York: Avon Books, 1994.

TV Commercials: The 50's and 60's, Vol. I and *TV Commercials Vol. II: The 60's and 70's*. Waltham, MA: CD Titles, Inc., 1996.

Chapter 8   Taking the Cue: Television and the American Personality

American Masters: Edward R. Murrow, This Reporter. Documentary produced by WNET-TV, 1990.

Astley, Amy. "Tube Tops." *Vogue*, March 1996.

Beckett, Kathleen. "A New Groove." *Vogue*, September 1985.

Blackwell, Mr. (a.k.a. Richard Selzer). "Mr. Blackwell's Fashion Guide: TV Stars to Watch – and Ignore – if You Want to Look Sharp." *TV Guide*, 22 July 1989.

Blasini, Gilberto M. *Survivor* entry. *Encyclopedia of Television*. New York: Fitzroy Dearborn, 2004.

Boorstin, Daniel. *The Image*. New York: Atheneum, 1961.

Brown, Les. *Encyclopedia of Television*. Detroit: Visible Ink Press, 1992.

Brown, Les. "The FCC proudly Presents the Vast Wasteland." *Channels of Communication*, March/April 1983.

"Candy Lightner: 'You Can Make a Difference.'" *Time*, January 7, 1985.

Carter, Bill. "An Earful the Public Didn't Hear But Guessed." *New York Times*, April 2, 1994.

– – . "MTV, Listening to Real World, Creates Spinoff." *New York Times*, July 8, 1996.

Cutlip, Scott M. *The Unseen Power: Public Relations, A History*. Hillsdale, NJ: Lawrence Erlbaum Associates, 1994.

Davidson, Bill. "The Farrah Phenomenon." *TV Guide*, May 21, 1977.

De Foe, James R. and Warren Breed. "Youth and Alcohol in Television Stories, With Suggestions to the Industry for Alternative Portrayals." *Adolescence*, Fall 1988.

Dean Martin Celebrity Roast (1977), Museum of Broadcast Communications archival collection, Chicago, IL.

Dempsey, John. "Producers/Writers to Influence Viewers on New Social Behavior." *Variety*, October 5, 1988.

Durslag, Melvin. "TV's Most Engaging Fraud." *TV Guide*, April 2, 1966.

Einstein, Daniel. *Special Edition: A Guide to Network Television Documentary Series and Special News Reports, 1955–1979*. Metuchen, NJ: Scarecrow Press, Inc., 1987.

Endrst, James. "Too Much of What's On Will Be Crasser than Ever." *Ann Arbor News*, August 27, 1995.

Feuer, Jane, Paul Kerr, and Tise Vahimagi, eds. MTM "Quality Television." London: British Film Institute, 1984.

Futch, Emily J., Stephen A. Lisman, and Marilyn I. Geller. "An Analysis of Alcohol Portrayal on Prime-Time Television." The International Journal of Addictions, vol. 19, no. 4, 1984.

Galbraitah, John Kenneth. The Affluent Society. New York: New American Library, 1958.

Gamson, Joshua. Claims to Fame: Celebrity in Contemporary America. Berkeley: University of California Press, 1994.

Greenberg, Bradley S. "Smoking, Drugging, and Drinking in Top Rated TV Series." Journal of Drug Education, vol. II, no. 3, 1981.

"Guest in the House." Newsweek, October 12, 1953.

Hauck, Dennis William. Captain Quirk: The Unauthorized Biography of William Shatner. New York: Kensington Publishing Corp., 1995.

Himmelstein, Hal. Television Myth and the American Mind. New York: Praeger, 1984.

"Imitation: A Welcome Form of Flattery When There Are Million-Dollar Profits." People Weekly, May 13, 1985.

Jennings, Dean. "It Makes Him Happy to See You Cry." Saturday Evening Post, February 4, 1956.

Karlin, Susan. "TV Standards Execs Say They've Seen It All Before." Electronic Media, September 11, 1995.

Kelly, Richard. The Andy Griffith Show. Winston-Salem, NC: John F. Blair Publisher, 1981.

Kolbert, Elizabeth. "Frank Talk by Clinton to MTV Generation." New York Times, April 20, 1994.

Lawrence, Jill. "Excuse Me, But.... Whatever Happened to Manners?" USA Today, December 16, 1996.

Liebart, Robert, and Joyca Sprafkin. The Early Window: The Effects of Televisions on Children and Youth. New York: Pergamon, 1973.

Leiby, Richard. "The Commander in Briefs." Washington Post, April 20, 1994.

"Like, Duh...and Other Words Nixed." Eastern Echo, January 10, 1997.

Lowry, Dennis T. "Alcohol Consumption Patterns and Consequences on Prime Time Network TV." Journalism Quarterly, Spring 1981.

Lytle, Lisa. "Short and Dangerous: What Works on TV Can Skirt Reality." Detroit Free Press, June 19, 1995.

Marin, Rick. "Absolut-ly Fabulous." Newsweek, November 20, 1995.

Medved, Michael. Hollywood vs. America: Popular Culture and the War on Traditional Values. New York: HarperCollins, 1992.

Monghan, Diane. "From the '50s Through the '90s, TV Has Mirrored the Dress of the Day." TV Guide, July 27, 1991.

"Monkee Do." Time, November 11, 1966.

"MTV Shuns Responsibility for Stunts in Show 'Jackass'." Arizona Daily Wildcat Online (http://wc.arizona.edu/papers/94/145/04_4_m.html), April 26, 2001.

Olmsted, Dan and Gigi Anders. "Turned Off – TV Survey: Sex and Vulgarity." USA Weekend, June 2, 1995.

Packard, Vance. *The Hidden Presuaders*. New York: D. Mckay Co., 1957.

Pedell, Kathy. "This is Murrow..." *TV Guide*, June 1954, reprinted in *TV Guide: The First 25 Years*, edited by Jay S. Harris. New York: New American Library, 1978.

Persico, Joseph E. *Edward R. Murrow: An American Original*. New York: McGraw-Hill, 1988.

"Poll: Lack of Civility a Problem." *Ann Arbor News*, June 12, 1996.

Powers, Ron. *The Beast, the Eunuch and the Glass-eyed Child: Television in the 80s*. San Diego: Harcourt Brace Jovanovich, 1990.

"Report Cites TV Influence on the Young." *Ann Arbor News*, October 17, 1995.

Rooney, Andrew A. *Not That You Asked*. New York: Random House, 1989.

Rosen, Gary Alan. "From Coonskin Caps to Farrah's Locks, TV Has Been America's No. 1 Fad Factory." *TV Guide*, July 27, 1991.

Rosenthal, Phil. "Tasteless Ads Bring Fox to New Low." *Ann Arbor News*, August 26, 1994.

Scanlan, Christopher. "Scholar Engineers Social Change through TV." *Detroit Free Press*, October 14, 1993.

Seplow, Stephen. "'Larroquette Show' Deals Deftly with Sobering Topic." *Detroit Free Press*, July 4, 1995.

Sperber, A.M. *Murrow: His Life and Times*. New York: Freundlich Books, 1986.

Spoto, Donald. *Marilyn Monroe: The Biography*. New York: HarperCollins, 1993.

"Television's Top 25 Stars." *People Weekly: Television's 50th Anniversary Extra Edition*, Summer 1989.

Tosches, Nick. "The Death, And Life, Of the Rat Pack." *New York Times*, January 7, 1996.

Twitchell, James B. *Carnival Culture: The Trashing of Taste in America*. New York: Columbia University Press, 1992.

Wald, Matthew L. "A Fading Drumbeat Against Drunken Driving." *New York Times*, December 15, 1996.

Wallack, Lawrence, Warren Breed, and John Cruz. "Alcohol on Prime-Time Television." *Journal of Studies on Alcohol*, vol. 40, no. 1, 1987.

Williams, Stephanie. "Must-Smoke TV." *TV Guide*, October 12, 1996.

Watson, Mary Ann. "How TV Sobered Up (But Is It Falling Off the Wagon?)." *Television Quarterly*, vol. 29, no. 1, Fall 1997.

Ziegler, Peggy. "Producers: Drunk Diving Plan Doable." *Electronic Media*, September 5, 1988.

Chapter 9   Deep Focus: Television and the American Character

Albom, Mitch. "Spitting Mad about Alomar." *Detroit Free Press*, October 2, 1996.

Bennetts, Leslie. "Jerry vs. The Kids." *Vanity Fair*, September 1993.

Blake, Howard. "An Apologia from the Man Who Produced the Worst Program in TV History." In *American Broadcasting: A Source Book on the History of Radio and*

Television, edited by Lawrence W. Lichty and Malachi C. Topping. New York: Hastings House, 1976.

Bolte, Bill. "Jerry's Got To Be Kidding." *Utne Reader*, March/April 1993.

Briller, Bert. "TV's Distorted and Missing Images of Women and the Elderly." *Television Quarterly*, vol XXXI, no.1, Spring 2000.

Bruning, Fred. "Trash Talk: Merely a Sign of the Times." *Maclean's*, June 20, 1994.

Dechant, Dell. *The Sacred Santa: The Religious Dimensions of Consumer Culture* Cleveland, OH: Pilgrim Press, 2002.

Del Valle, Christina. "Some of Jerry's Kids Are Mad at the Old Man." *Business Week*, September 14, 1992.

Delong, Thomas A. *Quiz Craze: America's Infatuation with Game Shows*. New York: Praeger, 1991.

"Disabling 'Jerry's Kids.'" *U.S. News and World Report*, September 14, 1992.

Duffy, Yvonne. "Telethons Only Undercut Progress." *Detroit Free Press*, February 4, 1996.

Fabe, Maxene. "The Big Quiz Scandals." In *TV Book*, edited by Judy Fireman. New York: Workman Publishing, 1977.

Gelman, David. "I'm Not a Role Model." *Newsweek*, June 28, 1993.

Giardina, Denise. "View from Appalachia," *Emmy Magazine*, January/February 1986.

"God and Television." *TV Guide*, March 29, 1997.

"Gray Power." *The Nation*, May 28, 1990.

Haller, Beth. "The Misfit and Muscular Dystrophy." *Journal of Popular Film and Television*, vol. 21, no. 4, Winter 1994.

Harrigan, Susan. "Jerry's Orphans." *New York Newsday*, August 28, 1992.

Hockenberry, John. *Moving Violations: War Zones, Wheelchairs, and Declarations of Independence*. New York: Hyperion, 1995.

Holbrook, Morris B. *Daytime Television Game Shows and the Celebration of Merchandise: The Price is Right*. Bowling Green, OH: Bowling Green State University Popular Press, 1993.

Janis, Pam. "God Pops Up in Culture." *USA Weekend*, October 11, 1996.

"Jerry's Kids." *The Nation*, September 14, 1992.

Kaplan, David A. "When Spit Hits the Fan." *Newsweek*, October 14, 1996.

Karp, Walter. "The Quiz-Show Scandal." *American Heritage*, May/June 1989.

Long, Rob. "Jerry Built." *National Review*, February 9, 1998.

Malone, Karl. "One Role Model to Another." *Sports Illustrated*, June 14, 1993.

Mankiewicz, Frank and Joel Swerdlow. *Remote Control: Television and the Manipulation of American Life*. New York: New York Times Books, 1978.

Marin, Rick. "Jerry Seins Off." *Newsweek*, January 12, 1998.

Miller, Ron. "Demographics Spell the End for Show with Over-50 Stars." *Detroit Free Press*, October 2, 1995.

Morreale, Joanne. "Sitcoms Say Goodbye: The Cultural Spectacle of Seinfeld's Last Episode." *Journal of Popular Film and Television*, Fall 2000.

Moyers, Bill. "America's Religious Mosaic." *USA Weekend*, October 11, 1996.

Nelson, Jack, A. *Disabled, the Media and the Information Age*. Westport, CT: Greenwood Press, 1994.

O'Connor, John J. "A Few Qualms from a Fan of 'Seinfeld.'" *New York Times*, May 30, 1993.

– – . "Labelling Prime-Time Violence Is Still a Band-Aid Solution." *New York Times*, July 11, 1993.

O'Hallaren, Bill. "Nobody (in TV) Loves You When You're Old and Gray." *New York Times*, July 24, 1977.

Pierce, Ponchita. "Whom Should We Admire?" *Parade*, August 6, 1995.

Real, Michael. "The Great Quiz Show Scandal: Why America Remains Fascinated." *Television Quarterly*, vol. XXVII, no. 3, Winter 1995.

Reilly, Rick. "Too Many Spoilsports." *Sports Illustrated*, January 11, 1993.

Riesman, David, in collaboration with Nathan Glazer and Reuel Denney. *The Lonely Crowd: A Study of the Changing American Character*. New Haven, CT: Yale University Press, 1950; second edition, 1961.

Robinson, Thomas E. *Portraying Older People in Advertising*. New York: Garland Publishing, Inc., 1998

Roof, Wade Clark. "The Baby Boom's Search for God." *American Demographics*, December 1992.

Smith, Vern E. and Aric Press. "Who You Calling Hero?" *Newsweek*, May 24, 1993.

Smythe, Ted Curtis. "Growing Old in Commercials: A Joke Not Shared." In *Images That Injure: Pictorial Stereotypes in the Media*, edited by Paul Martin Lester. Westport, CT: Praeger, 1996.

"Study: Elderly Are Scarce on TV shows." *Ann Arbor News*, September 13, 1993.

"Supermarket Sweep." *Variety*, December 22, 1965.

Swift, E.M. "Give Young Athletes a Fair Shake." *Sports Illustrated*, May 2, 1994.

Waters, Harry F. with Janet Huck. "A New Golden Age." *Newsweek*, November 18, 1985.

Watson, Mary Ann. "And They Said 'Uncle Fultie' Didn't Have a Prayer..." *Television Quarterly*, vol. XXVI, no. 3, 1993.

Watson, Mary Ann. "The Seinfeld Doctrine – 'No Hugging, No Learning' – Imprints the 1990s." *Television Quarterly*, vol. XXIX, no. 3, 1998.

"What Makes Heroes and Why We Need Them." *Detroit Free Press*, February 23, 1996.

Chapter 10   The Webbed Republic: Democracy in the Television Age

Allen, Henry. "The Gulf Between Media and Military." In *Messages 2: The Washington Post Media Companion*. Boston: Allyn and Bacon, 1993.

Andrews, Peter. "The Media and the Military." *American Heritage*, July/August 1991.

Barnouw, Erik. *Tube of Plenty*. New York: Oxford University Press, 1990.

Belkin, Lisa. "Death on the CNN Curve, The Life and Death of Robert O'Donnell, Baby Jessica's Rescuer." *New York Times Magazine*, July 23, 1995.

Carman, John, "CBS Shying Away from Coverage of Levy Investigation." *San Francisco Chronicle*, July 13, 2001

Chafe, William H. *The Unfinished Journey: America Since WWII*. New York: Oxford University Press, 1986.

"Connie Chung Nails Down Interview with Embattled Condit; Now What?" *Corpus Christi Caller-Times*, August 23, 2001.

Corporon, John. "The JFK, Jr. Coverage: It's as if Nothing Else Was Going On." *Television Quarterly*, vol. XXX, no. 3, Winter 2004.

Dominick, Joseph R., Barry L. Sherman, and Gary A. Copeland. *Broadcasting/Cable and Beyond*. New York: McGraw Hill, 1996.

Einstein, Daniel. *Special Edition: A Guide to Network Television Documentary Series and Special News Reports, 1955–1979*. Metuchen, NJ: Scarecrow Press, 1987.

Emery, Michael and Edwin Emery. *The Press and America: An Interpretive History of Mass Media*. Englewood Cliffs, NJ: Prentice Hall, 1992.

Frank, Jeffrey A. "Are There New Rules of History?" In *Messages 2: The Washington Post Media Companion*. Boston: Allyn and Bacon, 1993.

Goethals, Gregor T. *The TV Ritual: Worship at the Video Altar*. Boston: Beacon Press, 1981.

Gorer, Geoffrey. *The American People, A Study in National Character*. New York: W.W. Norton, 1948.

Heintze, Carl. "All-News Networks Sank to New Lows." *Los Gatos Weekly Times*, July 28, 1999.

Hill, Doug and Jeff Weingrad. *Saturday Night: A Backstage History of Saturday Night Live*. New York: Beech Tree Books, 1986.

Hilliard, Robert L. and Michael C. Keith. *The Broadcast Century: A Biography of American Broadcasting*. Boston: Focal Press, 1992.

Johnson, Peter. "Connie Chung Wins First Interview with Condit." *USA Today*, August 20, 2001.

Jurkowitz, Mark. "Networks Mull Challenge to Air McVeigh execution." *Boston Globe*, March 6, 2001.

Leab, Daniel J. "See It Now: A Legend Reassessed." In *American History/American Television*, edited by John E. O'Connor. New York: Frederick Ungar Publishing, Co., 1983.

Lichty, Lawrence W. "Watergate, the Evening News and the 1972 Election." In *American History/American Television*, edited by John E. O'Connor. New York: Frederick Ungar Publishing, Co., 1983.

Mankiewicz, Frank and Joel Swerdlow. *Remote Control: Television and the Manipulation of American Life*. New York: Times Books, 1978.

Margolick, David. "For Good or Ill, The Simpson Case Has Permeated the Nation's Psyche." *New York Times*, June 12, 1995.

Michener, James. "After the War: The Victories at Home." *Newsweek*, January 11, 1993.

Murrow, Edward R. "My Reply to Senator McCarthy." *TV News*, May 14, 1954.

Parachini, John V. "The World Trade Center Bombers (1993)." In *Toxic Terror: Assessing Terrorist Use of Chemical and Biological Weapons*, edited by Jonathan B. Tucker. Cambridge MA: MIT Press, 2000.

Rosteck, Thomas. *See It Now Confronts McCarthyism*. Tuscaloosa, AL: University of Alabama Press, 1994.

Sabadi, Jeanne. "The Gulf War as Popular Culture and TV Drama." *Communiqué*, May 1992.

Shales, Tom. "The Whole World Was Watching." In *Messages 2: The Washington Post Media Companion*. Boston: Allyn and Bacon, 1993.

Smolowe, Jill. "She Said, He Said." *Time*, October 21, 1991.

Spector, Bert. "A Clash of Cultures: The Smothers Brothers vs. CBS." In *American History/American Television*, edited by John E. O'Connor. New York: Frederick Ungar Publishing, Co., 1983.

Tucker, Cynthia, "The Role of the Press in the Post-September 11 World." Speech delivered November 14, 2001 as the annual Ralph McGill Lecture at the University of Georgia, www.uga.edu/news/september11/forums/mcgill.html

Epilogue

Carr, Steven. Entry on "2000 Presidential Election Coverage." *Encyclopedia of Television*. New York: Fitzroy Dearborn, 2004

Chunovic, Louis. "Will TV News – or Its Audience – Finally Grow Up?" *Television Week*, September 24, 2001.

Deveny, Kathleen. "The Electronic Hearth: Remember When Television Was the Bond that Brought Families Together?" *Wall Street Journal*, September 9, 1994.

Epstein, Michael M. "TV Journalism Under Attack!" *Christian Science Monitor*, September 20, 2001.

Feeney, Mark. "Sept. 11 May Bring Culture Shift." *Ann Arbor News*, September 30, 2001.

Fenton, Tom. *Bad News: The Decline of Reporting, the Business of News, and the Danger to Us All*. New York: HarperCollins Publishers

Feran, Tom. "Who Cares About 'Reality' TV Anymore?" *Ann Arbor News*, September 22, 2001.

Garner, Joe. *Stay Tuned: Television's Unforgettable Moments*. Kansas City: Andrews McMeel Publishing, 2002.

Mascaro, Thomas A. "Making Sense of the Noise and Nonsense the World Throws Up." *Television Quarterly*, vol. XXXIII, nos. 2 and 3, Summer/Fall 2002.

Schlosser, Joe and Susanne Ault. "Disaster Disrupts Prime Time." *Broadcasting and Cable*, September 17, 2001.

Scott, Karen. "The Unthinkable Happened: How 9/11 Changed Our Lives Forever." *Television Quarterly*, vol. XXXVII, no.1, Fall 2004.

Spigel, Lynn. "Entertainment Wars: Television Culture After 9/11." *American Quarterly*, vol. 56, no.2, June 2004.

Trescott, Jacqueline. "Talking about America, Federal Project Tries to Get People to Look at What Unites Us." *Ann Arbor News*, July 16, 1995.

"'Tribute' Telethon Raises $150 Million." www.nbc4.tv/news/969776/detail.

Whitney, Daisy. "Nation Hungry for News Takes Web Sites to Limit." *Electronic Media*, September 17, 2001.

"Why Ed Rates High." *Newsweek*, December 21,1953.

Index